SPARKS *from the*
COSMIC FLAME

Essays inspired by Dion Fortune's
The Cosmic Doctrine

edited by
WENDY BERG

SKYLIGHT
PRESS

This anthology first published in Great Britain in 2017 by Skylight Press,
210 Brooklyn Road, Cheltenham, Glos GL51 8EA

Designed and typeset by Rebsie Fairholm
Publisher: Daniel Staniforth
Cover illustration by Rebsie Fairholm

www.skylightpress.co.uk

Printed and bound in Great Britain by Lightning Source, Milton Keynes.

British Library Cataloguing in Publication Data:
A catalogue record for this book is available from the British Library.

ISBN 978-1-908011-86-2

About the cover illustration: The geometry in the image reflects the principles
of *The Cosmic Doctrine* and can be used for meditation. The design, taken from
a crop circle design which appeared on the slopes of Cley Hill in Wiltshire, is
structured around visible and invisible hexagons and hexagrams. The 'star' in
the middle is an isometric star tetrahedron and combines the symbolism of 3, 7
and 12 – it's made up of triangles, has 7 visible points and 12 edges. All the inner
circles are exactly half the size of the outer circles, with each type of circle double
the radius of the last.

CONTENTS

APPROACHES TO THE COSMIC DOCTRINE

WENDY BERG

If you have found your way to this book you will probably have read the text which inspired it: *The Cosmic Doctrine*, written by the twentieth century occultist Dion Fortune. You will probably also have some familiarity with the background and purpose of *The Cosmic Doctrine* but, briefly, it was communicated to her during 1923 and 1924 by a number of Inner Plane guides or Masters. For many years the text was circulated only amongst the members of her magical group (then known as the Fraternity of the Inner Light) who used it for study and meditation, and it was not made available to the general public until it was first published in 1949. A later edition containing some additional material was brought out in 1966 and was followed by several other editions.[1] Although it has been widely read, *The Cosmic Doctrine* has acquired a reputation for being obscurely worded and difficult to understand. It is not the intention of this present book to try to 'explain' the ideas described within it or attempt to re-write it in easy language: that would be impossible and in any case would defeat its purpose. The following essays show some of the many ways in which its teaching can be developed, adapted and put into practice. The chapters which follow this introduction have been written by men and women from all walks of life who have been inspired by its wisdom, and have applied what they have learnt to illumine their own diverse fields of work and interest.

The aim of the Inner Plane guides and teachers who communicated *The Cosmic Doctrine* to Dion Fortune was to help students of the wisdom of the Inner worlds form a working understanding of Cosmic Law: in other words the repeating patterns, rhythms and principles upon which the whole of our universe is based. The book teaches us how to discern the underlying influences behind the seeming confusion of life with all its complexities and apparently disconnected detail. The whole of life, it tells us, emerges from the One in a cosmic breathing out, a process in which the original unity and purity of spirit gradually develops into forms of increasing density, complexity and separation. Eventually, as the nadir of earthly manifestation is reached and turned, the cosmic breath is drawn in so that all will eventually return to the One in the evolutionary process which is characterised by synthesis, cohesion and unity. *The Cosmic Doctrine* helps us to understand how all this works so that we can become more actively and effectively engaged in the evolutionary journey.

A great deal has been written on 'life, the universe and everything'[2] and it might be argued that *The Cosmic Doctrine* doesn't actually tell us anything that hasn't been said before. For example, in the esoteric tradition of the West we have the wisdom of the Qabalah and the glyph of Tree of Life, the knowledge and practice of Alchemy and the numerous texts and cults associated with the many branches of Hermeticism, all of which have demonstrated how humanity can access the wisdom of the unseen worlds by a combination of esoteric knowledge and the development of the mind through meditation. In the later years of the 19th century – the period immediately preceding Dion Fortune – a flourishing of esoteric research and activity was enriched by the ease of foreign travel that opened the gateway to the Eastern religions, and their frequent reference to cosmic law was eagerly absorbed into Western esotericism. The work of Helena Blavatsky for example, who claimed to have travelled extensively in India and Tibet, culminated in the publication of *The Secret Doctrine: the Synthesis of Science, Religion and Philosphophy* (1888), this being a substantial description of the origin and evolution of the universe that includes many elements of Hindu and Tibetan Buddhist thought. In 1925 Alice Bailey, much of whose work was communicated by the Inner Plane Master known as the Tibetan, published her monumental *A Treatise on Cosmic Fire*, a text which combines an equally extensive cosmology with a more psychological approach to the underlying cosmic patterns that can be discerned within every aspect of life from a single atom, to human being, to an entire cosmos.

However, the approach taken by the communicators of *The Cosmic Doctrine* was significantly different to anything that had gone before or indeed has been achieved since. It too describes how the cosmos works, but it does so in an extraordinarily succinct manner which does not rely on any other occult exposition and makes almost no direct reference to any theology, philosophy or aspect of scientific thought. It conveys esoteric information that has long been available in one form or another, but it does so in a unique way. If you take a single paragraph, a sentence or even a short phrase from the text and hold it in your head in a meditative state of mind you will find yourself confronted with the marvellous achievement that lies at the heart of the book. It doesn't *tell* you how the cosmos works; it provides you with the means by which you can *experience* it for yourself and formulate your own understanding.

The Cosmic Doctrine is essentially an empowering work. It places the responsibility for our comprehension of the laws of creation into our own minds and imagination, and this is what distinguishes it from any other similar text. It contains a truly 'cosmic' depth of knowledge for which language is almost inadequate to express, yet rather than using more words, more detail and more examples in an attempt to describe what words ultimately cannot describe, it utilises the magical technique of metaphor. 'Magical', because a metaphor works like a visual symbol except that it uses words rather than images. Just as a magical symbol can become a gateway to an intuitive understanding of Inner qualities, so a metaphor uses the medium of words to suggest ways in which one thing is related at a higher level to another, apparently different thing. *The Cosmic Doctrine's* best known example of this technique is found right at the beginning of the book: "space moves."

Because a metaphor places two seemingly unrelated things in conjunction, you cannot comprehend its meaning at face value. If, however, you persist in your perplexity and resolutely hold the two concepts in your head, your mind attempts to build bridges between them by producing images or thoughts that help you to understand them at a higher level. In the text, the words "space" and "movement" initially appear between inverted commas to indicate that they are metaphors for something else that cannot adequately be described in words. How can 'space' also be 'movement?' How does 'movement' relate to 'space?' What does 'space moving' look like? How can it be felt or experienced? Is it 'out there' or 'in here?' Using your mind to hold together, simultaneously, two opposite states, enables you to reach above and beyond them into a higher truth, and the ability to do this is one of the fundamental principles of esoteric, Inner or magical work. *The Cosmic Doctrine* teaches you how to achieve this ability.

The creative process described throughout *The Cosmic Doctrine* hardly needs explanation: it is the coming together of two opposites – 'male' and 'female' – which create a third, a child of the union. The text constantly invites the reader to think about what lies behind the outer appearances of things. Behind the physical forms of man and woman are the principles of male and female, behind these principles are universal polarised qualities or attributes, behind these universal qualities are the concepts of force and form, behind force and form are the ideas of energy and substance, behind these is the apparent duality of 'movement' and 'space', and behind these is the ultimate Mystery of the Manifest and the Unmanifest. The implication is that even this duality is the outcome of a unique One-ness that might be called 'space-moved', although *The Cosmic Doctrine* refers to it as 'It.'

Of the many aspects of polarity that manifest throughout our universe it is probably the fundamental polarity between Spirit and Matter that most concerns us as students of the Mysteries. By trying to fathom this duality and discovering ways in which we can bring to light the hidden spiritual principles buried within the heart of matter, so we become an active part in the process of evolution in which the light of Life, dissipated and hidden, will eventually flow back to the One. "Man's primal loyalty is to the One – Unity."[3] In this way we ourselves become the mediators between Spirit and Matter.

The Cosmic Doctrine also uses the art of geometry as a dynamic metaphor. It invites us to think about the relationship between lines (moving energy) and points (stillness or inertia), to sense the cosmic forces that 'bend' a straight line into a circle and to consider the relationship between the relative position of forms. The first moments of creation are described in terms of circles, spheres, tangents and vortices. The intention is not to reduce the cosmos to a soulless mechanism but to employ the most abstract terminology possible while still conveying sufficient information for the mind to grasp a toe-hold in the meaning. The three Rings of Space, the Rays and the Circles, the centrifugal and centripetal force, the equilibrium and the Central Stillness are all expressions of patterns, tensions, reactions and relationships that are found at every level of the universe, not only in the first movements of creation but in our own life and personal connections: in our relationship with our partner and family, in office politics, the rise and fall of civilisations, war and peace, and the birth of stars. By using our own minds to comprehend the Mystery of creation we can discern the Mind of God and, simultaneously, discover more of our own Self.

Chapter One of *The Cosmic Doctrine* famously states that the purpose of the book is '...*to train the mind, not to inform it.*'[4] My own view is that this statement, often quoted in ironic despair by baffled readers, is not entirely helpful and not altogether true. It would be more accurate to say that the book trains the mind *and also* informs it. This may not initially be apparent because the first six chapters are concerned with the most abstract cosmic principles expressed through a metaphorical use of words that strains language to its limits. It is these first six chapters which are specifically designed to train the mind as described above, and the way to approach them is not to attempt to take them in all in at once but to study them slowly, one paragraph or sentence at a time, using a few words for further thought and meditation over an extended period of time. These chapters significantly avoid using words such as 'god,' 'spirit,' 'humanity,' 'world,' or 'sun' that would confine their meaning to any specific area of thought or world-view, or limit their application to any one level of manifestation. Later in the text, as the description of creation develops from its inceptive simplicity into increasing detail and complexity, so more specific information is given and the book becomes progressively easier to understand at a more immediate level.

The intention of the Inner Plane Masters in doing things this way is clear: you cannot properly understand the 'reality' of the material world about you unless you have some understanding of the energies and principles, or the 'real reality,' that lies behind it. A similar dilemma is encountered for example by those who write about the Qabalist Tree of Life: do you begin with matter or spirit? Do you begin with a description of the familiar world of Malkuth and risk your students missing the point because as yet they may not have sufficient awareness of the universal principles that lie behind it? Or do you begin with the spiritual world of Kether and risk baffling your students because this level may initially be too challenging to comprehend? The solution is to alternate between the two, between Kether and Malkuth, spirit and matter, and the very act of doing so helps to achieve the point of the exercise which is to 'realise' the life of the spirit within the world of matter.

Certainly not all readers of *The Cosmic Doctrine* find the text challenging. But to those who do, I suggest that approaching it in the conventional way of starting at the beginning, reading through it chapter by chapter and finishing at the end, is not the best strategy. It works well to alternate meditation on the 'mind-training' material of the first six chapters with reading and enjoying the subsequent, more accessible chapters. These need not all be read in the order in which they appear, and you might like to focus on whichever chapters speak to you at any moment. It can also be used as a book to dip into, a chapter or paragraph at a time, or even to open at random so that a single sentence or phrase can present itself to you for contemplation. Be flexible and creative in your use of this text.

In fact the last three pages are a very good place to start![5] These describe and explain the difference between the Planetary Entity, the Planetary Intelligence and the Planetary Being and, more importantly, describe humanity's relationship with the Planetary Being or Earth Mother. Any impression you may have formed of *The Cosmic Doctrine* as a difficult or abstract text is counteracted by the plain words and powerful earthiness of this section. Rather than dealing with the first moments of creation it brings you right into the here and now and includes some useful suggestions of how to put into practice what you have learnt from reading the book. These final pages remind us that everything we think, speak and do affects the Planetary Being, and the emphatic message which concludes the book is that just as we ourselves move forward in our lives by keeping in mind the image of our next goal or ideal, so we must also undertake this role on behalf of the Earth because, as yet, she is not capable of doing this for herself; only humanity is able to do this. Paradoxically, we are her 'parents.' "Therefore, whatsoever you do, let it be not only for your own gain or interest but also for the gain and keen interest of the Planetary Being."[6] This sentence might usefully be placed at the beginning of each chapter.

The material of this final section is usefully reinforced by a reading of pages 201–203 which describe the process through which the form of the earth has been constructed.[7] It contains some beautifully imaginative descriptions of the Lords of Form whose work is largely involved in the 'intensification' of the etheric body of the earth but which can also be discerned through the qualities of metals and precious stones which link the earth to other planets in the solar system. This section emphasises the importance of rhythm and repetition in the work of these cosmic 'Builders' and, almost as an aside, makes a useful comment regarding the importance of rhythm and repetition in the construction of magical ritual. These qualities, we are reminded, assist the Elemental beings in building the necessary astral forms while the ritual is taking place, something well worth keeping in mind by anyone involved in practical magical work. There is much in these pages that appeals to the imagination, and the material here can be used inspirationally in Innerworld work. This section is followed by some useful comments on the Archangelic forms associated with the Qabalah and the Tree of Life.

You may find that much of the material in the section headed 'Afterthoughts' helps towards an understanding of the earlier chapters.[8] For example, there is an elucidation of the important concept of the life 'swarms' which are described in more detail earlier in the text. The swarms are the rhythmic outflowing of wave upon wave of Sparks of Life emanating from the One which, over the ages, have gradually built up into the increasing complexity and density of the planes of creation as they emerge from spirit into matter. All living things begin as a Divine Spark of life, and this light endures forever, deep within our being. The word 'swarm' evocatively suggests a colony of bees winging out from the hive to gather nectar for the good of the colony. One of the important points to grasp in the description of the swarms is how each wave of beings can and should pass on its knowledge and experience to those who follow after. It is easy to see how this principle makes sense on every level of existence and in every area of our lives, particularly to those involved in esoteric work; it is how humanity learns, develops and evolves.

The first three waves of these cosmic Beings are described as the Primal Swarms: the Lords of Flame, Form and Mind. The Lords of Flame are responsible for establishing the different qualities of energy or vibration that develop into what we know as the laws of physics. The Lords of Form initiate the development of the substance and shape of forms that lie behind the laws of chemistry and, after a very long time has passed, the Lords of Mind appear, these being the powers behind the individual, active, reasoning, mediating human mind that can understand and interpret these laws. These are all sentient Beings however, not 'mere' principles, and it can be instructive to stretch the imagination and try to give imaginative form to the appearance of these Beings. As the text points out, we carry the seeds of our own beginnings, and as each of us came into contact with these great

Beings when our own Life-Spark began its journey from the Central Stillness into manifestation, so we still carry their influence within us.

Readers who are familiar with the work of Helena Blavatsky and Alice Bailey may find it useful to compare the descriptions of the first three Rays that are found throughout their writings with the three Primal Swarms of *The Cosmic Doctrine*. The first Ray, according to Theosophical interpretation, is that of Will, Power or Purpose or of undiluted intention, searing potency and absolute truth, and these same principles can be discerned in the work of the Lords of Flame. The second Ray is of Love and Wisdom, these being the principles behind the phenomenon of like attracting like, of cohesion and coherence and the activities that bind forms together. These principles can be discerned in the work of the Lords of Form. The third Ray is that of Active Intelligence (and/or Intelligent Activity) which is the ability to understand how the first two Rays work, to perceive the divine purpose working through them and to intelligently cooperate with them and incorporate them into your own life's work. These principles can be likened to the work of the Lords of Mind.

The 'Afterthoughts' are immediately preceded by the remarkable chapter which begins: "The Law of the Attraction of the Centre contains the secret of the Mystery of Love."[9] This opening statement alone is well worth pondering. There is some wonderfully evocative writing in this chapter, which essentially describes the quality of energy that is responsible for evolution: Love. (In *The Cosmic Doctrine*, the word 'involution' is used to describe the descent of spirit into fragmentation, complexity and matter; 'evolution' is the process by which all returns to Unity or to the One.) Creation began through God's desire to know or experience God, and this process is completed when each individual Divine Spark has experienced and absorbed every aspect of creation and there is nothing in creation which has not thus been perfected. (Still some way to go, then!)

But we should not think of evolution as a process in which the whole of creation gradually disappears as if into a sort of cosmic plug hole. "The approach to the Centre is not a movement in space, but a *unification*."[10] (My italics.) When all is perfected, the 'Centre' is now everywhere; not only at the centre but also the circumference and everywhere in between. The life-energy withdraws from the forms it has inhabited but its withdrawal enables the cleansing, restorative, spiritual energy of the Cosmic Night to flow, healing all imbalances and errors which still remain in the empty shells of the forms. "...as the daylight fades the spiritualising darkness of the Unmanifest flows over the fields of matter."[11] The process can perhaps be likened to what happens within our own selves during our hours of sleep, and the concept of the Unmanifest as the origin of all creation is one of the most significant points described in the earlier chapters.

What has this to do with love? *The Cosmic Doctrine* reminds us that it is *Life* which is perfected, not the impermanent forms – such as our own bodies – in which Life is temporarily housed. It is Life that flows back to the One, not the forms. Life manifests through the innumerable, scattered, apparently disconnected forms of creation but the process of evolution is one of unification, and it is only the *energy of love* that brings unity – or in the language of *The Cosmic Doctrine* it is love which brings one 'atom' closer to another. The text advises us in an unexpected moment of reassurance that it is not so important which type of love we express, whether it is physical unity on the plane of matter or a purely intellectual understanding of the subject, but that we express love as best we can in whatever way we can. "Whoever expresses Love, brings Spirit, which is One, into manifestation. To be separate is to be dead. Therefore choose Love and live."[12]

The chapters which deal with the various cosmic Laws – of Limitation, of Action and Reaction, of the Seven Deaths and so on – are all relatively easy to understand and a great deal can be gained from these chapters irrespective of how challenging you find the earlier sections. If you are involved in practical magical work you may find the chapters on the Laws of Limitation of particular interest. "It is necessary that those in the service of the Hierarchy should acquire a knowledge of the 'magical' arts, because these enable you to invoke and concentrate power effectively."[13] The Law of Limitation also offers a clear explanation of how the three cosmic Rings of Space described in Chapter One are at work when we bring any new project into birth, and demonstrates how these abstract, 'cosmic' principles actually apply to every moment of our lives. The initial movement of the Ring Cosmos which causes it to emerge from a single point and transform into a complete circle is likened to the process which occurs on a mental level when we are inspired with a seed thought and then 'think all round it' so that we are literally looking at it from all aspects.

When this 'thinking' stage is complete, the project can be transferred to the level of the higher emotions (love, joy and hope rather than anger or desire) which correspond to the Ring Pass-Not. This stage is important because "The object of immediate desire may be distinguished from the object of remote desire."[14] In other words, it allows you to discern whether you are interested in achieving something for short-term personal gratification or from an awareness of the greater good.

Finally, it is suggested that the driving forces of nature and the instincts should be applied to the project, a process which corresponds with the forces of the Ring Chaos.

It is no secret that much of the material in *The Cosmic Doctrine*, particularly the earlier sections, is attributed to the Greek philosopher Socrates. As Dion Fortune and her Inner plane contacts were at pains to emphasise, what really matters is whether the communicated material stands up to use rather than who was responsible for it. However, the approach taken by the main communicator does seem to accord with what we know of Socrates and his method of teaching which was based on the technique of asking a series of questions designed to help his students to distinguish what they knew and understood from what they did not know or understand. He taught them how to develop a system of self-questioning that enabled them to reach deeply into fundamental principles and to formulate their own answers. The key question was always 'What exactly does this mean?' His method was never to give out information – indeed he insisted that all he knew was that he knew nothing – but to encourage students to find their own way to the knowledge and understanding they sought. His methods instilled intellectual humility: he discouraged the assumption that he or anyone had the right or certain answer. This technique of teaching lies at the heart of *The Cosmic Doctrine*.

The authors who have contributed to this present book share a common enthusiasm for *The Cosmic Doctrine* as a source of inspiration and illumination, and have shown in this remarkable collection of essays just how wide-ranging the application of its teaching can be. The authors do not all agree with each other; in fact you will find a number of different points of view and one or two outright contradictions. This is just as it should be. There is no single correct interpretation of much of the material in *The Cosmic Doctrine* and it calls for the use of the imagination and intuition just as much as the reasoning mind. It is unlike any other book, and the guidance and inspiration of the Inner Plane communicators is still there to be contacted; the words are the catalyst. You have only to read a portion of the text and hold the images and concepts in your mind for the magic to work.

In a box somewhere in my attic is one of my first school exercise books: History Homework, written when I was eleven years old. Evidently the subject held absolutely no interest for me at the time because each exercise is rewarded with the advice that I should try harder. All, that is, except for an essay on the life and death of Socrates which extends to sixteen pages and was obviously written in my very best handwriting. I can still remember writing it as if I was there at the time, witnessing the events.

I have often discerned the power behind his teaching, never giving information but always urging the questions: 'Why do we do that? What is the purpose of this? What does this mean?' I hope that the following essays will help you to find that same inspirational energy behind the words of *The Cosmic Doctrine* which above all teach of love, wisdom and wonder.

1   Unless otherwise stated, all quotations from *The Cosmic Doctrine* correspond to the page numbers of the Red Wheel/Weiser edition of 2000
2   The phrase is Douglas Adams' *Life, the Universe and Everything,* the third book in the five-volume *Hitchhiker's Guide to the Galaxy*
3   Dion Fortune, *The Cosmic Doctrine* (York Beach, ME: Red Wheel/Weiser LLC, 2000), 209
4   *Ibid*, 19
5   These pages are headed 'Section 21' in earlier editions
6   *Ibid*, 211
7   This corresponds to Part II, Section 17 of earlier editions
8   This corresponds to Section II in earlier editions
9   This corresponds to Chapter XXX of earlier editions
10 *Ibid*, 181
11 *Ibid*, 183
12 *Ibid*, 185
13 *Ibid*, 154
14 *Ibid*, 154

2 THE MATTER OF PERSPECTIVE

M E BEARDSLEY

Silver geese flew past today, eight of them, their gleaming breasts sparkling with each beat of their wings. As I sat, unmoving, riveted by the stunning sight, I pondered how many others might be watching them. Very few, I suspect. I happened to be at the right position in relation to the bright winter sun to see the sparkle of light reflecting from the birds' breasts. I happened to be at the right place at the right time and happened to glance out of the window as the birds flew past. Another time or place, they would just have been grey geese.

How we perceive anything relates to the circumstances at the time, to where we are. Where we are includes not only our physical location, but also all we have experienced up to that time.

Often when I revisit Dion Fortune's *The Cosmic Doctrine* it is as though I am reading some part of it for the first time. How can that be? It seems unlikely the words have changed. The change must have been in me. I am interpreting the words in a different way. I am seeing the ideas in a different way. I have a different perspective.

Each one of us sees the world differently. Confined in our physical frame we each see the world from our own location. No two of us can be at exactly the same place at the same time in this three-dimensional world of matter. We gaze out at the things around us and we interpret what we see in terms of those things we have seen before and that we recognise.

The physical form with which we are all most familiar, from our earliest moment in this world, is the human form. That familiarity is perhaps the explanation for the frequent reports of folk seeing a human form or face in cloud formations, stones, even food. It would be unlikely that anyone would perceive, in some nebulous shape, a form with which they were not familiar. We cannot easily conceive that of which we have no experience. The mind appears to attempt to make what we see fit with what we expect to see, with that which is familiar to it.

So familiar and comfortable are we with the human form that some seem to have a desire to make other creatures conform more closely to that form. Some think it a good idea to dress their tiny canines in clothes of a type more normal for humans. Others think this an abomination. The differences in view are not based on different physical standpoints, but upon some other difference in perception.

As we gaze out from our physical frame at the world around us, each becomes a judge. Each has a perception of what they consider 'good' and 'bad', 'desirable' and 'undesirable', 'pleasant' and 'unpleasant', 'right' and 'wrong'. We each consider our own judgments to be correct. Yet how do we form those opinions? Are we consistent in the way we process information about what we see?

As time passes there appears to be an increasingly widely accepted view that the animals we exploit for food, clothing and companionship should be protected. But what aspect of their existence is it that we wish to protect, and from what? Any who have seen the Wild White Cattle of Chillingham in the northeast of England will be well aware that cattle are not naturally the dozy creatures with massive, ungainly udders that we often see grazing in the fields. The Chillingham Cattle are essentially wild, untouched by human hand. A glimpse of them is perhaps a glimpse of the cattle of the past, elegant beasts living in their family groups, bulls and cows together. Is it not appropriate to allow our domesticated creatures to live a life more akin to that of their wild cousins?

Take another look at the Chillingham Cattle. Many have the scars of battle. Some have lost an eye. Fights between bulls are common. None is treated should they fall ill. To treat them would be to handle them. They would no longer be wild. Doubtless many folk would rush to complain should they see a farm animal being 'allowed' to gore another, or see it bleeding in a field. But it is quite natural, essential, for those beasts in their near wild state. What is the difference between man's help and man's interference? Is it a matter of perspective?

Each of us forms an opinion of what we see. Some tend to focus on the positive, those things they consider 'good', 'desirable', 'pleasant' and 'right'. Some focus on the negative, 'bad', 'undesirable', 'unpleasant' and 'wrong'. Some take the 'good' with the 'bad'. Some seem to go through this life taking little notice of anything. Which are you? When you choose to speak with others, is it the positive or the negative that fills most of your discussions? Why?

Before we take those first, tentative steps to explore the unfamiliar, we might benefit from attempts to understand how we experience and interpret the familiar, those things we see around us and experience every day, and consider what effect we might have on those things around us, intentionally or unintentionally. We might then be better placed to comprehend the unfamiliar, should we encounter it, better able to distinguish between the thing we are perceiving and the impression of it that we might try to create based on our prior experiences and understanding. It may assist us to understand how we might be influencing what we see. If our mind persists in trying to force shapes and thoughts and ideas into the straitjackets of what is familiar to us, we might have some difficulty in assimilating the unfamiliar.

Our perception, even of the familiar physical world, is not always straightforward. We look out at the physical world from the limits of our three-dimensional bodies. We see the solid world around us and we see the solid things that inhabit that place. Largely, we see what we expect to see based on our prior experiences. We do not always perceive it quite as it is. Most of us know the stars are not fixed on the inside surface of a sphere that surrounds our world. They are not all the same distance from us. Yet, as we gaze at those constellations familiar to us, do we not tend to see a two dimensional array? We see the layout of the stars much as we would see them in a book, even though our mind knows that is not the physical reality.

We look at those things around us and we study them. We try to understand the things we see and we try to explain them and depict them in such ways as we can.

The scientist depicts aspects of the world and the cosmos through the medium of equations. Some claim that, because they can depict aspects of the cosmos in this way, because it appears to have some order, there is no basis for the mysteries and religions, there can be no divinity. Others disagree.

The artist depicts the things around us in oil, or pastels, or chalk. The artist does not profess knowledge of the validity of religions and beliefs simply because he can depict the world and skies in some way other than in the form in which it is usually perceived.

It has long been known by man that aspects of the space in which we live appear mechanical in nature. Much of what we believe to be important to us is predictable. We know when the Sun will rise and when it will set. We know when tides will be high and when they will be low. We know when the stars will be in a particular position in the skies. We know that spring will follow winter.

It has long been known that aspects of the space in which we live can be depicted or described by numbers and equations. Sometimes those equations and numbers have been used to explain or predict those things that are conceivable and understandable to some extent by all of us, such as the movement of the objects in the skies around us. Sometimes those equations and numbers have been used in an effort to explain or convey ideas of things that are outside normal comprehension.

Equations are used by modern scientists and engineers in their work. That work is esoteric in that it is not understood by all. The symbols and manipulation of figures in science and engineering allows the adept in those areas to calculate, with varying degrees of accuracy, the particular aspect of the physical world with which that adept is involved. The symbols in those equations are effectively shorthand. They represent, for example, some type of force, form or constant. When numbers appear in the scientist's or engineer's equation, they usually represent a quantity or an amount of something. The number is not representing a physical thing. It is a symbol to represent an aspect of something else.

Numbers and symbols are used as easily understandable representations of something else. They can also be used as a stepping stone to help in making the unfamiliar more understandable to us, a stepping stone between the familiar and the unknown.

The use of numbers persists, to a greater or lesser extent, in most modern belief systems, though arguably at a lower level than was the case with earlier traditions. The Gnostics and Pythagoreans, amongst others, perceived number relationships in the tangible and the intangible. Much that was written by such thinkers was destroyed by folk who thought the ideas wrong, but such as does remain seems to suggest that numbers were used not only to describe quantity but also in an attempt to describe that which was inconceivable and impossible to describe using the words and images generally applied in the exoteric world. Each number was understood to have a reality of its own. It was a way in which the human mind could attempt to understand or know that which it was not currently equipped to conceive.

Unity was the divine number. The further one moves from Unity, the less perfect is the number and all it represents, and the closer one moves to form, to the material. The closer one approaches Unity, the more difficult it is to perceive, understand and know. All else emanated from that One. There was no beginning and end, so some numbers were conceived of as circular or spiral. All goes through a number of cycles/incarnations and all returns to Unity. All can be represented by the numerals of 1 to 10. Greater numbers can be reduced to those numbers. So 10, 100 and 1000 were all reflections of Unity, conditions of return after each cycle, similar conditions, but not quite identical. Finally there is a return to the first Unity, though there has been a connection throughout, by virtue of all emanating from that Unity.

That might ring bells with those familiar with the symbolism of the Qabalah. Ten Sephiroth are arrayed on the Tree of Life. The Tree of Life exists in each of the four worlds of Assiah, Yetzirah, Briah and Atziluth. The ten Sephiroth on each Tree are the same 1 to 10 but, at the same time, they are different. Each Sephirah has a different nature in each of the four worlds, from the material world of Assiah to the divine world of Atziluth. Whilst the nature of each Sephirah on each Tree of Life might be considered, or meditated on, in isolation, each is part of a whole, the sum of all the Sephiroth in all four worlds together being Unity. Sometimes it is suggested that the four Trees may be visualised arrayed vertically, each interlocking with the one above. This forms a ladder that can be used to climb from concepts of the material world, arguably those most easily grasped by the human mind, through ever more abstract ideas in an effort to achieve understanding of the whole.

In the above thought systems, numbers and geometric shapes are used to aid the mind in reaching outside its usual limits, to conceive of what it has no prior remembered experience.

Our familiarity with our current existence, physically constrained within our three-dimensional frames is arguably the principal impediment to our ability to think outside that form and to think of things coexisting, or existing in the absence of space or time. We tend immediately to think of the limits of three-dimensional space and time as we generally conceive it. It is hard to envisage more than one thing being/existing, unless each is separated from others by space or time.

The Cosmic Doctrine is, I believe, aimed principally at assisting us in developing the ability to think outside the limits to which our thoughts and understanding are currently limited, and to comprehend something of that which we would normally consider unknowable.

Those often repeated words "These images are designed to train the mind, not to inform it", reflect that idea.

Some initial concepts in *The Cosmic Doctrine* are described in terms that seem readily understandable to our minds. We can visualise Discs and Rings, Circles and Rays and Vortices and we visualise them in the context of the dimensions and progression of time with which we are most familiar. We can imagine progression, travelling out from a centre along the rays, passing through the circles on the way and back again, spiralling back and forth until returning to the centre and finding that centre to be the one we left, but changed in consequence of the developments within the system as a whole.

We can visualise these things in terms of the physical concepts with which we are familiar, but I suspect we are not intended to hang on too hard to those simple shapes and movements. Rather those images are a spring board to attempt to perceive thoughts and ideas outside our previous experience. The intention is for us to move on from that to consider how such concepts might be in a dimensionless, timeless state, and how they might come to be, to determine where we are in that system, and where we might want to be.

It is perhaps our relatively 'advanced' state in evolution that makes these concepts difficult. We are used to learning through the medium of the spoken or written word. We are used to the written word being intended to be taken at face value (though a brief comparison of "the truth" represented in a sample of any day's newspapers may cast doubt on the validity of that). We are unused to encountering allegory and symbolism in our everyday lives.

Perhaps those who went before us had something of an advantage there. A brief look at the ideas of the philosophers of the High Middle Ages shows how adept they were at assimilating new concepts. As eastern ideas became translated into Latin, so the thinkers of the time were presented with ideas quite alien to them. Some assimilated them readily enough and found ways to integrate them with previously existing understanding and knowledge.

Those who could read and had the time and means to obtain copies of the written tales of the time would be wholly familiar with the concept of allegory. Almost all stories of the age were allegorical in nature. De Lorris and de Meun's *The Romance of the Rose* is a fine example of the use of allegory, the two authors showing rather different levels of subtlety.

Those who could not read would be likely to be exposed to tales told round the fire. Many such tales would be likely to be packed with archetypes and allegory, still available to us, should we choose to look, in the folk tales that have come down to us. Most folk at that time would have been used to visual representations. Ideas of heaven and hell and the bible stories were depicted in glorious colour on the walls of the churches. Should the churchgoers draw themselves from the gossip to be had and the deals to be made with their neighbours as they gathered in the church, they may hear the words resonating from the other end of the building. Those words would be incomprehensible to most, Latin words. They had no idea of the meaning yet they knew them to carry some power.

Most folk at that time lived close to the land. They saw the turn of the seasons. They knew one poor season could be their ruin. They knew of the need to care for the land, to be a part of it. They may well have been a step closer than us to being able to conceive of what Dion Fortune intended when referring to 'the Planetary Being'. It may have been a little easier for them to see past the purely physical.

Our forefathers were more familiar with a world of images, symbols and allegory than most of us. In that respect, some might have been more able to assimilate and comprehend esoteric ideas.

In general, we have more time to pursue such matters than those who went before. Unfortunately, it seems we may have lost much of our ability to assimilate abstract ideas. We are aware of the turn of the seasons but we are, perhaps, more likely to mock the inaccuracy of the weather forecasters' predictions than take a serious interest in the potential impact of the weather on our livelihoods.

When weather related problems do arise, deluges engulfing homes built on flood plains, or travel at a standstill because of inappropriate winter precautions, many appear to react as though surprised at the potential impact of the seasons on our lives. Perhaps most folk see their wellbeing more closely related to the cost of a barrel of oil than the turn of the seasons (though folk responsible for getting offshore rigs on station, and keeping them there, will be well aware of the importance of the seasons and the weather).

We should not expect to be able to comprehend readily the unfamiliar if we are not aware of the way we perceive the things around us in our everyday lives. A little time spent taking a look at our surroundings, the 'good' and the 'bad', and coming to terms with our places in it, can give a sound base from which to launch our quest to understand those things less familiar to us.

Once we understand where we are and how we see those things around us, we might start to exercise our minds with the less familiar. All of us are familiar with the depiction of the three dimensional world in two dimensions. At the simplest level it might be a photograph, an idle doodle or some great masterpiece. More complex representations are used by the likes of the geologist and crystallographer, depicting directions and planes in two dimensions so they can make records of the orientation of features, from the clearly visible, to the atomic scale. Simple exercises based on thinking of the representation of the three-dimensional in two dimensions may make our comprehension a little more flexible, a little more able to negotiate the steps to conceive those things of which we have no prior experience.

Imagine a direction in space, a line in space. Imagine a sphere sitting on that line so the line runs through the centre of the sphere. Imagine that you had to draw what you are imagining. The drawing would be a circle with a spot at some location within it, corresponding to where the line emanates from the sphere on the side nearest to you. The line becomes a spot within a circle but that symbol has all the information required to determine the precise direction of the line that you imagined.

Think of a plane, a surface, in space. Imagine a sphere placed so the plane cuts through the centre of a sphere. Consider the shape made on the surface of the sphere where the plane passes through it. Imagine how you would draw the sphere and plane on a piece of paper. The plane becomes a curve within a circle, yet that simple two dimensional symbol again gives all the details necessary to describe the orientation of the plane in space.

These are just very simple mind exercises but they might help the mind to think in ways it would not normally think, to make it more flexible, more able to grasp those things with which it is unfamiliar and to understand that simple symbols can be used to convey more complex ideas.

The Cosmic Doctrine is, I think, there to help us extend our ability to seek out and comprehend those things outside our current understanding, to help us find those things we might seek. It is a system of signposts, or perhaps it might better be seen as a way of servicing the mind to prepare it to attempt to travel over new terrain.

How we interpret the signposts and how we might conceive that new terrain could well differ depending on our previous experience and understanding. One person might even find quite different ideas and understanding on each rereading. Each of us develops within our own 'lifetime.' We are influenced by every experience. There is, I think, no 'right' and 'wrong' in how we interpret what we might find along the way.

The Cosmic Doctrine may help us to assimilate ideas outside our previous remembered experience. It will not tell us what to think. It might, perhaps, help us free our minds from the strictures we might unconsciously impose on it, tending to limit its scope to the readily comprehended, three-dimensional mundane, locking it inside the material human form, that with which we feel safe and comfortable.

It is not an easy read. It will not correlate readily with the familiar but it might well help you on your way. Do not seek to rely wholly on some flotation aid that has helped another on that path. What has worked for others might not work for you. What might appear to be the 'top', the 'bottom', the 'best', the 'worst', the 'easiest', the 'hardest' and so on may be quite different for different people. It does not matter. Once we know where we want to end up, we can pick our own route. If it seems we are not at a good place to start, we can try to move towards a better place. In doing that, we will have started our journey.

Bibliography

de Lorris, Guillame and de Meun, Jean, *The Romance of the Rose*, (translated by Dahlberg), 3rd edition, Princeton University Press, Princeton, 1995

Fortune, Dion, *The Cosmic Doctrine*, Red Wheel/Weiser LLC, York Beach, ME, 2000

Hopper, Vincent Foster, *Medieval Number Symbolism*, Dover Publications, New York, 2000

Kieckhefer, Richard, *Magic in the Middle Ages*, Cambridge University Press, Cambridge, 2000

Lawlor, Robert, *Sacred Geometry Philosophy & Practice*, Thames & Hudson, London, 1982

Lisle, Richard J and Leyshon, Peter R, *Stereographic Projection Techniques for Geologists and Civil Engineers*, 2nd edition, Cambridge University Press, Cambridge, 2004

Thorndike, Lynn, *History of Magic & Experimental Science*, Columbia University Press, New York, 1934

www.chillinghamwildcattle.com

3 THE LORDS OF FLAME, FORM AND MIND

GAINING A NEW RELATIONSHIP TO OUR ELDER BRETHREN AND THE BEINGS OF NATURE

JAMES NORTH

"For the earnest expectation of the creature waiteth for the manifestation of the sons of God. For the creature was made subject to vanity, not willingly, but by reason of him who hath subjected the same in hope, because the creature itself also shall be delivered from the bondage of corruption into the glorious liberty of the children of God. For we know that the whole creation groaneth and travaileth in pain together until now. And not only they, but ourselves also, which have the firstfruits of the Spirit, even we ourselves groan within ourselves, waiting for the adoption, to wit, the redemption of our body." (*Romans 8: 19-23*)

"The Lords of Mind are the Initiators of our present evolution, and as such will receive much reference in the course of these teachings. They it is, who, able to react upon all planes of manifestation, range up and down the planes, performing adjustments by exercising compensatory stresses when the faculty of epigenesis has disordered an evolution." (*The Cosmic Doctrine*)[1]

In the name of the Three who are One,
Peace!
And by the will of the King of the Elements,
Peace! Peace!
(from *Under a Dark Star* – Fiona Macleod)[2]

I. The Cosmic Doctrine and the Lords of Flame, Form and Mind

The Cosmic Doctrine's teachings about the Lords of Flame, Form and Mind remain a hidden treasure in the history of twentieth century esoteric teaching. One wonders whether Dion Fortune realised how unique and timely the teaching that she channelled would soon become.

As with *The Cosmic Doctrine* as a whole, it is possible to trace influences upon the teachings about the 'Lords.' (From here onwards, the Lords of Flame, Form and Mind will be referred to collectively as Lords.) The language and basic framework of these teachings owe much to the teachings of the Theosophy of H. P. Blavatsky, filtered through the 'Adyar' revision of Annie Besant and C. W. Leadbeater. Less obvious but perhaps more important is the influence of Qabalah, although the deep structure of the teaching about the Lords owes less to the Hermetic Qabalah of the Golden Dawn than to the deeper and more primal Jewish roots of the tradition. Finally, we must not discount the influence of her first occult teacher, Theodore Moriarty, who was very much concerned to link Eastern and Western teachings in his own Universal Theosophy.

However, if we try to read other systems into *The Cosmic Doctrine's* teaching about the Lords – including even the standard views of the so called Western Mystery Tradition and twentieth century Magical Qabalah – we will miss the essence of the text. *The Cosmic Doctrine* is not a commentary or intellectual synthesis of other systems but an original, inspired work authored by one or more spiritual entities. The best approach is to forget most of the detail of what you may have studied in other systems, and dive straight into the text. We are fortunate that the teachings about the Lords, which are mostly contained in chapters 16 to 18, with additional material in chapters 19 to 23, are exceptionally clear. Some parts of *The Cosmic Doctrine* require much 'unpacking', especially the earlier chapters, and occasionally one suspects that something was 'lost in translation' during the process of communication. But with the teachings on the Lords, all one has to do is read closely, in a state of focused meditation, and follow this through from the relationships that emerge to a more imaginative approach using certain key images. This study is fundamental to working with *The Cosmic Doctrine* as a whole, because it is the teaching about the Lords that opens up the relationship between the cosmic mysteries of the beginnings of things, and the elemental and material reality in which we live on earth.

1.1 Who are the Lords of Flame, Form and Mind?

Before discussing these beings in detail, it may be helpful to make some introductory remarks and clarifications.

⊙ The language of *The Cosmic Doctrine* is somewhat dry and technical, and often focusses on presenting clear concepts and characterisations of relationships. Yet it must be remembered that we are discussing whole classes of glorious beings who undergo their joys, sorrows, evolutionary triumphs and tragedies. We also owe an immense debt of gratitude to the work of the Lords who with the Logos are the co-creators of our planet. They are not uniform collectives, but species with their own characteristics and specialisms within each rank.

- The closest analogy to an appropriate way of thinking about them in the Western tradition is in the works of angelologists like Dionysius the Areopagite; there is also some useful material in the Jewish Qabalah and Muslim Sufism but pursuing these connections is beyond the scope of this essay.

- There is much less material directly relevant to the Lords themselves in the Magical or Hermetic Qabalah, in particular when this focuses on planetary cosmology and astral magic. It is true that the systems of magic were right to connect the planetary spheres and realms of nature in their understanding of the Hierarchies. Yet, in practice, modern ritual magic often seems to equate the planetary forces with the Archangels – based on a one-sided and materialistic understanding of the Tree of Life.

- At its extreme reduction ad absurdum, Gabriel is simply seen as a name for the energies of the Moon, and Zadkiel for Jupiter etc. This is emphatically not the case, and this belief poses dangers to magical work. Nor are the Angels merely forces waiting to be commanded by humans to meet their desires!

- The world's spiritual traditions often differ over fundamental questions: is God changeless or does the Divine change? Are the laws of nature fixed, or do they change, more like habits? Is God basically outside the universe, within it, or simply identical to it? The genius of *The Cosmic Doctrine* is that it embraces all of these creative tensions to produce a teaching that is a genuinely new, stimulating and 'initiatory' text.

- The Angelic Hierarchies bear a deep relationship with the Divine Mind, as does humanity – but this does not mean that the Angels are mere thoughts in God's mind (or human minds). Angels are not just states of consciousness, or concepts. They have an existence as objective and important to the cosmos as any other being, and are real in a higher sense even though the Divine Mind has been reduced to thoughts by philosophy, and often ignored by mystics.

⊙ The various beings which natural or passive clairvoyants may encounter in a receptive state are not usually the Angelic Hierarchies or the Lords to which *The Cosmic Doctrine* refers, but other forces, connected with the Lords, of an elemental nature. There is a deep relationship between the Hierarchies and the various involutionary beings that work in nature and the matter of the solar system, but if we cannot distinguish them we will misunderstand how evolution works, and will be unable to play our correct role on Earth.

⊙ In this sense, *The Cosmic Doctrine's* teaching about the Lords contains an urgent spiritual task that is particularly relevant at the present moment in time.

1.2 Three Ways in which we may approach understanding of the Lords through *The Cosmic Doctrine*

Because of the way in which *The Cosmic Doctrine* was transmitted, it may seem a little more abstract and disconnected from our real life concerns than is actually the case. The Lords are expounded by three complementary approaches – although the third of these is less obvious in Dion Fortune's original transcription and comes to the fore with Margaret Lumley Brown's later amplifications. These are:

1 Cosmic *a priori* meditation on the origin of things, which ultimately reduces to the relationship between the Three and the Four. Although this is not explicit in the text, the key to this approach, and the deepest understanding of the Lords and of humanity, comes through meditation on the Holy Name of God.

2 Scientific and philosophical observation of Nature which reveals the Divine Mind working in it, ultimately through the different spiritual hierarchies.

3 Contemplation of certain imaginative symbols which become keys to an inner relationship with the Lords and the principles they represent.

We will use each of these approaches, although in a slightly different order.

2. The Cosmic Doctrine's Unique Relationship to the Lords

2.1 Who are the Lords and what do they have to do with us?

Who then are the Lords? The first approach, from the perspective of the Western tradition, is that they are another term for the Angels and Archangels that are described in different systems of religion, magic and philosophy. They can also be compared to 'other world' beings, or to the myriad beings called Devas which Hindu and Buddhist esoteric teachings see as going through their own forms of evolution analogous to humanity. For present purposes, we will keep these teachings in the background and simply think of the Lords as our Divine-spiritual elder relatives. They are co-creators of our solar system along with our common ruler the Logos. And so are we.

One very natural and honest question that the casual student or even the serious devotee of the Mysteries may ask is: "Why should I care about these abstruse teachings about previous evolutions and transcendent spiritual beings. Isn't this just dry and irrelevant intellectualism?" It is highly important that we ask ourselves this. Any truly spiritual text is not given to humanity just to pique intellectual interest for armchair occultists. Unless merely produced out of the brain of a rational thinker, cosmological teachings are a projection of spiritual energies into the framework of the rational mind, sometimes even to the point of seeming like a round peg in a square hole! But the mark of spiritual contact is a deep, moral and service-oriented need, answered through revelation and sensed as such in the heart, and its ability to trigger similar realisations and actions in others.

Any serious student of the spiritual traditions of East and West will be aware that, historically, the lineages placed great store in the study of complex metaphysics, and that students were expected to absorb a great detail of cosmological theory before they might aspire to 'high voltage' practical magical or mystical work. After the preliminary work of mastering a rational spiritual framework which enabled the student to think about the Invisible and relate it to the Visible, much of the work was in study and meditation on profound and often impenetrable texts.

Experience proves that the more is put into this kind of work – whether the material is the Upanishads, Vedas and Tantras in Eastern teachings or Platonism, Qabalistic texts or Rosicrucian mysteries in the West – the more coherent and powerful any later practical work is. Whereas to simply dive into 'chakra meditations', random psychism or various rituals either produces no particularly impressive results, or dubious and counter-evolutionary ones.

Although cosmological insights may seem abstract, they are penetrations or crystallisations into the human mind of spiritual beings; by decrystallising them through meditation and imaginative contact, they can put us in contact with the Cosmic Word from which they originated. However, at the present time it is important that we learn to relate cosmological principles to the practicalities of our everyday lives: this is indeed the cutting edge of esoteric spirituality. By the end of this essay, I hope that you will have a vivid sense of the reality of the Lords of Flame, Form and Mind, initially through their effects, their residues in the world around us and, increasingly, through aspiring to contact with them in their reality.

2.2 Pleroma

One key principle present in most spiritual philosophy, but often overlooked because it is so basic, is the fullness of the cosmos. Modern humanity looks out into space and believes that (s)he sees emptiness, while the material world is full of beings. Yet from the spiritual perspective this is an upside down view of reality. The cosmos is full of spiritual beings and what appears so solid and material to us is in each case the ephemeral expression of the consciousness of a spiritual being, whether just our own or the collaboration of many others, fundamentally including the Source, whether thought of as a personal God or an Absolute.

There is a wonderful Greek word for this – Pleroma. This is usually translated simply as 'fullness' but it can carry a host of other connotations in the original Greek, including that of a ship or its crew. The Gnostics spoke of the Pleroma as the collective complement of spiritual beings that emerged from the primal source in ranks upon ranks of hierarchies, each an essential part of the spiritual cosmos.

God's spiritual work, in expression, is seen in the rainbow-like harmony of different qualities – a unified multiplicity of spirit – not just a mere dot in infinity. St. Paul, in line with John's gospel, says that "the fullness of the godhead dwelt in Jesus bodily,"[3] and we must remember that this means that the entire range of spiritual consciousness, power and memory lived in and worked through Jesus.

Meditation upon the word 'fullness' and the Cosmic Pleroma can take one a long way towards communion with the Lords.

2.3 The Laws of Physics, Chemistry and Biology

The Cosmic Doctrine's simplest teaching about the Lords of Flame, Form and Mind – a groundbreaking one – is that they are the Laws of Physics, Chemistry and Biology respectively.

In many respects this represents the culmination and re-visioning of the Platonic tradition and it forms a link in a chain going back from Plato to earlier Mysteries and forwards to the Mysteries of the future.

The earliest angelology of which we have detailed knowledge in the Western tradition is that of Zoroastrianism. In its classical form, the God of Light, Ahurah Mazdao (God of Light, Great Aura) is attended by the Six Amshaspands, who are Vohu Manah (right thought) Asha Vahishta (supreme virtue) Khshathra Vairya (desired empire), Spenta Armaiti (generous surrender), Haurvatat (health), Ameretat (immortality). These beings in turn stand above countless lesser spiritual beings in a graded hierarchy.

Zoroastrianism is a particularly important religious tradition in this context, for it is in some respects a common ancestor for the monotheisms of Judaism, Christianity and Islam, and in particular for their angelologies. Its dualism between the two beings of Ahura Mazdao and Ahriman (the Destructive Spirit) is also deeply connected with the teachings of the Ring Cosmos and Ring Chaos in *The Cosmic Doctrine* and with what Gurdjieff called the Holy Affirming and Holy Denying forces.

Thus, the Angels that accompany God are at the same time moral qualities and active concepts. Here we see an early form of a teaching that is worked out in the Qabalistic scheme of the Sephiroth, and also in Plato's World of Ideas or Forms. The average common sense thinker is likely to say: "A concept is just an idea in my head, how can it also be an Angel?" But this common sense idea is only a relatively new and unimpressive attempt by science to obscure its own origins, for all of Western science and philosophy, at least in its theoretical underpinnings, is unthinkable without Plato. From a Platonic perspective, both ordinary sense perceptions and our thoughts about them are ultimately unreal. Things are shadows of reality, and the laws we conceive are likewise shadows of shadows – or sometimes direct reflections of higher truths. In other words, 'roseness' is a quality we understand in our minds even though it doesn't exist merely as a thought in our minds. It exists in roses in the real world but it cannot be 'seen' with the eyes, so it must exist in a realm beyond that of the physical senses.

Thus the thought relationship we discern must originally have been created as living thought, and to the extent that these creative thoughts are vessels of the Hierarchies, Angels are Living Laws, who patterned in consciousness the archetypes of our earthly life. This was more or less an open secret in the Platonic and Hermetic traditions, though it was lost to academic philosophy.

Just as there are no absolute boundaries between physics, chemistry and biology, the work of the Lords of Flame, Form and Mind overlap. Likewise, *The Cosmic Doctrine* states that the result of earlier evolutions is already available to those coming later. In the same sense, the energies and matter of inorganic nature are present in living beings from plants to humans, but reworked according to the laws of biology. Human bodies only behave purely like inorganic nature when they die.

This is our first clue. The healthy approach to the Hierarchies is through life. The universal force closest to us is best contacted through Mind and its ability to structure life. Just as chemical existence has already mastered the physical, internalising its electrical and energetic properties in the creation of patterns of reaction in the earth and atmosphere, so the Lords of Form can be invoked to master the powers of the Lords of Flame. (A little thought should reveal that this is one of the basic purposes and justifications of ritual magic).

First Meditation

Let us pause and meditate on the way in which the Lords of Form have followed an evolution which already includes the results of that of the Lords of Flame, such that their laws take up those of the Lords of Form and include them in their chemical interactions. We can symbolise the Lords of Flame by fire and the Lords of Form as water and earth. So we meditate on the secret fire contained within the Stone, and the mystery of fiery water.

Likewise, biological existence has already mastered the chemical: the living body exists through respiration, various secretions, the maintenance of temperature and so on, just as the Lords of Mind can be invoked to master the forces of the Lords of Form. In human terms, there is a deep connection between consciousness and our life forces, though much of it happens in the subconscious and is aptly symbolised by the eighteenth Arcanum of the Tarot, the Moon. The connection between incipient consciousness and the biological forces of the body is also at the heart of the Biblical story of temptation of Adam and Eve by the serpent in the Garden of Eden – one meaning of which is that the patterning energies of the Lords of Mind rose from representing the forces of reproduction to become mental consciousness itself in physical beings, with all the consequence of 'good and evil' that brought.

It follows logically that it is through our own spiritual nature that the Lords of Mind's energies shall be mastered and raised up to a higher use than that left by the Lords of Mind. In this sense life is not a riddle to be solved by the mind, for Mind itself will be transmuted and assumed into a higher set of laws, those of sociology – or true HUMANITY.

We left the garden of Eden, but we shall return to the Tree of Life in the New Jerusalem.

The Lords of Mind gave individuality, the Lords of Humanity will give synthesis, and thus without losing our individuality we shall be united in one Being. The prototype of this experience in the Bible is the event of Pentecost, and its outworking is pictured in the Book of Revelation. We shall have a better idea of what this has to do with cosmology by the end of this article.

If the reader wants to take the slow but sure path to the Lords, (s)he could simply immerse him or herself in the teachings of physics, chemistry and biology and at each stage offer up this scientific meditation to the higher consciousness through meditating along the lines suggested above. Ultimately this will give rise to a kind of updated alchemical philosophy. But we should remember that things must be understood backwards. If we try to start from basic physics, we will be seeing things upside down; we will be using our own minds but without having understood and mastered them. Instead we must start from our humanity, working back through biology, chemistry and physics and seeing all life as the product of Spirit. But not the illusory projection of our own spirit of course – life in our world is a symphony of the creative work of countless spiritual beings.

This means that spiritual teachings, philosophy, contemplation and an intuitive approach to life are essential. Materialistic science is fundamentally an evasion of the nearest knowledge available to us – that of ourselves, the light we are and through which we see.

3. The Cosmic Doctrine's deeper Teachings about the Lords

3.1 Self-Knowledge as the True Gateway to Knowledge of Hierarchy
When meditating on the Lords it is important to remember that we are essentially the same kind of being. In the scheme of evolution that *The Cosmic Doctrine* presents, the Logos whose physical image and manifestation is the Sun, is the ultimate ruler of our solar system. We exist in only one particular solar system of all those that exist on the physical plane of the Cosmos – the so called seventh and lowest Cosmic Plane. There are innumerable other solar systems in physical reality, and *The Cosmic Doctrine* assures us that there are many others on subtler planes of the Cosmos, nearer the Central Stillness. Yet our deepest essence, as human beings, is no different to that of the Solar Logos itself. The Solar Logos has formed His system to realise, know and express Himself and in doing that he calls into service many of the lesser Divine Sparks that were also born in the Cosmic phase of evolution. As He forms his system, He recapitulates in many respects His own Cosmic experience and memory (although it may be called subconscious by analogy with the human subconscious mind). So it is that, as 'swarms' of Divine Sparks are released into the originally unformed basis of the solar system, their work, evolution, relationships with each other and with the Logos reflect the earlier stages of Cosmic 'time' (which is no time as we understand it).

Thus our Solar Logos exists on the seventh Cosmic plane, which is the furthest from the Central Stillness and therefore the densest, most formed and solid Cosmic plane. Likewise, we will see that our Logos forms seven planes (which may be called sub-planes of the seventh Cosmic plane) and sends forth seven swarms of Divine Sparks. It is the first three of these swarms that *The Cosmic Doctrine* calls The Lords of Flame, The Lords of Form and The Lords of Mind.

Study of different passages of *The Cosmic Doctrine* may give the impression that humanity is the fourth swarm, or the seventh, or collectively the fourth through to the seventh. In fact, these are all valid interpretations that do not really contradict each other, but in this essay we shall think of humanity as archetypally the fourth swarm including the remaining three.

As the Lords undertake their evolution they in turn are shaping the solar system, creating a system of seven 'planets'. Confusingly, *The Cosmic Doctrine* numbers the *planets* in the same way as the Cosmic planes, that is from the first planet which is the subtlest, to the seventh which is the densest, but it numbers the *sub-planes*, i.e. the actual planes of the solar system in which we exist, from 7 to 1. That is to say the first planet is on the seventh plane, the second planet on the sixth plane, right through to our Earth which is the seventh planet on the first plane! The reason for this is doubtless that most of us are conscious (or perhaps better, self conscious) on the first plane of our solar system which is the physical world, and it requires us to raise our consciousness through successive stages to reach the seventh plane. Divine manifestation occurs from above downwards, but human evolution occurs from below upwards.

In line with the teachings of Theosophy, particularly Adyar Theosophy, the highest three planes are those of the so called Individuality and may be termed Spiritual Will, Intuition and Higher Mind (sometimes called Atma, Buddhi and Manas which are terms slightly adapted from traditional Indian metaphysics). Dion Fortune related these to the Abstract Spiritual, Concrete Spiritual, and Abstract Mind. We have all had experience of Oneness, spiritual conscience and higher thinking that goes beyond the rational brain – these are experiences of our Individuality. The remaining four planes of concrete intellect, higher emotions, lower emotions (or instincts) and the physical make up the personality.

The Divine Sparks that went forth from the Logos in swarms develop in the first place as Individualities and only secondly as Personalities. This is of course the basis of the doctrine of reincarnation, and reorientation to the spiritual path and the way of Initiation requires us to clearly distinguish our intuitive realisations and higher aspirations from our instincts and our rational thoughts, and to bring the former into harmony with the latter.

Having gone forth later than the first three swarms, humans represent a more complex and thus less primal form of force than the earlier evolutions. Yet though we are younger, less evolved and at times seemingly something of a disgrace to our Divine origin, it is absolutely true that we are the same kind of being.

This means that the first and best approach to the Lords is through self-knowledge. One only really understands a family when one sees its different members, and can recognise similarities and differences. Likewise we only understand mammals as a whole when we know the different range of mammals from human to rodent. We are of the same Cosmic 'family' as the Lords. Such self-knowledge will be grounded in an understanding of ourselves as bodies, minds and spirits and very much rooted in a vivid realisation that the energies of previous swarms continue to work in our bodies.

3.2 Involution and Evolution, Our Solar System and the Logos

The Cosmic Doctrine gives us this very useful table which explains that each swarm goes through an evolution successively on each of the

Three Emanations of the Logos. Based on Figure 19 in *The Cosmic Doctrine* seven planets in the solar system. This is a concept from Theosophy (also found though in revised form in the teachings of Rudolf Steiner) but is quite differently developed.

The idea of involution and evolution is one of the most important teachings of Theosophy and *The Cosmic Doctrine* is broadly in line with the Theosophical idea. In simple terms, the first act of Spirit is to form increasingly dense material realms and to take them on as sheaths, becoming as it were 'buried' within them. From the inside, this corresponds to a Divine Spark having more and more concrete and graspable objective experiences, but finding its own primal light confined by more and more sheaths or 'coats of skin'. Evolution, by contrast, occurs when we have gained the essential experience of material existence and progressively slough off our inclinations and any sense of needing to continue having the same kind of experiences.

Each of the seven planets has a special relation with one of these 'coats', although each of the seven planets is in time clothed with substance of each of the seven sub-planes. Thus, just as the human being has seven 'bodies', so does each of the seven planets. For example, Mars is essentially a planet of the second sub-plane of instincts, the more concrete emotions of defence, attack, sex and self preservation, although it has each of the seven kinds of 'matter' in its planetary aura.

The Cosmic Doctrine also shows that the Lords of Flame have a special relationship with the highest two planes of Spirit, the Lords of Form with the Emotions and Instincts, and the Lords of Mind (unsurprisingly) with the planes of Mind.

This shows that Humanity (who will one day be called Lords of Humanity) have their own special relationship with the earth plane itself. In addition, we can see that:

⊙ The results of each planet resonate on each planet of the solar system.
⊙ Earth is the master planet for the physical matter throughout the solar system.
⊙ Humanity's special evolutionary role is to do with the Earth itself.

As even its name suggests, humanity is very much a being of earth, of physical form. This is anything but a lowly or unspiritual calling. For our Solar Logos is a being on the seventh Cosmic plane and thus the seventh planet corresponds directly to His own Cosmic existence. As He is to the Cosmos, so we are to Him in the solar system.

Dion Fortune was always at great pains to emphasise the special and paradoxical closeness of the highest and lowest Sephiroth of the Tree of Life, Kether and Malkuth. *The Cosmic Doctrine* justifies this, and as we shall go on to see, sheds new light upon it.

[NB – The order and correspondence of the planets and planes may seem strange although it bears a certain relationship to the esoteric scheme given by Blavatsky and used as the basis for her esoteric school.]

3.3 The Relationship between Spiritual and Elemental Forces

For clarity of expression, and also to avoid getting too near the chaotic aspects of evolution, we can assume that the Lords have largely completed their 'round' of solar evolution, have worked through the involutionary and evolutionary experiences possible on the seven planets based on their own potentialities and the work done by previous swarms, and have reunited with the Logos, contributing all that they have learned and experienced to the Logos as a basis for further evolution.

The Lords of Flame gave the basic energetic structures of each planet – its subtle forces, lines of power, potentials – and also work on the later swarms of divine sparks.

The Lords of Form gave it its shape, its basic physical characteristics and reactive tendencies

The Lords of Mind developed freedom and reflective Mind on the planets, thus bestowing individuality.

The Cosmic Doctrine very sensibly tells us that it will focus on the effects of Cosmic evolution on our own Earth planet, which makes it much easier to understand the Lords in terms of our own experience. For we must understand that although the Lords originated the laws of nature on each planet including Earth, they do not continue to direct and express what happens on a given planet, because when their evolution on each is complete they move on, eventually to reunite with the Logos. Instead, their will and intention continues to be expressed as 'laws of nature' on each planet through their creation of elemental beings. Thus, the beings that live in and directly bring about every physical, chemical and biological process on earth are not the Lords themselves, but their children, the "creations of the created" as Dion Fortune liked to call them.

This is one of the most important aspects of the teachings and a whole book could easily be written about elemental beings and *The Cosmic Doctrine's* teachings in relation to other systems. Suffice it to be said that the Western magical tradition generally talks only about the four classes of beings who live in and through the four elements, namely the Salamanders of Fire, Sylphs of Air, Undines of Water and Gnomes of Earth. Yet in the strict sense, these are only one particular part of the totality of elemental beings that exist even in our world. This is often ignored in spiritual teaching because 'involution' is such a complex and potentially dangerous area of teaching. Yet it is essential to realise that we have absolutely nothing to do directly with the Lords of Flame, Form or Mind in the normal functioning of the planet, which is simply the reverberation of their creative work in the continued reactions of the elementals, who are like projected thought-forms of the Lords.

In fact, it must be pointed out that for many centuries people had increasingly less to do directly with the Lords, and this was part of humanity's evolutionary journey. However, the seeming absence of the Lords from our normal experience and the awakening of an interest in the primal and elemental aspects of our planet and its subtle energies creates a dangerous moment in evolution.

One of the prophetic purposes of the Communicator behind *The Cosmic Doctrine* was to prepare Initiates and those of dedication to meet the challenge of the chaotic unleashing of the elemental energies of our world, as we shall see later.

3.4 Evolution of the Lords within the solar system as a clue to their role on Earth

The Cosmic Doctrine's description of the involution and evolution of the swarms is, to my knowledge, unique in all occult literature. Whilst it is perhaps closest in spirit to Rudolf Steiner's Occult Science, it goes one better than that. The *way* in which each swarm experiences its evolution is unique and bears the stamp of its analogue in the Cosmos. Let us start by reflecting on the polarity of the Lords of Flame and the Lords of Form.

- ◉ **Lords of Flame** – proceed and return as it were in a line, going slowly, building up the Group Mind of each Planet.

- ◉ **Lords of Form** – focus essentially on the material envelope of each planet.

The first evidence of their characteristic behaviour occurs when the Lords of Flame have descended from the sixth plane and its planet (Jupiter) to the fifth (Mercury). At this point the Lords of Form have proceeded to the sixth Plane and the Lords of Mind enter onto evolution on the seventh (the Sun). The effect of being 'surrounded', as it were, by these evolutions causes the Lords of Form to shed their envelopes of matter of the seventh and sixth planes and to return to the Logos.

We can see how simplicity and progress are the hallmarks of the Lords of Flame whereas cyclical formation and dissolution are typical of the Lords of Form. We may reflect on the teaching of "the Lamb that was slain before the beginning of the world" – the primal sacrifice described in many creation myths. Lords of Form labour constantly to build up form, yet their work is repeatedly shattered – although this is to the good as their experience is repeatedly returned to the Logos.

The Lords of Mind have quite a different experience, self contained in a way that (as we shall see) reflects the Ring Pass-Not. The evolution of the Lords of Flame is slow because they have to do the primal work of structuring and impulsating the solar system; the Lords of Form go through the repeated experience of forming and shedding their bodies of matter. The Lords of Mind, however, have benefited from the evolutionary work of the previous swarms and thus on each planet they have surplus time where they no longer need to coordinate themselves with the outer evolution, but can thrive inwardly. *The Cosmic Doctrine* gives this the telling term epigenesis, thus connecting to early debates in the theory of evolution. In the materialistic philosophy of the late nineteenth century, mind itself was sometimes regarded as a mere 'epiphenomenon' of matter. Although this is a distortion, it suggests the sense in which mind can prefigure, overrun and surpass the physical necessities of its environment. Mind ramifies and convolutes in the most fascinating ways, like a tree which, having reached the limit of its necessary growth, enfolds and seeks ever new possibilities of growth.

This tendency to being self contained and not directly affected by the prime impulse of the Lords of Flame is a distant echo of the Ring Pass-Not's tendency to be drawn into a spherical motion by the action of the Ring Chaos. This is shown in the characteristic moment in which, when the Lords of Flame are returning from their deepest experience of materiality and return from the seventh planet (Earth), they meet the Lords of Form on the sixth planet (Mars). There, the Lords of Flame and Lords of Form have their first and seminal meeting from the point of view of the solar system. The Lords of Flame are fully aware of this meeting, now being on the evolutionary arc, although the Lords of Form are not aware of this encounter with the Lords of Flame until the end of their period on this planet, after which they progress to Earth to reach the nadir, while the Lords of Flame press on to the fifth planet (Venus). At this point the Lords of Mind *leave* the fifth planet to move on to the sixth planet and so, according to *The Cosmic Doctrine*, they never meet the Lords of Flame.

3.5 How have humans come into contact with the Lords? (and why don't more of us?)

As we have seen, the purpose of each swarm is not to linger on a planet when it has completed its evolution, but to press onwards until it reunites with the Solar Logos. Our sense that the world is predictable, a world of rules rather than endless supernatural miracles, is a testament to the formative intelligent work that the Lords have done on each sphere.

In the normal run of things on the return phase of the evolutionary arc, each of the swarms is likely to move ever further away from physical natural evolution. And this has crucial consequences for humanity's relationship with them. To begin to grasp this, let us consider the question "how do we come into contact with the Lords?" To approach this vital matter, we can divide the traditional means of contact with them into three broad categories.

1 By invoking their power to have some effect on visible nature, or on our own human existence in the Earth sphere.
2 By entering the Sea of the Spirit and experiencing various states of consciousness, which in reality make contact with the Lords inevitable (though not necessarily conscious).
3 By perceiving them directly through various forms of psychic vision.

- ⊙ The first way is that of Ceremonial Magic and the post-Renaissance Magical Qabalah.
- ⊙ The second is, broadly speaking, that of Yoga, Mysticism and Mystical Theology.
- ⊙ The third is that of natural clairvoyance, especially the traditional clairvoyance possessed by many ancient peoples.

We stated above that the golden key to communion with the Lords is the unflinching quest for Self-knowledge and a desire to serve. However, human beings are by nature one-sided and tend to show a bias for one of the three primary 'Rays', and this poses dangers:

Ceremonial Magic – the great danger in the ceremonial approach to the Lords is that we regard them, unconsciously or even consciously, as a kind of natural or blind force that we can manipulate. Say the correct 'words of power', draw certain sigils and work certain rites, and the Angelic beings will 'automatically' stop what they are doing and direct spiritual power to help us achieve our worldly ends!

As well as being essentially blasphemous, it is all too easy to miss having any actual contact with the Lords on this path. Many magicians do not develop sensitivity to levels beyond the Astral/Yetziratic so it is understandable they do not distinguish between the Lords and psychic/psychological forces of will or elemental energy. Even worse, Ceremonial can embody the intent to block out and replace the forces of Grace and Angelic radiation streaming from above, turning the Earth into a prison of magic and the lesser human will.

The Western way had a strong bias to magic, and a deep calling to work in and to transform the material world. Thus it built in extensive safeguards against the kind of dangers mentioned above. However, the lack of direct contact with the Angels was a notable feature of latter-day magic. Ritualists from at least the time of John Dee often made use of mediums whose clairvoyance would substitute for their own lack of receptivity, although one of the most noticeable and progressive features of the Golden Dawn was the role assigned to scrying and travelling in the spirit vision. Dion Fortune knew of these techniques, and that of 'rising on the planes'; however, I would argue that the theory and practice of her work took spiritual contact to a much higher (or deeper) level than that of the Golden Dawn.

Ascent of Consciousness – a much more direct way to come into contact with the Lords inwardly is through various forms of Yoga and meditation enabling the ascent of consciousness. The more purely this approach is followed, the less it is concerned with power or objective manifestations, and the more with inwardly experienced states of pure consciousness.

Perhaps the most developed examples of this way in the East and the West are Buddhism and the Platonic tradition which both developed a clear philosophy which, as a counterpart to meditative ascent, showed the clear link between meditative ascent and states of consciousness and discernment. Buddhism describes a series of *Jhanas* or experiences of *Dhyana* (according to tradition and terminology) which are not in the first instance bodies or material planes, but progressively refined states of consciousness. Likewise, Plotinus' Platonism is very much one of elevation of consciousness through Soul and Intellect to The One. (If we have spoken of Buddhist meditation rather than of Raja Yoga this is not to imply any lack in Hindu Yoga, but simply because the link between Buddhism and Neoplatonism is particularly suggestive, historically and spiritually.)

This approach became foundational to Christian angelology through the work of Dionysius the Areopagite, later developed by such geniuses as St Thomas Aquinas and St Bonaventure. For example, Bonaventure's work *The Triple Way* (*De Triplici Via*) explains that humanity may experience the Hierarchies in the path of purification, illumination and union in the process of progressive approach to the absolute Truth that is God.

- The first Hierarchy of Angels, Archangels and Archai (or Principalities) are specially connected with the work of purification.
- the second Hierarchy of Powers, Mights and Dominions (Exusiai, Dynameis, Kyriotetes) with illumination.
- the third Hierarchy of Thrones, Cherubim and Seraphim with perfection.

It can be seen that this scheme has many similarities with *The Cosmic Doctrine* and with Qabalist tradition. In particular, the scheme of a 3 × 3 manifestation of the spiritual world, deriving from Dionysius the Areopagite and the Neoplatonic tradition, is closely linked with the Sephirothic scheme of the Tree of Life. However, whereas the Tree is particularly useful for charting the descent into manifestation of the Divine Qualities, Bonaventure's scheme emphasises the process of ascent, which is why he calls the lowest Hierarchy and that closest to humanity the 'first Hierarchy', whereas it can be called the 'third Hierarchy' in descending process of emanation from the Source.

The Triple Way explains that such practices as prayer, study and preaching involve work in the realm of the first Hierarchy: this bears a close relationship to *The Cosmic Doctrine*'s teachings about the realm of the Lords of Mind.

To enter the domain and develop the faculties appropriate to working with the second Hierarchy, we must develop the more emotional qualities of veneration, zeal and selflessness. This gives a clue to the way in which the realm of the Lords of Form should be approached.

However, the realm of the third Hierarchy can only be reached through qualities of sacrifice, ecstatic contemplation and fiery spiritual love. These again are the inner qualities that fit one to draw near to the Lords of Flame. (The interested reader will find more information on medieval Christian angelology and its deep links with the Qabalah in the anonymous work *Meditations on the Tarot*).[4]

For present purposes, I suggest that we consider the Lords of Flame as equivalent to the 'third' and highest hierarchy of the Seraphim, Cherubim and Thrones; The Lords of Form to the 'second' hierarchy of Dominions, Virtues, Powers; and the Lords of Mind to the 'first' and lowest hierarchy of Principalities, Archangels and Angels. (There are other patterns or resonances, each of which has its use, but this is the simplest.)

The point to grasp about this way of developing consciousness is that the Yogi or the Mystic may be raised through successive elevations and yet have no incentive to have psychic meetings with particular Angelic beings, let alone to invoke their powers to make positive changes to the Earth sphere. The mystic is focused on becoming increasingly one with the Divine – becoming like an Angel inwardly – why would they wish to spend time talking with Angels about their particular tasks? The mystic may become so enamoured by his Father (or perhaps his inner self who he may believe to be his 'Father') that he risks forgetting his myriad brothers and sisters – yet they are just as important to the Father as he. The path can become all 'Vertical' without the 'Horizontal' of God's creation as a whole.

One can see that this mystical approach has the opposite danger to the Ceremonial approach, namely that we lose interest in the material world and God's creation as a whole. Mysticism can become a drunken revelling in the dissolution of barriers and the 'oceanic' feeling of oneness. This is why the great Mystical teachings of East and West keep intellectual work and often hard physical labour as part of the spiritual life.

Buddhism, Neoplatonism and Western angelology thus have the effect of linking with the Hierarchies through states of understanding, not just nebulous spiritual bliss. The way to spirit is through the Mind, and as mind has gradually become a property of most of the human race and represents humanity's current 'centre of gravity' spiritually speaking, this means that the Mystical-spiritual approach to the hierarchies has remained open as a general – rather than esoteric – path to Angelic awareness, when the other two have largely closed. We will see why that is, in considering the third traditional path. However, it must be remembered that a danger on this path is that of forgetting the reality of the Spiritual World, and this is one reason why Hermetic Qabalah is still so valuable; it is a philosophy "of the three parts of the wisdom of the whole world" as the Emerald Tablet of Hermes Trismegistus has it.

Natural and Objective Clairvoyance or Psychism

For many people, the most direct way in which to come into contact with spiritual beings is simply to have met them in the normal run of life. This may happen spontaneously in a state of absorption, light trance or day dreaming, or even in the dreams of the night. Instead of tuning the consciousness through Yoga or tuning the intent through magic and occult science, we simply become receptive to hidden aspects of reality. It is clear that ancient human beings had these experiences much more often than modern people, and to this day urban and intellectual individuals tend to have less of them than those that live according to the slower rhythms of the countryside and traditional life.

However, the challenge here is that as the centuries have passed, fewer and fewer people have met the Angels or gods (there is some overlap between these categories). As explained above, this is partly a consequence of the Lords themselves hastening to complete their evolution in the solar system and partly through changes in human consciousness and our particular work on Earth. As we survey recorded history, we can see that Angelic consciousness receded, until people were at most aware of the elemental beings behind nature and human souls. Sometimes, the attempt to contact these forces in the old way led to meetings with dark or chaotic beings.

Humanity's business, having turned the nadir, is to look up to the Hierarchies, not to pursue them in the old and indirect fashion. This is best done through in-depth study of the descriptions of the Lords in *The Cosmic Doctrine* and through means we will introduce at the end of this article.

In this context, it is fascinating to note that most of the vast explosion of material about Angels that is rife in the New Age derives essentially from the second generation of Theosophical material, the Adyar revision of Besant and Leadbeater and all those authors it influenced, which was vastly concerned with Involutionary beings. These are without doubt real beings, but it is absolutely clear that they are not the Angels of the Western tradition nor are they the Agnishvattas of Eastern Theosophy. They are various forms of elemental being, thought-forms projected by the Lords or sometimes even by humanity. (We cannot here go into Faery evolution, which is a different and complex matter.)

In other words, the danger here is that the passive or earth-fixated psychic thinks they are meeting Angels, but they are meeting a different kind of being. This would not necessarily be problematic except as described below; we live at a time when elemental energies are re-emerging with great force, while their Angelic parents move further away in their own evolution.

3.6 The Three Open Ways to Communion with the Lords
From the above it follows that prior knowledge of the Lords of Flame, Form and Mind through magical practice or elemental instinct is not necessarily an advantage, particularly if they have been pursued against the grain of evolution. There are and will be three paths emerging from the philosophical-yogic way, i.e. the development of the potentialities contained within our own consciousness, which anyone can follow and through which they will inevitably come into true and healthy contact with the Angelic Hierarchies, even if this contact is not at first fully conscious:

1   Scientific contemplation of nature and its laws. This must lead ultimately to the realisation that nature is not a dead machine like a clock, but is a collection of instinctive and more or less conscious reactions and patterns which ultimately derive from beings. This leads to understanding the Angels as agents of the Divine Mind.

2   A deep sense of how the energy that underlies all things is identical with the energy of our own soul and inner being. This leads, under a regular path, to understanding how the consciousness within us is one with the energy of all creation. This leads to understanding the Angels as ministers of Divine Will.

3   A therapeutic and religious feeling for how the Earth is a battlefield of sickness and health and how the indubitable divine intentions sometimes come to fruition and sometimes wither on the vine. This leads to the desire to help God through cooperation with Angelic beings so that the amoral or chaotic patterns of nature eventually will become expressions of Divine Love.

(NB these paths are not placed in order of their connection with the Lords, and ultimately they merge into one great Path).

3.7 Further Images for Meditation and Magical Approach

Before we move on to the second part of this approach to the Lords, I invite you to gather up the information *The Cosmic Doctrine* provides about the Lords and the modes of movement and evolution of each swarm, and to use the basic images the text gives as a basis for meditation. (We can elaborate very slightly, but it is for the reader to put flesh on the bones). It is advised that readers take a moment to meditate on the image given and see whether connections with the laws of physics, chemistry and biology present themselves:

Lords of Flame – radiant motion in a straight line, dynamic force, a ray of energised light.

Lords of Form – formation and dissolution of matter in an ever increasing scale – a pyramid, or stupa repeatedly built up, torn down and built higher.

Lords of Mind – epigenesis – turning and ramifying – a tree spreading, or like mistletoe growing on a tree, the growth of new life upon the old; the crystallisation of many microcosms out of one macrocosm; the nervous system; the stars reflected in a pool.

- ⊙ Note the qualitative differences between the three kinds of symbols given.
- ⊙ Note how the symbols embody the qualities of intellect, devotion and spiritual will

PART 2

4. The Cosmic Pattern and the Holy Name of God

Whether or not Dion Fortune was aware of this (I suspect she must have been, as she already had a good understanding of Qabalah in 1923/24), her communicator gave the clue to much when (s)he said: "The Ray Exemplar presiding over each evolution is a Lord of Mind, and as he is of the third evolution he will have the aspects of the earlier evolutions in his nature. Therefore while three is the prime symbol of this evolution, because its Christ is three-aspected, four is the ultimate symbol. The Trinitarian aspect is the basic, but the Tetragrammatonic is the completion. This is the clue to much".[5]

It is indeed the clue to much, though this must be taken on faith at first in studying Qabalistic theory. The relationships the Communicator has in mind are fairly evident to a student of Qabalah but there must have been original members of the Fraternity of the Inner Light who needed further elucidation, as later transmissions received through the mediumship of Margaret Lumley Brown made most of these correspondences explicit.

4.1 The Three Rings as Prototypes for the Qualities of the Lords of Flame, Form and Mind

According to *The Cosmic Doctrine*, existence begins with three kinds of motions in space, without there being any matter (as we understand it) to move. These are as we know (in the geometrical analogical language of Part One):

Ring Cosmos – a motion that goes out, ultimately returning on itself after a vast curve.

Ring Chaos – a motion at right angles to the Ring Cosmos, forming a circle which stands outside and around the Ring Cosmos and as it were checks it.

Ring Pass-Not – the result of the attractive, repulsive and containing action of the Ring Chaos on the Ring Cosmos, leading to the formation of a Sphere.

Unlike Euclidean geometry which begins with a point at the centre from which planes and solid beings are built up, *The Cosmic Doctrine* proceeds more in the fashion of Projective Geometry which Rudolf Steiner identified as a kind of mathematics that was much closer to describing the Inner Worlds of spiritual experience. Thus we begin from the periphery and a spherical turning form, and the forces generated then cast importance on the Centre of this Space – which is known as the Central Stillness.

4.2 The Semi-Heretical Theology of *The Cosmic Doctrine*

The Cosmic Doctrine says something extraordinary – and from an orthodox Christian point of view, wildly heretical – in comparing the three Rings to the doctrine of the Holy Trinity as explained in the Creed. To see how daring this was, bearing in mind that Dion Fortune was deeply involved in Christian mysticism at the time of *The Cosmic Doctrine's* transmission, consider:

if the Ring Cosmos relates to the Father
does this mean that the Ring Chaos relates to the Son?
And then the Ring Pass-Not to the Holy Spirit?

The Son, then, would be associated with forces of dissolution and the ultimate origins of evil in the Cosmos. Christ would be the denying force compared to the Father. If this idea is strange and unthinkable now, it is not hard to imagine how it would have been received in 1923.

However, if one takes the time to reflect on many metaphysical schemes, it is clear that there are two main kinds of Trinity:

1. Positive, Negative, Neutral – which spatially can refer to Top, Bottom, Middle in that order, or to Top, Middle, Bottom depending how we diagrammatise it!

1.	$+$		1.	$+$
2.	$-$		2.	∞
3.	∞		3.	$-$

This abstract scheme is similar to the family Trinities of Father, Mother and Child such as Osiris, Isis and Horus in Egypt, which has a definite application to *The Cosmic Doctrine*. It can also be represented as right, left and middle.

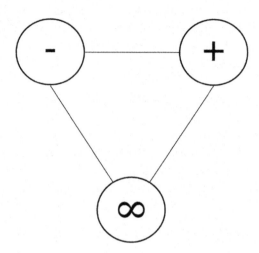

2. Source, Expansive, Contractive – this is more the connotation of the Christian Trinity and bears a relationship to the first three Sephiroth of the Tree. This is contained within the imagery of Christ and the Holy Spirit being as it were two 'hands' of the Father sometimes found in Orthodox theology.

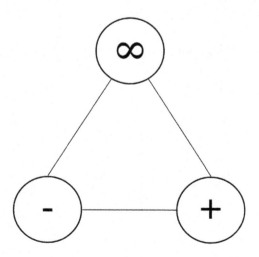

Though they are helpful if used creatively and with common sense, juggling these images intellectually can lead to mental congestion. For example, the confusion between these two kinds of scheme is one of the reasons for the expanding literature that tries to claim that the Holy Spirit is really the Mother. Be that as it may, it is worth reflecting on the heretical implications of the Communicator's theology.

Is the Word, the Son, really an opposing or chaotic force compared to Cosmos? In a way, yes, because it is a limiting form which acts as a challenge. The idea that God might have a Son was unacceptable to Muhammed for a similar reason.

Gurdjieff spoke about the three primal forces he called Holy Affirming, Holy Denying and Holy Reconciling forces in a way which bears an interesting resemblance to *The Cosmic Doctrine*. The Ring Chaos is the Holy Denying force although it emerges directly from the Ring Cosmos. One may remember that Jesus, the fiery Incarnate Christ who brought a sword to humanity, said: "None is good but God alone", a distinct pre-echo of the foundational statement of Islam: "There is no God but God." The fact of multiplicity, of the duality of form and inner spirit, and of God and Creation, underlies the tragedy of the sting of death which is prefigured by the evolutionary experience of the Lords of Form and ultimately by the Ring Chaos. Yet without it, the world could not exist.

4.3 The Advantage of Qabalistic Teaching over Exoteric Religious Imagery

As we have noted, theological thinking based on mythic images can be enlightening but it can also tie the mind up in confusions and contradictions rather than leading us directly to spiritual experience. Do we need to think of the Son, Word or Christ as actually being the same force as the Mother? Many logically minded beginners on the occult path tie themselves in intellectual knots trying to think through these issues until they realise such schemes are generally only meant to be helpful images to lead the rational mind beyond itself.

In this context the Qabalistic doctrine of the Name is perhaps more helpful.

Yod – Father
He – Mother
Vau – Son
He – Daughter

The English-speaking occult lines and the Western Mystery Tradition have largely ignored meditation on the Holy Name as represented by the 'Family' of Father, Mother, Son and Daughter, yet how suggestive it is of the imbalance in the Christian terms for the Trinity. But there are traditions that see Motherhood and Daughterhood as part of God. For example, with the addition of the Holy Spirit and what some Russian theologians have called the Holy Soul (the feminine counterpart of the Holy Spirit) we have the Most Holy Trinosophia which began to emerge in eighteenth century Rosicrucianism and was formulated in a work of this name in a famous work attributed to the Comte de Saint Germain.

This scheme represents a sequence of
1 – active
2 – passive
3 – an active kind of neutral
4 – a passive result (that will become active to a further reality)

Students of Tarot will notice that this pattern reflects the continental understanding where the second Qabalistic world, that of Creation (Beriah), relates to the suit of Cups and the element of Water.

We can see that the Name teaches that the result of the union of Yod and He is the neutral (yet male) son or Vau, but that there is a second He, a feminine child. The way in which the second He of the Name in turn becomes the Yod of a new sequence can be studied in the metaphysical literature of Hermeticism: for example, one can see this scheme worked out in perhaps pedantic detail in Papus' book on the Tarot.

If we place the first three 'persons' on the Supernal Sephiroth, this gives a rather different picture to that of Christian Qabalah which relates Kether, Chokmah and Binah to Father, Son and Holy Spirit (which thus also becomes equated, only partially correctly, to the Mother). However let us note that the Daughter, as second He, relates to Daath. The veiled teachings of Rosicrucianism speak of a fourth addition to the Holy Trinity, which they called the Persona. For Jesus Christ was not just a Cosmic archetype but a flesh and blood individual who went through a special destiny on earth as a personality. Indeed if there were no value in personality, if we were just Individuality, there would seem to be little value in incarnating at all and certainly not in reincarnating! The Personality is a Holy Mystery, yet one whose evolution is not complete. The Lords of Humanity have much to do with bringing it to completion.

4.4 How the Cosmic Archetypes manifest in the Lords

Let us synthesise various aspects of what we have learned to develop our understanding of the relationship between the Lords and the origins of Cosmos. We know that each original movement or pattern in the evolution of the Cosmos becomes the prototype for all later manifestation, even if this operates largely in the 'subconscious'.

Thus when the Logos comes to organise its own system, the first swarm to emerge, the Lords of Flame, very much have the quality of the Ring Cosmos. They press on through the solar system, forming the stresses that pattern matter, proceeding down and up the planes of manifestation. Then the Lords of Form go forth, who pattern matter which is a check and challenge to the free expression of Spirit. Finally, Intelligence is given to the solar system by the Lords of Mind who embody the affirming and denying forces of the previous swarms, building on their previous work to develop the seeds of freedom and individuality – this mirrors the primal action of the Ring Pass-Not in specifying the basic parameters of existence within the Cosmos. Returning again to our images for the Lords but seeing them in a slightly more conceptual form:

Ring Cosmos/Lords of Flame – dynamic movement in a straight line for a purpose, unimpeded and pure. Yod.

Ring Chaos/Lords of Form – matter, the seeming opposite of spirit, confining and giving shape to the formless thrust of spirit. He.

Ring Pass-Not/Lords of Mind – turning motion within parameters (usefully imagined as being of spiral nature) with the scope of individuality and every kind of free expression. Vau.

We can well illustrate the connection of the Lords with humanity by the image of the three supernal Sephiroth and Daath, but perhaps a better illustration is the triangle which can also be seen as a tetrahedron (it is well known that Daath can be seen as lying in another dimension to the rest of the Tree).

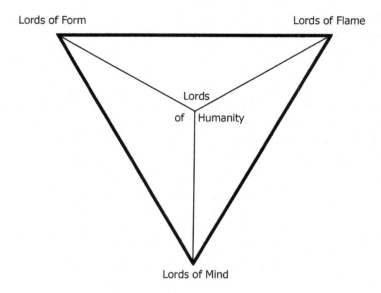

Thus in one sense humanity – or perhaps better, Divine Humanity – is the entire goal of the original system of Rings and Rays. For if the three Rings relate to the Holy Trinity, the fourth is the Central Stillness, (along with the whole system of rays, planes, tangentials, atoms and so on).

The Lords of Humanity, that is ourselves, are in a way the focus of all the work of the preceding Lords since they build the material reality which in a special sense humanity inhabits.

And this is one of the deepest symbolism meanings of Jesus Christ, the carpenter and son of a carpenter, being crucified on a wooden cross which is itself a human reformation of a tree, that prime symbol of the Lords of Mind.

5. PART 3

5.1 The Opportunity and Challenge of the Elemental or Druidical Rebirth

We have gathered enough material to begin to understand the Lords, and their relationship to humanity and the rest of nature. But we have not yet grasped the way in which we are meant to work with them and join the great co-creative work of evolution and redemption.

At this point, let us reflect on two fascinatingly prophetic passages from *The Cosmic Doctrine* which I quote at length:

> "For instance, where the Druidical cults built up their powers these powers will remain in evidence ... while this method of bathing in the mental atmosphere is valuable for adjusting the balance of the individual who is lacking in this respect it is injudicious for those who already have an overplus of it..."[6]

> "On the evolutionary arc, as he goes up the planes, man no longer looks straight to the Logos but to his immediate hierarchical superiors; but on the involutionary arc he neither looks back to the Logos, nor on towards matter, but across the diameter of the plane to his gods..."[7]

Somewhat buried in the learned terminology of early twentieth century occultism, the above thoughts contain a *serious warning*, and a task for Initiates in the stream of the Communicator. Let us ponder on another quotation which explains this further:

> "...when we touch the Earth Soul we touch its most primitive aspects first, and it is not until we have penetrated deeply into its sphere that we realise of what it is capable."[8]

In brief, it is clear that the Communicator foresaw the massive growth of the pagan revival. Importantly, despite the strong pagan influence that Dion Fortune represented, the tendency to be too preoccupied with the Earth-soul, the elementals and the past to the exclusion of the Lords and the Cosmos is uncompromisingly criticised.

There is a special resonance here in that Dion Fortune's group was establishing itself in Glastonbury in the early 1920s. At that time, Glastonbury was very much perceived as a centre of Esoteric Christianity and while Dion Fortune was personally sensitive to the Green Ray forces (as witnessed by the famous incident on Glastonbury Tor leading to the reception of the Chant of the Elements), the specific nature of the warning and challenge in these words appear genuinely prophetic because the intent to separate the elemental energies from the work of evolving in harmony with the Logos and the Lords is more obvious than the path the Communicator is advocating (and that Dion Fortune followed). The fact that this is probably due to mass disenchantment or even disgust with institutional Christianity does not make it any less tragic.

As we contemplate the magical revival of the twentieth and twenty-first century, it is important to be clear that while this naïve and basically materialistic approach to the Mind side of Nature through atavistic cults of Nature and the instincts was justifiable in the past, it is not so today, except in dealing with pathologies. However, this is no excuse for prudery or judgemental rejection, for the global imbalance in the nature forces of our planet and the associated human reaction mean that this pathology has risen in prominence. This means that there is a lot of work waiting to be done by Initiates who want to help:

> "It will thus be seen that each of the Primal Swarms, after it has achieved oneness with the Logos, performs the part of 'Compensator' or 'Counterpoise' in the work of evolution, for, with the coming in of Epigenesis, comes also the risk of developments out of harmony with the Logoidal Nature".[9]

In plain English, this means that although the Lords do not normally interfere in the day to day running of the laws of nature they established in each planet, they do have a particular mandate – in human terms one might say a duty and also the power – to balance the results of chaotic evolution in the spheres with which they are connected. And on this planet, that work must largely be done through humanity – led by the Masters and served by their cooperatives in physical incarnation.

The present moment in evolution is one where the blind stimulation of the Earth soul and atavistic looking back to ancient Nature cults, in combination with the chaotic and overstimulated subconsciousness in humanity created by current conditions, is likely to lead to an ever increasing growth in what we can only call black magic and ecological chaos. If successful, this would either make the planet uninhabitable or make humanity's further evolution almost impossible for the majority of Sparks passing through this evolution. It must be remembered that Earth is the densest of all planets in the solar system, and its Group Mind is on the physical plane. When we speak of Gaia, the reality we are normally addressing is the Planetary Being (or Planetary Spirit in Dion Fortune's original, Golden Dawn influenced terminology).

5.2 The Ecological Awakening and the Green Movement

In retrospect, the ecological or green awakening was perhaps the most significant spiritual event of the twentieth century, closely connected with the revival of respect and veneration for the feminine principle, in humanity and divinity.

The nightmarish spectacle of two World Wars and the cumulative awareness of the horrors of industrialisation and the mechanisation of war, agriculture and society inevitably cast human minds back on Nature, which a limited perspective had considered a primitive principle from which we should aim to escape.

Awareness of the spirituality of nature was resurging through various channels from the late nineteenth century onwards, including the influence of the Romantic movement, the rise of Vegetarianism, Theosophy, the Celtic Twilight movement and Rudolf Steiner's Anthroposophy.

Rachel Carson's 1962 book *Silent Spring* was enormously influential (Carson was a student of Steiner's Anthroposophy). 'Back to Nature' became one of the rallying points of the Hippy Movement and the 1970s saw further contributions such as Schumacher's *Small is Beautiful*.

All extremes promote a backlash, and perhaps inevitably, centuries of insensitive and aggressive exploitation of our planet and the beings of nature by technological materialism led some members of the Green movement to develop a form of hatred for humanity, even glorying in visions of Gaia punishing humanity in a backlash of nature. These commit the same error as their opponents in thinking of nature as basically separate from humanity. We have also seen the often sentimental and commercialised valorisation of traditional peoples, such as the Native Americans and Aboriginal peoples, as if all cultures that developed beyond the primal beliefs of many thousands of years ago are useless.

These ways of thinking cannot help humanity balance the current forces of chaos.

The spectre of climate change is particularly unsettling. Visions of polar ice caps melting and sea levels rising evoke the memory and fear, deep in the subconscious, of the end of Atlantis which is the same event as Noah's Flood described from a different perspective. The argument between climate change believers and deniers – which the public can only enter by taking one of these set of experts on faith –

masks the subliminal knowledge that changes in climate are basically due to humanity's instinctive connection with the nature forces.

The lack of consciousness – and conscience – with regard to our own inner climate can be seen in mass responses to climate-related policy. For example, fracking (the extraction of shale gas by hydraulic fracturing deep underground) is a controversial technology, and some green-minded magicians have responded by enacting magical rituals against it. The irony is that much current green spirituality is engaged in the exact spiritual equivalent of fracking – namely, in burrowing into buried levels in the Earth-soul and trying to draw their energies to the surface when they are in general best left alone and 'underground'. In fact, from the perspective of *The Cosmic Doctrine*, these atavistic forms of magic are dangerous and toxic in exactly the way that fracking is feared to be in physical terms.

5.3 Initiation and Joining the Lords in the work of Compensation

From all that has been said, it is axiomatic that, on the evolutionary arc, we come into contact with the Lords through awareness that they are behind the laws of physics, chemistry and biology, by a deep desire to help and join in the work of evolution, and through inner spiritual work. When developed, this becomes the will towards Initiation and to work with and as part of Hierarchy.

Because of the state of the universe and the role of the Lords in compensating any imbalance in the evolutions they originated, it is inevitable that if we work in the sincere effort to balance conditions on Earth, we will come into increasing contact with the Lords.

In the first instance, this will usually be with the Lords of Mind. Many of our immediate challenges, even natural ones such as climate change, are bound up with the misuse of freewill we know as evil. Since the possibility of this kind of individual evil and karma began with the Lords of Mind, it is logical that our work involves aspiration to link with their redemptive work.

From the connection of the Lords of Mind with the laws of biology, we can see that there is a mysterious inner relationship between human evil and disruption in the biosphere – one that is the fundamental truth behind somewhat simplistic traditional ideas that floods and volcanic eruptions are responses to human sin.

To be fit for this work, it is clearly important that we purify and illuminate our own thinking – hence the emphasis on thought in *The Cosmic Doctrine*.

It should also be noted that, while many students of magic aspire to raw power, this is not necessary. The deepest elemental powers derive from the Lords of Flame. In Qabalistic terms, these are a reflection of the powers of the Supernal Sephiroth. But on the Path we begin by anchoring ourselves through development of the connection between the lower mind and the higher Intuitive mind (sometimes called the Antakharana). This correlates our personality with the Mental Plane or world of Briah at its link with the psychological realm of Yetzirah, because humans are beings that can think, uniquely in the individual aspects of the realm of Malkuth.

Next comes a penetration deep into the subconscious and dreaming mind relating to the world of Yetzirah, which is pervaded by the powers of the Lords of Form. Finally, a foundation exists which can bear the input of the Lords of Flame. This involves the deep regeneration of the instincts so that together Mind and Form are in harmony with the fundamental and potentially destructive powers of the Lords of Flame – powers of the Spirit which are akin to the Stars and are expressed as our dedication and intent, not just as limited personalities but as Divine Sparks co-evolving on the Earth.

Thus it is not to be expected that our spiritual work will necessarily lead to spectacular occult fireworks! If it does, this will be an effect of the pre-existing evolutionary relationships between the Lords. For example, the particular Lord of Mind involved in an aspect of redemptive work may itself have a deep connection with a Lord of Flame, and the activation of this connection under spiritual law may lead to remarkable changes in the subtle and physical levels of the Earth. In Jesus' case, the particular nature of His work meant that he had a relationship to the whole range of Hierarchical beings. We know that "the fullness of the godhead dwelt in Him bodily" but even in Jesus' case it was only after the purification of forty days in the wilderness followed by temptation that "the devil left him and angels ministered unto him." After this, His miracles followed directly and in an increasing sequence of power, from turning water into wine at Cana to the seventh and greatest miracle which was the raising of Lazarus. (Of course, the eighth miracle was beyond revivification, namely the actual resurrection of Jesus – a deed whose full meaning will only become apparent far in our evolutionary future.)

The Spirit of Planetary Service

If we focus on our moral and spiritual evolution, all the powers we need to serve our evolution will be given to us. Taking these ideals to heart and acting on them will be of great importance:

- ⊙ Try to make Nature a matter of conscience.
- ⊙ Ask for opportunities to help.
- ⊙ Be willing to balance evil and to purify your own thinking.

5.4 *The Cosmic Doctrine* and the Evolution of Qabalah

The next link in our chain of understanding involves understanding the evolution of Qabalah itself.

The way in which the Western Hermetic tradition currently uses this wonderful tradition is quite a far cry from its medieval Jewish roots, and from contemporary Jewish Qabalah. Many students of the Western Mystery Tradition do not read the foundational texts like *Sepher Yetzirah* or the *Zohar*, nor do they relate to them through immersion in Jewish culture and the scriptures. Instead, the focus is on one particular use of the diagram called the Tree of Life.

A clear and essentially traditional approach to the foundations of Qabalah can be gained from the many books of Warren Kenton (Z'ev Ben Shimon Halevi). In essence, in the classic Qabalistic way of thinking, the universe as we know it began when from the primal mystery of God (which to us is Limitless Light which seems to be Nothingness) ten fundamental principles emanated. These were the so-called Sephiroth which constitute the World of Emanation. They can be understood as ten primal attributes of God or ten Divine Names and are related to each other in various ways. They are both distinct from God and inseparable from Him as a kind of reflection of His mysterious essence in the Divine Mind which we may dimly understand as God's concept of Him/Herself. The relationship between the World of Emanation and the Absolute bears a deep connection with the relationship to the Creator God and the Logos – who was *with* God and *was* God, and was the pattern through which all things were made.

The diagram of the Tree of Life is holy because it actually and essentially represents the realm of Atziluth.

Next arose the World of Creation, Briah or Divine Thought, which is more distinct from God and constitutes what we can think of as

Platonic Ideas or Archetypes of things rather than the pure existence of Names or emanations. This too can be envisaged as a Tree. In human terms this is the Spirit and is a form of intelligence and existence that is beyond the changing tides of thought and feeling of normal human experience.

After that came the World of Formation, Yetzirah, which brings us into the realm of the human psyche, of emotions and thought-images, of the concretisation of archetypes such as 'rose' into particular roses of different colours and scents. This too can be envisaged as a Tree of Yetzirah.

Lastly the World of Action, Assiah, which contains the entire physical universe.

A simple, traditional and effective scheme places the Archangels in Briah, the Angels in Yetzirah and humans in Assiah. (However, in another sense we can see the entire Angelic Hierarchy as relating to Briah, or in another and different sense, in Yetzirah.)

Thus, the Tree of Life is not fundamentally a picture of the Cosmos; it is a picture of the Emanations of God revealing his Divine Qualities – and the human body is an image of that Divine Pattern. However, for reasons too complex to go into here, Western Hermetic Qabalah gradually mutated or even displaced this 'top down' understanding of the four Worlds and used the Tree as a picture for the Cosmos as a whole.

The point is, that to an older mindset, the four-fold nature of Creation is primary, and the ten-foldness of the first of these four Worlds, the world of Emanation, is secondary because it emerges from the four (this relationship was also studied in the tetractys).

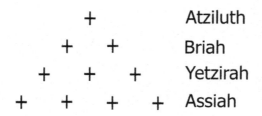

However, once the Tree started to be seen as an entity in itself, it was natural that a more materialised vision of the world would develop. This does not fit very well with medieval Qabalah, but it does mesh with the revival of pantheistic systems such as the Stoicism of the Renaissance which gradually inserted itself into the Western Hermetic Tradition, not least through innovators such as Giordano Bruno.

There is a strong pantheistic streak in Theosophy (particularly Adyar Theosophy) and so it was inevitable that Dion Fortune would have absorbed this somewhat non-traditional form of Qabalah. (It must be noted that the Golden Dawn generally kept to a somewhat purer understanding of the Qabalistic tradition which owed more to Jewish and Rosicrucian Qabalah and less to Theosophy.) Yet the great popularisation of Hermetic Qabalah in the twentieth century probably owed more to Dion Fortune's book *The Mystical Qabalah* than to any other text. This masterwork of experimental occult theory was so successful because it shared language and presupposition with the Theosophical terminology that essentially underlies the whole New Age. It also presents a view of the world that is fundamentally reconcilable with science, being materially based and dynamic rather than dualistic and static.

Gareth Knight's book *A Practical Guide to Qabalistic Symbolism* further popularised the monistic and basically pantheistic approach of *The Cosmic Doctrine* and the fundamental status of the ten-fold scale based on the Emanations (though Knight later changed his standpoint to the Creationist standpoint of traditional Judaism, Christianity and Islam).

For all these reasons it is easy to see why Dion Fortune's Qabalah is controversial and inevitably regarded as unimpressive by guardians of earlier and more rigorous esoteric tradition. However, the basic impulse of *The Mystical Qabalah* represents an important development in the history of the Qabalah itself. We have seen that its development into Christianised and then occult forms involved a gradual move away from an Atziluthic focus on the Tree of Life that revealed the Sephiroth as an alphabet of Holy Emanations and a prototype underlying the whole Book of Nature. Instead, the progressive analysis of the relationship between the Divine Mind and the World led to a change of focus through which European Qabalah became an occult system which was essentially cosmological and almost materialistic. Nonetheless, the Tree of Life embodies a failsafe in that we are told that Kether is in Malkuth and Malkuth in Kether. This is emphasised through the image of the Holy Living Creatures as the Angels of Kether and the presence of a four lettered Name of God: AHIH.

In other words, *The Mystical Qabalah* is based on the cosmology of *The Cosmic Doctrine*. It represents the first signs of an attempt to recast the Tree of Life and the Qabalah into a form suitable for evolutionary ascent past the nadir, rather than a portrayal of the involutionary process whereby transcendent forces built and ruled in matter. It is a form of Qabalah that represents the new way in which humanity will need to learn to relate to the Lords, and to the nature forces, and is best seen as the beginning of a dynamic process rather than a static masterpiece.

Traditional Qabalah saw the four elements as lower reflections of the powers of the Holy Living Creatures, grounded in the mystery of the Divine Name, the Tetragrammaton. As we turn the nadir and work upwards from Malkuth, we start instead from the four elements as they are known to us in Nature and work back upwards to the Source. Much like the presuppositions of Tantra (which shares with Qabalah the vision of the rising serpent as a symbol of evolution), we must start where we are, at the bottom, where the energies are to be found, and work up. We know from the Tradition that the elemental energies of nature are themselves analogues of the Highest. This knowledge is a privilege of the Earthly consciousness of the nadir – but to take it further, we must proceed to relink our relationships to the elements with a new connection to the Lords. No longer imprisoned in Malkuth, we shall gain the ability to ascend the Tree and bring higher forces to bear in transforming and transmuting our world.

5.5 The Particular Mission of *The Cosmic Doctrine* – The Spirit in Nature

If we envisage the relationship between God, Man and Nature as a triangle, we can see that three relationships are highlighted – that between God and Man, between Man and Nature, and between God and Nature.

The emphasis of *The Cosmic Doctrine* is very much on the God-Nature aspect, and that is the lens through which the Lords are seen. As suggested above, this tendency was probably strengthened by the way in which the text was received by Dion Fortune, who raised herself to the Mental Plane and disengaged from her personality. This procedure, especially when undertaken in a state of deep trance, would tend to minimise the human aspect and the imaginative richness of the human personal subconscious.

Yet the gain far outweighed the loss, because in Dion Fortune's time, and still in our own, we are awaiting the remembrance of the work of the Hierarchies in nature. This is the work of the Archangels, even in the earthly elements. Although in modern Western ritual (or those forms deriving from the Golden Dawn) the four Great Archangels are often invoked, it perhaps remains to awaken to their full Archangelic status and not just imagine them as elemental lords (which limits our awareness of them, though it may make ritual safer).

The elements themselves embody the foundational stellar powers of the Lords. It is helpful to meditate on how the elemental beings – Salamanders, Sylphs, Undines and Gnomes – are often experienced, and contrast this with the way in which *The Cosmic Doctrine* characterises and meets the elemental world at a deeper and more fundamental way. Something of this attunement (which still awaits the successors of Dion Fortune to unfold to us) is captured in this passage, although it shows the consequences of the tragic situation in which the human personality is displaced by elemental consciousness in a kind of possession:

> "…and of such it may be said that they have a stone of the earth, or a wave of the sea, or a wind of heaven, or a flame of fire for a heart, for human heart they have not; and because of the strength of the Elements they call unto the Elemental in mankind with a profound calling, and such have always troubled the sons and daughters of man. For they come as beings of a strange and Elemental power that knows not the bonds that bind humanity…"

This of course was one of Dion Fortune's preoccupations in her occult fiction, and features strongly in the original Dr Taverner stories. It is also one of the few passages in modern occult literature that comes close to capturing the mood of experience of the faery realm (or part of that realm).

5.6 From Atlantis to Golgotha to New Atlantis

Fundamentally, all in our universe is in motion, although in another sense the core and backdrop of this motion is a profound peace and stillness. What we perceive as motionlessness is either something moving too slowly or too fast for us to perceive as motion. As the first part of *The Cosmic Doctrine* makes very clear, the primal atom is created as a locking up of the force of two tangentials, whereby they oppose each other's motion and thus swirl around a common centre. Each successive manifestation involves a concreting, a locking up of force. In general this occurs through the pattern shown in the top diagram on page 50. Each stage of manifestation therefore involves a stepping down of power, and to incarnate necessitates the sacrifice of a certain degree of freedom and energy in exchange for the gain of operating within limits and the discipline of definiteness.

The last great change in humanity's energy levels occurred with the end of Atlantis, when that sea-based or basically etheric civilisation made way for the dry land of our present epoch of evolution. In some ways this was a step forward as it allowed us to pass the nadir and make direct contact with the Logos, yet it also brought forgetfulness and loss of magical powers.

It is quite evident, looking at the history of Western philosophy, that philosophers and theologians gradually lost sight of the elements and the cosmos in motion. Looking at this over the long term, we have a sense of a gradual slowing down, like a spiral turning in on itself, or a spinning top losing momentum. The exact point at which the cosmos reached a minimum stillness as far as the seeing consciousness can discern is up for debate, but in the Rosicrucian tradition it is identified with the Incarnation of Christ, the Mystery of Golgotha or Turning Point of Time, as the most important recent theoretician of Christian Esotericism, Rudolf Steiner, called it. (In many respects our theories still embody the mindset of our predecessors just before and after the Incarnation; this may have been temporarily necessary, but it does not need to continue.)

It was as if at this moment of stillness, the seed power of the fullness of the Elohim was 'dropped down the chute' so that it could begin to regenerate the Earth from within. Remembering that the inner spirituality of Earth is actually most active through humanity (and its relationship with the other kingdoms of nature), we can see that the regeneration of Earth is only just beginning and that we cannot palm off responsibility for this onto God, the Logos or the Lords, for they have given a key role in this work to ourselves! The first signs of our returning awareness of and connection with the inner levels of nature are the sense of the speeding up of time and evolution, the recurrence of memories of Atlantis and the stirring of the elemental energies which now, for human evolution, are definitely behind us. They have thus become our responsibility as we begin the arc of ascent.

The great scientist and teacher Sir Francis Bacon liked to quote the prophet Daniel's words as signs of what Bacon foresaw as the path to the New Atlantis: "But thou, O Daniel, shut up the words, and seal the book, even to the time of the end: many shall run to and fro, and knowledge shall be increased."[10]

The dawn of the modern era was the age of the ship and the practical mastery of the elements. With the reawakening to the fundamentally alchemical doctrine of evolution, we see pioneers from Giordano Bruno to Francis Bacon to the Communicator beginning to lead the Esoteric Tradition back into the waters. Perhaps in the future we may know them to be the waters of heaven and our ship will be a spaceship!

PART 4

Conclusion - Images

As becomes increasingly evident when we study *The Cosmic Doctrine* deeply, creation is holographic. The basic patterns laid down 'in the beginning' are replicated, regenerating themselves throughout all successive acts of sub-creation. One of the best ways to enter the 'feel' of the Lords is to meditate on the linked series of images we are given. So let us close by moving up a level from philosophical reflection to union with the Lords in contemplation.

The Three Rings

The Ring Cosmos corresponds to the Lords of Flame.
The Ring Chaos corresponds to the Lords of Form.
The Ring Pass-Not corresponds to the Lords of Mind.

We have already studied these relationships above (in Section 4).

Meditation on the three Rings and the Lords

- See the Ring Cosmos as pure thrusting yet harmonious energy, moving in a vast curve through space until it forms a spinning ring.
- See the Ring Chaos surround the Ring Cosmos, modifying and confining it, while drawing the Ring Cosmos outwards from the centre to the periphery both up and down until it gains the suggestion of a sphere. When the Ring Chaos has reached its optimal 'speed' the relationship between these rings is stable.

⊙ See the Ring Pass-Not mediate the forces of the preceding Rings, setting a boundary to the centrifugal effect of the Ring Chaos on the Ring Cosmos.

The scene is now set for the Cosmic evolution of Rays, atoms and travelling atoms.

Holding the flavour of this image like a chord, now contemplate the word of the Lords in our solar system

⊙ The Lords of Flame pattern the fundamental forces of each planet on the seven planes of our first Cosmic Sub-plane
⊙ The Lords of Form act on the form side of these planets. This confines and opposes the spiritual energies of the Lords of Flame but sets the essential material framework for their energies.
⊙ The Lords of Mind are now able to bring epigenesis and freedom to each planet which is its own reason to exist and its means of expressing itself in the universe.

Our ability to have any understanding of universal law relies on our connection with the work of the Lords of Mind – whose role itself echoes that of the Ring Pass-Not.

Meditating on the state of harmony and balance between Force and Form, we meditate on how Mind is born in the creative relationship between Spirit and Matter. We sense the freedom and light that is born as a beginning and as a question. Is it awaiting an answer?

Next we feel how from the three great impulses of the Lords a fourth reality begins to arise. It is that of deep physical reality, which is a manifestation of the combined and mutually functioning energies of the Lords, which in turn reflects that of the three Rings, and the Rings, Rays and Atoms.

We stop and feel the linkage and resonance of all these levels of God's world.

The Earth-state, the Malkuth of the Qabalists, is the world of sense. Whilst in one sense it is the deepest of worlds, in another it is less deep than the 'foundational' realm of the Lords of Form. It is an end and a new beginning. It is humanity's home. We see the signs and out-pressings of the previous evolutions in the world that surrounds us. Our first act as magicians is to symbolise them and gather together our consciousness of their different energies.

Meditation on the Sun, the Earth, the Living World and the Lords

- ⊙ Let us meditate on the Sun shining down, casting a spear of golden light into the Earth, impulsating the elements – the work of the Lords of Flame.
- ⊙ Let us see Matter respond instinctively from its very depths – Mother Earth, changing into the form of the Goddess or the Virgin Mary. She who gives sleep, death and yet new life – the work of the Lords of Form.
- ⊙ As the Sun beats down upon the Earth we become aware of a Tree, pristine as the dawn of our world, and in it the subtle yet radiant Cosmic Christ; whom we see opposed by, yet mysteriously linked with, the spiralling serpent.

We hear the same chord resounding up and down Jacob's Ladder.

And now let us meditate at the junction point between these levels of creation in order to ponder more deeply on the relationships between the Lords. From among many images, we may initially work with the following:

- ⊙ At the boundary of the pure Force of the Lords of Flame and the formative work of the Lords of Form we see a radiant white diamond energetic structure crystallising into form as a perfect revelation of the hidden forces of nature.
- ⊙ And at the boundary of Form and Mind we see the Living Stone, soft and malleable, iridescent with hints of rainbow colours and giving rise to tree-like formations.
- ⊙ At the boundary of Mind and Humanity we see the image of the Crucified Lord on the Tree, balancing force pouring out from Him in all directions as we see His risen form prefigured in his suffering.

"the stone that the builders rejected…"

Contemplating the mystery of the Philosopher's Stone, we move a step nearer to our own human experience and development, and symbolise these mysteries in terms of our own evolution.

Meditation on the Grail Hallows and the Lords

◉ Meditating on the Spear, and feeling in it the primal thrusting power of being, we connect with the forces of the Lords of Flame.

◉ Meditating on the Chalice we feel the primal mystery of Form – the life of the Spear must be gathered into the Chalice, must die and give up its ghost – the mystery of the Lords of Form.

◉ From the tragic tension and anguish of this moment we take up, in imagination, the knife or sword.

"My word is a two-edged sword" – we discern dark from light, we shape life intelligently, we alternately grow and shed – the mystery of the Lords of Mind.

And now we pause, for we are at the heart of the mystery of the Three in One.

What is the meaning of the Cosmos formed by the three Rings? How do we take up the work of the Lords? How do we live in harmony with ourselves as beings of Spirit, Mind and Body? – the mystery of the Lords of Humanity.

And from this mystery, subtle as a fading memory of a dream, we see an image of the whole of creation forming itself into a pattern of shining, living crystals, of human beings that shine with blue-white light and themselves form vast constellations.

There are no words for the intuition that arises at this point, but we contemplate the image of the Heavenly Jerusalem and know that She is both Sophia, the star-crowned Bride of Christ and the collective awakened relationship of all humans on Earth – and in time, in the solar system.

Sophia in her vast blue crystal form is the Planet Earth and she is gazing at the Solar Logos, returning His outpourings with 'interest'.

We stop to meditate on how the relationship of Lords of Humanity to the Logos resonates with the Logos' own relationship to the Central Stillness, and indeed the mystery of the attractive centre that is the Central Stillness to the three Primal Rings.

We allow images of the love match of Earth and Sun to glow in our awareness – the Hexagram, Golden Rain, the rainbow. We draw these together in contemplation of the hexagram.

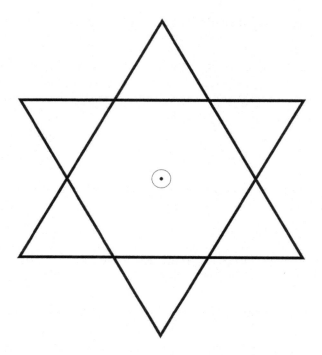

We have no word for this synthesis between our Spirit, Mind and Nature but we can be sure that by balancing these three at each stage of our path, we will be fulfilling our appointed task.

Who am I?

What becomes ever clearer is that between God and Nature stand the Hierarchies, the swarms or Lords. And that is essentially what we are.

If we think only of God, we can only imagine a static and mechanical world, mirrored by thoughts in a disembodied divine mind.

If we think only of Nature, we blind ourselves to the presence of intelligence which is not mere instinct but evolutionary and coordinated, and we condemn the Earth and all that is on it to an evolutionary dead end.

If we think of man, we have a being with images which may be mere fantasies of a better world (a humanistic New Jerusalem), that have no reason to exist, no hidden gold within the Earth that will become the seed of a future sun.

Through Wisdom alone, we reach only the concept of the Creator God, though we are tempted to descend into Ceremonial Magic. Yet here we only contact elemental beings, not the Angels.

Through Will, we reach only the spirit within, though it may raise us to the hidden spiritual levels of ourselves and our world. Yet we do not reach the actual Hierarchies who have gone beyond us into the higher spheres.

Yet through the heart, we are linked with all those who work for the alchemical perfection of our planet, the growing of all things in line with their archetypes.

Through a constant heart connection with Hierarchy we enter a much more expanded realm of spiritual experience, because it is only by looking 'down' to their work, especially in spiritualising and freeing elemental nature, that we rise to oneness with their parents.

The Lords of Humanity are also the Lords of Synthesis. We have the honour of being Malkuth to the Logos' entire system, of embodying and grounding the purpose of it all; Lords of the Nadir, we paradoxically enjoy the privilege of a unique relationship with the Logos, one more direct than that enjoyed by many of the mighty Lords that went before us. Unique not least because we are to Him as He is to the Cosmos.

The nature of this synthesis is actually inconceivable except as a kind of hypergeometry. Perhaps the most relevant symbol is the one that emerges for each person as they meditate on it.

What is the fourth that emerges from the three as its centre, result and synthesis?

The fourth that is to body, soul and spirit as its 'I'?

Experiencing your own body, with its elemental life within, the earth below and stars above, becoming aware of the chain of Lords of Mind, Lords of Form and Lords of Flame and the Logos, aware of yourself in your wholeness, ask yourself:

Who am I?

Visita Interiora Terra, et Invenies Occultum Lapidem.

1   Dion Fortune, *The Cosmic Doctrine* (York Beach, ME, Red Wheel/Weiser LLC 2000) 112
2   Fiona Macleod, from *The Amadan* in *The Dominion of Dreams* and *Under a Dark Star* (London: William Heinemann Ltd, 1910) 424
3   Colossians 2: 9
4   Anonymous, *Meditations on the Tarot: A Journey into Christian Hermeticism* (New York: Jeremy P. Tarcher/Putnam, 1985)
5   Dion Fortune, *The Cosmic Doctrine*, 134
6   *Ibid*, 143
7   *Ibid*, 133
8   *Ibid*, 142
9   *Ibid, 113*
10 Daniel, 12:4

4   THE PLANETARY BEING, THE EARTH AND THE COSMIC DOCTRINE

STUART DELACEY

Then the Old Man of the Earth stooped over the floor of the cave, raised a huge stone from it, and left it leaning. It disclosed a great hole that went plumb-down.
"That is the way," he said.
"But there are no stairs."
"You must throw yourself in. There is no other way."

(George Macdonald – *The Golden Key*)[1]

The concept of the Planetary Being is one that we must urgently throw ourselves into, irrespective of our interest in the mysteries of *The Cosmic Doctrine*. We have lived blindly and recklessly by treating the Earth's plentiful resources as infinite, without regard or gratitude for the Being who nurtures us. We have extinguished species at a much greater speed than the steady, background rate of extinction; we have altered, over-harvested and poisoned key habitats and, since the industrial revolution, we have poured more and more greenhouse gases into the atmosphere. Consequently, we have reduced the ability of the Earth's life systems – the very physical body of the Planetary Being – to respond to the deleterious and unsustainable effects which are now altering the global climate. This period of accelerated extinction has been described as 'the Holocene Extinction' and began some 12,000 years ago when our dominance, and our abuse of the stewardship of the Earth (described in so many major world religions) first manifested. In the past hundred years or so, as our global economic and technological development has rapidly increased, the effect of the human-induced Holocene has increased exponentially to push the Earth's life systems towards an irreversible tipping point.

Bearing in mind our relentless follies, when we approach our Mother – the Planetary Being of *The Cosmic Doctrine* – we would be wise not to expect complex intellectual communication or wordy arguments. Instead, we may have to accept direct instructions, without any hint of care or compassion for our personal welfare. This Being is ancient; she is truly red in tooth and claw, and her love emanates from a perspective and paradigm in which true compassion, utterly eclipsing our sentimental and comfortable conception of the word, originates. Ultimately, the study of the Planetary Being demands not armchair philosophy but a response that rises to the challenge through right choices and right action.

The Nature of the Planetary Being according to The Cosmic Doctrine

"The Planetary Being is as it were a vast Elemental composed of the consciousness (using the word in a wide sense) of each one of its children – the children being all the lives upon the earth, humans, beasts, birds, reptiles, fish, insects etc. In the great Elemental, the Planetary Being, all these are, or should be, one: and so they are, or should be, one in their relationship to each other; it is because that relationship has been shaken, broken and betrayed that so many ills have come to pass."[2]

There are many references to other Planetary Beings within *The Cosmic Doctrine* but the following pages are mainly concerned with the Planetary Being of the Earth. Most of the relevant material is found in the final section of the text which was not transmitted through Dion Fortune but through one of her successors. Two other terms are used in *The Cosmic Doctrine* that are closely linked to the Planetary Being. First, the term 'Planetary Entity' is the 'Logoidal Idea' of the planet, this being the spiritual state which it will reach at the end of its evolution, following conditioning by the Planetary Being and by those who dwell in and upon it. This spiritual state is notably described in the Lord's Prayer as the coming of the Kingdom. Our role in 'right action' is central to the ultimate union of the Planetary Being and the Planetary Entity, the former thereby rising from a lowly form of manifestation to a spiritual existence. The second term is the 'Planetary Intelligence' which describes an Archangelic guide who assists the Planetary Being. We will return to this term later in the chapter.

According to *The Cosmic Doctrine*, a planet is composed of matter from all the preceding planes of manifestation and thereby resonates with all the descending forces of existence. This is represented in the physical world not only in the myths and cosmologies that link back into the forces that dominated the previous planes of manifestation but also in the fact that our Earth – and indeed our own bodies – are not made solely of elements formed in the cauldron of the Sun. Many elements crucial to our lives are derived from super-novae and other cataclysms that took place in the early Universe following the destruction and transformation of entities far greater than our own star. The Planetary Being, however, is formed from "the stresses of the plane" on which it subsists and it must awaken solely within that plane. Hence its destiny is closely linked with ours.

The Earth's Planetary Being is described as an 'etheric double' without conscious intelligence. By analogy, it therefore works at the level of the autonomic nervous system of the human body. *The Cosmic Doctrine* makes it clear that the higher self of the Planetary Being depends on the lives "dwelling on it for its development" as it reaches towards a spiritual existence conditioned by the lessons of life. Thus the Planetary Being is the 'Earth Mother' or 'Mass-Mother' and the 'personality' of the planet, built of its experiences and realisations which are derived from the sum of the consciousness functioning within the planet. It has thereby become a Group Soul, and much archetypal knowledge is accessible to us concerning this great soul within the myths and cosmologies of all the cultures that have developed – and vanished – throughout our history.

As the Planetary Being develops through the evolution of our lives, she remains one step behind us. This delay in her development also acts as a drag on our own evolution and conditions our development and progression, forcing us to test and be tested through generations of toil just as we were warned when we left the garden of Eden. This is evidenced in many ways but particularly in small, rural, long-evolved indigenous cultures, and by the slow testing of human aspirations through repeated errors and agonies to ultimate victories. This delay in absorption may also partly account for why the Planetary Being does not immediately react to the distortions that we are currently inflicting upon it. Perhaps the state of the earth has to decline to its darkest hour before the finger of judgement writes on the wall that we have been weighed and found wanting.

One of the most important messages of *The Cosmic Doctrine* is that the path of regeneration for our Planetary Being is irrevocably wrapped up with the direction that the human race takes in its own journey of evolution. To date our record has been abysmal and the future is now on a knife edge. We are irresponsible, and rarely turn our mind from short-term, utterly selfish goals that lack the greater perspectives that are required to enable wise choices to be made. If we cannot be faithful stewards in the world how can we expect to lead the planetary Being to ultimate fulfilment and its spiritual totality?

The Planetary Being is not, however, entirely alone and completely at the mercy of the vagaries of the human race. Each Planetary Being has assigned to it an Archangelic Intelligence which operates as a guide, providing consciousness to an otherwise unconscious and initially, at least, reactive being. These guides are of the first evolution described in *The Cosmic Doctrine* as the Lords of Flame and are called 'Archangels of the spheres'.

We will next examine the scientific description of the current state of the physical body of the Planetary Being. But in doing so we must remain aware that *The Cosmic Doctrine* asserts that "Orthodox science studies the materials of which the body of the Earth is made and their composition, but the 'deeps' of the inner Earth, the make-up of the Planetary Being is what is most important to esoteric studies."[3]

The state of the world

On looking at the Earth from the Moon:

> "If you could look long enough, you would see the swirling of the great drifts of white cloud, covering and uncovering the half-hidden masses of land. If you had been looking a very long, geologic time, you could have seen the continents themselves in motion, drifting apart on the crystal plates, held aloft by the fire beneath. It has the organised, self-contained look of a live creature, full of information, marvellously skilled in handling the sun."[4]

The Planetary Being derives its evolutionary direction and empowerment from the life and consciousness that is on and in the Earth. In recent Ages this has been represented by organic life but *The Cosmic Doctrine* is also concerned with pre-organic life, and its definition of consciousness is wider than that which is generally understood. Consciousness was manifest before the tumultuous volcanic upheavals that preceded the first stirrings of rudimentary organic life. Hence the mythological memory of beings such as the Titans who embodied those 'pre-conscious' forces.

In terms of the present, however, we must understand where the path of involution towards manifestation meets the path that we are currently taking on Earth, and examine the legacy of our stewardship. The history of the Earth takes us back to the origin of the Universe, approximately 13.8 billion years ago. Organic life, from the first, rudimentary bacterium containing only RNA (which comprises only one half of the double helix of the life-transmitting molecule of DNA) to the present complex diversity and sophistication of life, has persisted on our planet for 3.6 billion years or roughly one quarter of the life-time of our universe. During this time there have been long periods of comparative peace in the development of life on Earth alternating with cataclysms that have been described as 'extinction spasms.'

There have been at least five 'mass extinctions' on Earth. One of the most commonly recalled of these is the Cretaceous–Tertiary extinction which occurred about 66 million years ago, when the reign of the dinosaurs finally ended and three-quarters of the species on Earth were extinguished, including all land creatures weighing more than a kilogram.[5] Some believe this may have been caused by the impact of the meteorite Chicxulub into the area that is now close to the landmass of the Yucatan of Mexico.[6] The impact created a compromised atmosphere that would have restricted the access of the sun's rays and caused a drastic global cooling on the Earth which had the effect of removing the domination of a variety of related species that depended on the climatic pattern of their epoch. This extinction was drastic, and to many it was an irrevocable disaster. Nevertheless, it paved the way for a wholly new development of species from a small, mouse-sized predecessor of some of the mammals of today which was able to hide away in the dark years and ultimately radiate into a branch of phylogenetic sophistication culminating in the hominid species. In consequence, the cataclysmic 'disaster' gave rise to new growth on the biological tree of life which culminated in the authors and the readers of this book.

The spasm that destroyed the reign of the Lizard Tyrants seems from a geological perspective to be a sudden event but when examined from the human perspective it was a slow affair. Geological records suggest, although the evidence is not conclusive, that the period of decline of

the dinosaurs took around 25,000 years to come to a conclusion –
almost five times the length of what we can safely describe as human
history. Other mass extinctions were similarly sudden in geological
terms (compared to which the span of human life is merely the life of
an ephemeral mayfly) but they extended over a length of time which
is beyond our ability to grasp.

Many scientists now acknowledge that we are in the epicentre of
another mass extinction: the sixth global event of this nature. But
this time events are moving with a speed of extinction that eclipses
any comparison with the past. According to some observers we are
extinguishing species at a rate more than 1000 times greater than
the ordinary, background rate of extinction of life on Earth and are
therefore in danger of defeating the ability of species to evolve and
adapt quickly enough to ensure the survival of life on earth.

We tend to perceive climate change caused by anthropogenic
emissions of greenhouse gas as the sole issue of concern, and it receives
a great deal of notice from the media compared to other environmental
concerns. But this is not the correct perspective. The matrix of organic
life on Earth, according to Lovelock in his *Ages of Gaia*,[7] has protected
us from the time when it first gained a lasting foothold on the world,
against all that has been thrown at the Earth. Gaia, as he puts it, "is as
old as life." Ultimately, therefore, had we not devastated life on Earth
in the very recent geological period we might scarcely have noticed
the effects of climate change because the networks of ecosystems and
meta-systems, as Lovelock beautifully describes in *The Ages of Gaia*,
have been able to buffer, moderate and resist virtually all challenges
directed at the Earth for many millions of years.

And this is the point at which scientific theories, observations
of climatologists, palaeontologists, ecologists and meteorologists all
begin to accord with the description of the Planetary Being of *The
Cosmic Doctrine*.

Gaia and the Planetary Being

"There is no thing on Earth, no thought brought through to earth which
does not concern the Planetary Being – however great or lofty, however
(unfortunately) mean or base. You have a very great responsibility not
only to yourselves and to each other but also to the great Group Soul of
the Earth, the great mass-Mother of you all."[8]

The concept of the Planetary Being does not yield its secrets easily. But we are given unequivocally clear and easily accessible guidance: assume responsibility, take right action and make correct choices. Indeed, the Planetary Being's future depends upon such right action: we are given *"a great responsibility."* We need to work with the fully manifested aspect of this Being and seek to understand the deeper meaning of its more subtle manifestation so that we can make the correct response.

In this regard, we also need to understand the role and power of the Planetary Being's Guardian which *The Cosmic Doctrine* names as Sandalphon, and we are urged to seek guidance from this great Archangel. The text tells us that Sandalphon is not the greatest in stature of the planetary guardians, nevertheless he swims in the same starry sea as the other Planetary Intelligences who have seen planets lose their atmospheres and water – the very foundation of organic life – and no doubt has witnessed other, greater tragedies. C. S. Lewis assists us with images of these planetary guardians in his mythopoeic space trilogy[9] in which he describes how the planets are nurtured and guided by Archangel-like beings known as 'Eldila' who are subject to a hierarchy and possess characteristics and qualities typical of the Gods in our ancient cosmologies. Reading this trilogy may indeed be a useful strategy to gain imagery and symbols which can enrich our study of our Earth's guardian or Planetary Intelligence.

The Planetary Being, as an unconscious elemental made up of all life on Earth, has learned to protect its children and, as Gaia, will sometimes even eat them in order that their fruit may persist and survive. Indeed, in Lovelock's words: *"Gaia theory arose from a detached, extra terrestrial view of the Earth, too distant to be much concerned with humans,"* which he goes on to indicate is actually consistent with the true meaning of our *"values of kindness and compassion"* in that it enables us *"to reject sentimentality about pain and death, and accept mortality."*[10] This ethic derives from a perspective in which our brief lives appear almost invisibly ephemeral.

We are told in *The Cosmic Doctrine* that the Planetary being *is of immense age,* and Lovelock attempts to describe when the fully material aspects of Gaia came into existence. He believes that Gaia could not have come into existence until rudimentary bacteria were spread across the planet, altering the biosphere in such a way that, if allowed to persist, would have threatened the very fragile beginnings of the great journey. He argues that from then on she would relentlessly resist changes that would be adverse to a sustainable and optimum life existence, which sometimes required the destruction of her own offspring. He describes how, for example, life itself created a blanket of carbon dioxide in order to begin the process of maintaining an optimum temperature. This layer of CO_2 was very like the one we are now creating but much more suited to that time in ages past when the Sun was a cooler star. Lovelock is a scientist and does not readily commit himself to express views that cannot be corroborated, but he does propose that Gaia may well have finally 'awoken' or gained some sort of lucidity when life created a great crisis on Earth due to the dominance of photosynthesizing plants producing oxygen. Oxygen in large quantities acts as a poison to life, and its output needs to be carefully controlled to constitute no more than approximately one fifth of the gases in the atmosphere. Hence, at that point she intervened to create a system that supported a balance of plants and animals in order to protect the wider radiation and development of life.[11]

Gaia also worked with the commodity of immense time to allow life to radiate and multiply. In this endeavour she deployed all the increasing interrelationships that began to make up her own physical body in order to maintain the optimum global climate. Thus Lovelock's Gaia is an inspirational and authoritative description of the Planetary Being.

However, according to *The Cosmic Doctrine*, the Planetary Being is not only composed of the consciousness of organic life but also the consciousness of inorganic and Inner-plane beings. It might be said that Gaia is therefore a projection into our incarnate dimension of the totality of the Planetary Being. Lovelock was expressly avoiding ideas that strayed into the numinous, and named his idea "Gaia" following the inspired advice of a poet and attached the word, as a symbol, to a complex scientific theory describing planetary homoeostasis.

We must remember also that *The Cosmic Doctrine* is designed to open our minds to ideas that will move us and assist us to perceive, to see and to grow. It requires us to experience the knowledge it discloses with as much of our being as we can muster, even if that means throwing ourselves into the cavern revealed in the ground by the Planetary Being – expressed as the Old Man of the Earth by George Macdonald in the quotation at the beginning of this chapter. We must also consider the relationship of guidance between the Archangelic

Lord of Flame with the Planetary Being in terms of the events that are transmitted down the planes to be witnessed by those in incarnation. Are the mass extinctions part of a design or a product of the evolving symbiosis between the Planetary Being and the Guardian?

Finally, we must return to responsibility and right action. *The Cosmic Doctrine* makes it very clear that our own choices will dictate the route that the Planetary Being's evolution will take and we must presume this can mean either utter destruction or a path which, in the end, will rise towards Divinity to where even the Angels will bend their knees. To date our choices have not been exercised well. But we, as humans, have one more chance to make our choice.

1   George Macdonald, *The Golden Key*, first published in 1867 in '*Dealings With the Faeries*', available as an e-book at: http://www.george-macdonald.com/etexts/fiction/golden_key.html

2   Dion Fortune, *The Cosmic Doctrine* (York Beach, ME: Red Wheel/Weiser LLC, 2000), 210

3   *Ibid*, 198

4   Lewis Thomas, *The Lives of a Cell: Notes of a Biology Watcher* (New York: The Viking Press, 1974)

5   Richard Fortey, *Life: An Unauthorised Biography, A Natural History of the First Four Billion Years of Life on Earth* (New York: Vintage, 1997)

6   L.W. Alvarez, W. Alvarez F. Asaro, H.V Michel, (1980) *Extra-terrestrial cause for the Cretaceous–Tertiary extinction*, Science 208 (4448): 1095–1108

7   James Lovelock, *The Ages of Gaia: A Biography of our Living Earth* (Oxford: Oxford University Press,1995)

8   Dion Fortune, *The Cosmic Doctrine*, 211

9   C. S. Lewis' Cosmic Trilogy comprises: *Out of he Silent Planet, Perelandra,* and *That Hideous Strength.* They were written partly in response to a challenge set with his friend J.R.R. Tolkien to write up their respective myths in the form of a trilogy.

10 James Lovelock, *The Ages of Gaia,* Supra note 8 at p. 236

11 James Lovelock, *The Ages of Gaia,* Supra note 8 at p. 78

5 QABALAH AS THE CONCEPTUAL MATRIX OF THE COSMIC DOCTRINE

DALE KENDRICK

A first reading of *The Cosmic Doctrine* may soon leave the reader feeling disorientated, as though lost in a computer-generated fractal animation. We are used to being given information, to being taught, but *The Cosmic Doctrine* makes us work for our knowledge. The fractal analogy is not out of place for the potentially infinite, iterative replication of a metaphorical pattern of movement which is *The Cosmic Doctrine*. Characteristic of a fractal are both replication and irregularity: a paradoxical non-identical repetition, the dimensions of which, mathematically speaking, exceed its topographical context. Characteristic of *The Cosmic Doctrine* is a creative emanationism: the flowing forth of the divine creative nature from which all reality, subjective and objective, emerge.

'Little by little,' says Dion Fortune, 'like a rising tide, realisation is concreting the Abstract, assimilating and expressing in terms of its own nature things which belong to another sphere.'[1] This is an interesting statement, presenting a cosmological unity by combining the process of emanation, as set forth in certain teachings of Qabalah, with a sort of Gnostic realisation. Emanation, then, signifies a process by which not only the world comes into being, but by which human beings may expand their consciousness and approach the unknown origin of that emanation.

The process, it seems, works by means of analogy whereby the Divine consciousness is understood to emerge as human consciousness, through a process of emanation, and the principles of emanation are understood to be reflected in the actions and reactions of human life. *The Cosmic Doctrine* presents a schema for infinite complexification: a cosmic itinerary which is also a map of human psychology. By approaching the text from a philosophy of process rather than substance, it is possible to assess Dion Fortune's recursive emanationism according to a theology of movement which achieves an integrity with regard to her overall metaphor, rather than a theology of system which – though it may provide insights into both her cosmology and her understanding of psychology – would not address what I contend is evident as the purpose of the text and the way it works as a psycho-cosmology. Presented as an *a priori* revelation, *The Cosmic Doctrine* functions as an *a posteriori* realisation; revelation and realisation become coterminous as both a development in consciousness and as a 'making real' in a physical sense.[2]

The metaphor Dion Fortune develops in *The Cosmic Doctrine* constitutes the creation of a coherent reality embracing, primarily, a pragmatic theory of truth rather than an empirical one.[3] The psycho-cosmology is functional, in accordance with her understanding of magical praxis and with the authorial methodology by which the *The Cosmic Doctrine* is said to have been received in the first place. In other words, the text demonstrates that which it describes. The divine movement towards manifestation and revelation described in *The Cosmic Doctrine* is reflected in the magical journey of the reader's assimilative realisation. Like *The Cosmic Doctrine*, *The Mystical Qabalah* also provides a concept of emanationism which embraces divine creativity within an arena of infinite possibilities; as an organising principle, the Tree of Life is presented as a 'diagram' of the macrocosmic universe and the microcosmic human soul.[4] An exploration of the way Dion Fortune's Qabalistic ideology, presented in *The Mystical Qabalah*, functions as the conceptual matrix of *The Cosmic Doctrine* will serve not only to provide foci on concepts of emanationism and of process thinking implicit therein, but also of methodological participation, which is foundational to the stated textual intention of 'training the mind'.[5]

It makes sense to consider well Dion Fortune's methodology, for – if the reader of *The Cosmic Doctrine* is being put to work – an appropriate method of labour needs to be adopted. The following exploration does not seek to provide exegesis, but to enable a new reader to begin to engage with the fractally recursive extension of the central metaphor in *The Cosmic Doctrine* and to encourage such a reader to remain open, thereafter, to the possibilities of a participative epistemology which underpins Dion Fortune's definition of magic. If the task seems arduous, the reader would do well to remember encouraging words from *The Mystical Qabalah,* that "unless we make a start we have no hope of a finish".[6] Little by little, the tide will rise.

Qabalistic emanationism

In *The Mystical Qabalah*, the divine emanation is shown geometrically as a 'descent' from nothingness, according to the pattern of a lightning flash, which displays various vertical and horizontal polarities as it descends from spirit to matter. In addition to the cosmos, the Tree of Life is also taken to represent the human individual, or any unit of manifestation. The spheres are connected by twenty-two paths which delineate the relationship between them. These paths are said to represent the 'subjective' import of the Tree, connecting as they do the 'objective' Sephiroth; the symbolic Serpent of Wisdom may be shown 'rising' on the Tree, connecting the paths in an order which may be understood to represent the raising of consciousness from the terrestrial to the celestial.[7] Aspects of cosmological and psychological information can be associated with different Sephiroth on the Tree and considered in terms of the schematic relationships which emerge thereby.

The Tree can be considered according to threefold and sevenfold structures; it may also be divided into Four Worlds, broadly representing stages in the divine emanation as well as the spiritual, mental, emotional and physical aspects of a human individual. Each World contains within itself a Tree, as does each Sephirah on the Tree. The whole, therefore, functions as an infinitely complex psycho-cosmological schema wherein emanation is not considered in terms of distance from source, but according to increasing complexity.

According to Dion Fortune's Qabalistic cosmogony, emanation from the 'Unmanifest' gives rise to the initial manifestation of unity (Kether) which emanates into a duality (Chokmah and Binah); this is represented on the Tree of Life in the three named Sephiroth forming the 'First Trinity', or the 'Supernal Triangle'. The series of emanations, therefore, even at its simplest level, may be identified as a fractal replication of a 'root concept'.[8]

The cosmological and the psychological content of *The Cosmic Doctrine* and *The Mystical Qabalah* describes a replicating pattern of 'development' which must be thought of as non-identical repetition in the same way that certain types of fractal images (such as the

Koch Curve) develop recursively, containing within themselves endless replications of the whole as they 'emerge' mathematically in a repeating pattern which produces infinite variations.[9] Fractals are irregular in that they exhibit stochastic self-similarity, not replication; they may, therefore, be said to display non-identical repetition as do Dion Fortune's non-deterministic (creative) Cosmic processes.

The term 'fractal' has a precedent in academic occult study, for S. A. Farmer uses it as a synonym of Pico della Mirandola's 'correlative ontology'.[10] In accordance with Pico's first principle that 'whatever exists in all worlds is contained in each one', Dion Fortune says: 'We shall find that a thing which is true on any plane of the cosmos is true through the whole of its system of correspondences'.[11] Her concept of correspondence points, then, to an ontological correlation which signifies more than a mere interlocking of disparate elements.[12] Spirit crystallises as matter in the process of involution and matter returns to spirit in the process of evolution; the latter is an unfolding of the former (that which was 'infolded').[13] That the completion of the Great Work is a state of 'the *commencement* of Whirling Motions' illustrates that Dion Fortune's concept of regeneration implies a process of genesis, as a 'coming into being', whether epigenetic, palingenetic or agamogenetic; even though, as she says, 'That which has been comes round again on a higher arc, and nothing opens up in evolution whose germs are not implicit in involution', that which is the Great Work of 'regeneration' is its completion in Kether as 'generation'.[14]

The Cosmic Doctrine presents the development of movement (which is considered to be eternal) in the formation of universes as 'the formation of an infinite number of minute centres of stability of various types, and the continued organisation of the reactions among those centres'.[15] These 'universes' are said to be built upon the same principles as the three Rings of moving space which constitute the Cosmos within which they develop; the concept of the three Rings, then, is repeated throughout the emerging miniature 'Cosmoi', or 'universes' in a fractal process of infinite possibilities similar to that expressed by the Tree of Life where each aspect reflects the whole.[16]

In *The Mystical Qabalah*, Dion Fortune says that 'The Qabalistic system is explicit concerning the doctrine of Emanations, whereby the One unfolds into the Many, and the Many are reabsorbed into the One.'[17] She also says, regarding the relationship between psychological microcosm and cosmological macrocosm, and implying a recapitulation of ontological evolutionary patterns in conscious development, that 'Certain aspects of consciousness were developed in response to certain phases of evolution, and therefore embody the same principles; consequently they react to the same influences'.[18] It is in this relationship between the 'One' and the 'Many' (noting the use of capitalisation), that God is understood to be an evolving God. In *The Cosmic Doctrine*, also, God (the Logos) is not an impassible, unchanging *Deus ex machina*, but an involved and developing entity. Because, in *The Cosmic Doctrine*, one of the key aspects of what may be considered as a single process of involution and evolution is expressed as the reciprocity between the consciousness of the Creator and that of the emanated Creation, the text can be read as a metaphor which shows something of both a transcendent, Deist view of 'the grip of Divine Law upon the whole of manifestation', whilst retaining the concept of an immanent, loving God in an intimate, reciprocal relationship with Creation (implicit in the last sentence of Part One of *The Cosmic Doctrine*, 'Therefore choose Love and live').[19]

The concept of God presented in such an arena of infinite possibilities is panentheist rather than pantheist; God – as a developing 'being', or state of being, in relationship with that which God has emanated or created – cannot be merely the totality of the created world.[20] When considering how Dion Fortune understands the relationship between God and the Creation, however, the language she uses to describe one is the same language she uses to describe the other. This use of language, in a panentheist context, not only establishes the basis for analogical thinking, but expresses a psychological and cosmological understanding of a complementary development between God and Creation. Given that the Tree of Life is described in *The Mystical Qabalah* as both a dramatisation of the Divine Mind and as a schema of human consciousness and that the emanating units of manifestation in *The Cosmic Doctrine* are described as projections of the Logoidal Mind according to a pattern which serves to plot the development of human consciousness, analogy (wherein analogical cognition may be understood in terms of recapitulation) takes on a specific theological significance in the psycho-cosmology presented in the two texts.[21]

According to Dion Fortune's emanationist thinking, Creation is the manifestation of God; given that the evolution of human consciousness exists in a continuum with the involution (or emanation) of God, participation by the magician in the Great Work of regeneration is participation in spiritual generative power.[22] In *The Cosmic Doctrine*, the Logoidal projection of the Universe is a manifestation of archetypal Cosmic force. The method of magical participation is described in this process by means of the 'Law of Limitation'; the reader is told that, 'having circumscribed the task you have set yourself, see it in relation to the Cosmos. By seeing the Cosmic Archetype you will draw in the force of that ideal and by seeing the circumscribed form which it is desired to manifest, you will focus that force.'[23] The 'task' is mundane and the force invoked transcendental; the process of 'drawing in' or 'invoking' the force, in this context, begins with meditation.[24]

The 'unbroken chain of associations' which the mind ranges over when it contemplates the Tree of Life is the framework of evolutionary experience whereby the grades of initiation, as 'condensed evolution', are established.[25] In terms of the Western magical tradition, Dion Fortune understands the development of 'supernormal consciousness' (which may be assumed to refer to 'superconsciousness' as a characteristic of initiation) as a 'Rising on the Planes', which elevation of consciousness can only occur after the densest plane of physical manifestation, the nadir, has been passed.[26] In *The Cosmic Doctrine*, emanation is plotted from archetypal patterns, to the earth as an atom, and on to the initiate who becomes the matrix of a new emanation (or 'system'); commenting on this emanatory process, Dion Fortune says that: 'The 1st plane is the only plane upon which the Initiation of the Logos is given, but it is this Initiation of the Logos which marks the transmission from the involutionary to the evolutionary arc, for it wakens the Divine Spark which has well and truly been called the "God within" and which evolves into union with the "God without".'[27] Such an understanding of the relationship between God and Creation allows metaphysics, psychology and spiritual action to be linked centrally in the description of the process of self-development as self-regeneration which culminates in self-divinisation.

Qabalistic ideology

Dion Fortune describes Qabalah as 'the Wisdom of Israel' and considers her presentation of it in *The Mystical Qabalah* to be an adaptation evolved by adepts or initiates of the 'Western Tradition' of occult teaching for the purposes of their 'evolutionary destiny' (an aspect of which being 'to conquer the physical plane').[28] Evolution, which she states was 'explicitly taught in the Mystic Tradition of Israel', and the relationship of Westerners to physical reality are important themes in both *The Mystical Qabalah* and *The Cosmic Doctrine*, for each book shows the author's concern with the practical implications of its subject matter.[29] Remarks made in the concluding chapter of *The Mystical Qabalah* clearly express the importance placed by its author upon occultism as an active art, as distinct from a merely theoretical philosophy; she says:

> In these pages I have given the philosophical basis on which this art rests. Its practical application depends not only upon technical knowledge; but upon the development of certain powers in the mind by careful and prolonged training, of which the first is the power of concentration, and the second the power of visual imagination. It is concerning the power of the visual imagination that we are so lamentably ignorant in the West. Coué just missed the turning when he sought in prolonged attention a substitute for spontaneous emotion.[30]

From the outset, in *The Mystical Qabalah*, Dion Fortune considers her book to be a 'practical' guide, stating that the mysticism of Israel 'forms the theoretical basis upon which all ceremonial is developed' and presenting her guide as part of the reinterpretation and reformulation of Qabalah necessary for what she refers to as 'the present dispensation'.[31] In both *The Cosmic Doctrine* and *The Mystical Qabalah*, she talks about causing changes in material reality by influencing elemental forces; in the former text, for example, she says: 'it is the knowledge of the method of manipulating ... the elemental essences of each kingdom – which is the basis of practical magic.'[32] That she considers the elemental forces to be 'beings' (albeit relatively unintelligent beings) is coherent with an understanding of magic whereby the interaction between the magician and the elemental forces is presented not just in terms of magical manipulation, but also as magical relationship; in other words, a magical methodology is presented not merely as a mechanical, esoteric science, but as the art of entering into relationship with an animate universe by means of the creative imagination.[33]

In *The Cosmic Doctrine*, the statement of its revelatory nature may be thought to be problematic given that it claims to train the mind rather than inform it.[34] It was, however, of little concern to Dion Fortune whether the contents of such revelation came from 'discarnate entities' or originated in 'dissociated complexes' of her own subconscious mind. She says: 'The manner of their obtaining is a psychological question and has no bearing on the problem of their truth'.[35] It is interesting that, describing the nature of *The Cosmic Doctrine* as a received text, she says that 'Transmitters cannot transcend the mental content of a medium; only those ideas already in the mind can be used but they can and do combine them into new patterns'.[36] The phrase 'new patterns' suggests that, in *The Cosmic Doctrine*, new analogical insights are being received; the implication here is that the analogical technique in which the mind is being trained by reading the text is the technique by means of which it was written in the first place. Dion Fortune's retreat from a distinction between 'utilising' the dissociated contents of the subconscious mind and the method of contacting discarnate entities is a practical one; she says that if organised systems of forces are responded to as sentient beings, rather than as 'a fortuitous concourse of uncorrelated incidents', powers of dealing with them will be extended.[37] It is clearly stated that there is a possibility that the 'response' may not, in fact, be mutual, but Dion Fortune holds that if belief in a hypothesis yields results, then it makes sense to believe.[38]

It is in this pragmatic sense that statements in the text about the 'truth' of the metaphorical cosmology may be evaluated; the nature of the entities is a moot point, because the reason for considering such entities as sentient beings is justified primarily by the benefits of analogical cognition, gained thereby, in terms of a performative 'system of psycho-spiritual development' functioning as an initiatory process.[39]

Dion Fortune considers the emanation of manifestation out of the 'Unmanifest' to have been an act of will, the potential to exercise which is present in all aspects of manifestation, and the actual exercising of which depends upon evolutionary development (of consciousness).[40] Accordingly, then, by means of a trained and concentrated visual imagination, forces may be personified; thereafter, the relationship between cause and effect may be understood as purposive. Dion Fortune's concept of magic is the same as her understanding of evolution (albeit, as practiced by initiates, *condensed* evolution').[41] She defines evolution as the unfolding of Logoidal consciousness and points, more specifically, to the goal of evolution as unification of developed human consciousness with Logoidal consciousness; magic is defined, accordingly, as co-operation with the divine Mind.[42] Because such co-operation is reciprocal due to the recursive nature of the context of its development (evolution resembling 'a series of duplicating mirrors'), it can be understood as *participation* in the divine Mind whereby evolution is co-Creative and the goal of evolution, as extended involution, is self-divinisation.[43] The system of psycho-spiritual development is, therefore, potentially regenerative.

In *The Cosmic Doctrine*, the lack of an absolute distinction between ontological reality and epistemological experience is evident in the application of the extended metaphor to both cosmology and psychology; an understanding of the 'unbroken line of development from movement to thought' informs the psycho-cosmology and facilitates a consequent definition of magic.[44] Dion Fortune does not, however, treat mind and matter as synonymous, for – in *The Mystical Qabalah* – she is careful to state a differentiation between epistemological and ontological reality, between imaginary forms and the cosmic forces they represent, necessary in order to prevent the magical practitioner from becoming 'hallucinated'. She says:

> The gods are emanations of the group-minds of races; they are not emanations of Eheieh, the One and Eternal. Nevertheless, they are immensely powerful, because by means of their influence over the imaginations of their worshippers they link the microcosm with the macrocosm.[45]

Dion Fortune's use of process thought, inherent in her Qabalistic emanationism, suggests the terms of a theology which facilitate an approach to *The Cosmic Doctrine* by way of a participative metaphysics. Magic, therefore, is considered effective, not because reality is imaginary, but because the imagination is 'real.'

The 'method' of the Tree of Life

Dion Fortune's emphasis in *The Mystical Qabalah* is on how the Tree of Life is used in order to attain knowledge.[46] It is important, in this context, not to confuse the attainment of knowledge with the gathering of information; the process of assimilating the metaphor of *The Cosmic Doctrine* or the Tree of Life is that of analogical cognition.

The Tree of Life and the cosmology of *The Cosmic Doctrine*, even if the metaphorical images which are used to depict the emanationist cosmology cannot be verified as corresponding with cosmic reality in a wholly empirical sense, circumscribe fields of vision within which reality may be 'created' in a performative sense. The central metaphor in *The Cosmic Doctrine*, however, is essentially 'unthinkable'; 'space moving' is not something the conscious mind can grasp.[47] In *The Mystical Qabalah*, it is said of such metaphors that 'although ... [the] words do not tell us all that we would like to know, they convey certain images to the imagination; these sink into the subconscious mind and thence are evoked when ideas enter the conscious mind which are related to them. Thus knowledge grows from more to more.'[48]

The accumulation of knowledge by association of ideas, according to Dion Fortune's 'method' of using the Tree of Life, is primarily one whereby symbols are allowed to incubate in the subconscious and hatch into consciousness.[49] In describing this 'method', she says: 'A vision evoked by the use of the Tree is, in fact, an artificially produced waking dream, deliberately motived and consciously related to some chosen subject whereby not only the subconscious content, but also the superconscious perceptions are evoked and rendered intelligible to consciousness.'[50] Magic, for Dion Fortune, if compared with the 'stuff of dreams' in the Shakespearean sense, is not 'rounded with a sleep', but is a more enduring 'realisation' of the contents of the subconscious.[51]

In her esoteric psychology, Dion Fortune expresses her understanding of the human psyche as a vehicle for spiritual force; an exploration of this concept of 'psycho-spiritual development' will show that to describe her metaphysic as analogical may not, in itself, provide sufficient insight into the scope of *The Cosmic Doctrine*.[52] The text is written analogically, not merely because it deals with subject matter that is incomprehensible, but also because analogy is foundational to the nature and purpose of practical magic within the Great Work of evolutionary regeneration.[53] In order to show how the content of *The Cosmic Doctrine* is not just analogical, but performative, consideration needs to be given not only to how Dion Fortune's psychology informs her cosmology, but also to how her concept of the nature of the universe underpins her reformation of psychology according to spiritual principles for the purposes of her magical practice.

In *The Machinery of the Mind*, she talks of the unknown being known by means of a correlation of superconsciousness and the subconscious in the conscious mind; this concept of super-consciousness is a primary principle of her development of esoteric psychology particularly as it is described in terms of an evolutionary cosmological development.[54] In *The Mystical Qabalah*, she says: 'We may personalise natural forces in terms of human consciousness; or we may abstract human consciousness in terms of natural forces; both are legitimate proceedings in occult metaphysics, and the process yields some very interesting clues and some very important practical applications.'[55] Such 'clues' and 'practical applications', when considered in terms of 'superconsciousness', point to a methodology of magic which develops a practice of evolutionary recapitulation from a foundation of analogical cognition.[56] Dion Fortune not only uses the same vocabulary to describe the 'thought-form projected by the mind of God', which is a universe, as she does to describe the original structure of the Cosmos, she also clearly describes the divine *fiat* in the same terms she uses in her description of her Qabalistic methodology.[57]

An example of, and a key factor in, Dion Fortune's concept of 'superconsciousness' is her understanding of the way symbols 'work' according to the collective, transpersonal nature of the subconscious and the implication that the 'experience' of others is accessible through 'symbol'. Pertaining to the use of symbols in her psycho-spiritual system, *The Mystical Qabalah* states that it is the 'polarised function' into which consciousness and the subconscious are brought by the initiate which effectively yields 'super-consciousness'; this 'polarised function' reflects the reciprocity between the Logos and the universe, presented in *The Cosmic Doctrine* as initially occurring due to the integrated reactions of the whole universe, and what is described as the 'reciprocal reactions of the group consciousness and the Logoidal consciousness'.[58] It is this reciprocal consciousness which constitutes the relationship between the universe and the Cosmos, between phenomenal and noumenal existence.[59] According to Dion Fortune, much subconscious thought is irrational and can only be expressed in terms of symbolism; part of her emphasis on training the mind appropriately is in order that the meaning and significance of such symbolism may be accessed by rational consciousness and applied purposively.[60]

In *The Mystical Qabalah*, gauging the value of psychology according to a broader purview of the human mind than is suggested by the practice of psychotherapy merely as a means of personal well-being, Dion Fortune is explicit about the scope of her esoteric psychology in terms of the spiritual dimension of mental training; she says, with reference to the spiritual practices of various religions: 'They are the callisthenics of consciousness, and aim at gradually developing the powers of the mind. The value does not lie in the prescribed exercises as ends in themselves, but in the powers that will be developed if they are persevered with.'[61] Given the statement of design with regard to the training of the mind, in *The Cosmic Doctrine*, it is reasonable to assume that it is just such powers of the mind (including superconsciousness) which may be developed by contemplating, and thereby imagining, the symbols in the text; in this way, the spiritual dimension of the scope of textual intention begins to emerge. For Dion Fortune, 'the causes and springs of being' behind the forces and factors of the manifested universe are more deeply penetrated by the use of the creative imagination than by science.[62] The necessary co-ordination and synchronisation of all aspects of the individual nature, given the nature of the subconscious and the 'potentialities' which the Divine Spark comes to possess, may be considered to constitute the primary purpose of her esoteric psycho-cosmology which is, effectively, a technique of developing superconsciousness in service to the Great Work of emanationist regeneration and divine union.[63] It is because conscious discrimination is considered an ontological correlative of manifest differentiation, that her well-known qualification of Crowley's definition of magic may be read as being without diminution or restriction, her concept of consciousness being one that embraces both epistemological and ontological reality.[64]

Dion Fortune states, in *The Cosmic Doctrine*, that 'the first process in the invocation of power is the rejection of that which is irrelevant. This is another name for concentration. The Law of Limitation means the concentration of power by the rejection of the irrelevant. This is not sufficiently understood. In all undertakings the prime requisite for success is to know what you cannot do. This is discrimination.'[65] This emphasis on concentration and discrimination coheres closely with the way she describes the method, or technique, of using the Tree of Life. Involutionary manifestation is considered impossible without differentiation (the One emanates the Many).[66]

The conscious discrimination to which Dion Fortune refers (as integral to analogical cognition) may, therefore, be considered to be an evolutionary correlative of differentiation and, described as it is according to the same involutionary pattern of development, as a recapitulation of it.[67] Discrimination requires concentration, which is identified, in *The Mystical Qabalah*, as the first stage in a two-stage process of practising magic; concentration is followed by the use of visual imagination, both of which are clearly requisite in any serious attempt to assimilate the meaning of *The Cosmic Doctrine*.[68] Concentrating the mind is formative, both in the sense of signifying the production of 'form' and as signalling the occasion for 'development'. Imagination is both creative and co-creative. Both concentration and imagination, as Qabalistic methodologies, are consistent with the pattern of Cosmic development outlined in the first Section of *The Cosmic Doctrine*.[69] That power is referred to as being '*invoked*', may initially suggest that the mind is trained as a conduit for some 'other', external power, but in the context of the Hermetic understanding of microcosm and macrocosm, the distinction is ultimately irrelevant. In Dion Fortune's esoteric psychology, the functions of the human mind, such as 'the concentration of attention' and the use of the creative imagination, produce enduring 'thought-forms' which, as effective recapitulations of Cosmic processes, may be considered ontologically.[70]

Qabalistic psycho-cosmology

Dion Fortune's remark, in *The Cosmic Doctrine*, that 'God cannot be seen by any unit of the manifested universe during a manifestation. He can only be deduced', carries an implication that such 'units' may transcend manifestation.[71] This point of view is important for a Qabalistic understanding of the development of the individual self in relation to its unknown, though 'knowable', origin, and to the nature and extent of any cognitive relationship between visible and invisible realities.[72]

With reference to involution as the outgoing arc of the metaphorical circle of 'space moving' which describes manifestation, and to evolution as the returning arc, Dion Fortune says that thought (which may be assumed to be either in the mind of God or in the mind of a unit of manifestation) must move within this delimiting circle. When she says that 'thought must move in a circle, returning whence it originated. Starting with a concept it must proceed logically from that concept, reasoning from the general to the particular upon the outgoing arc, and from the particular to the general on the arc of returning, thus envisaging both sides of the question and correlating them', she is expressing her metaphorical mapping of the Cosmos as a way of understanding human psychology.[73] Her esoteric psychology, in turn, is used to construct a cosmology within which the individual may be contextualised. In this sense, involution is deductive and evolution inductive and esoteric philosophy must employ both types of logic.[74] The significance here is not merely, as she remarks, that what the 'ancients' could know only by way of deductive reasoning, comes within reach of the inductive natural sciences (psychology being among them), but that the deductive process of cognitively assimilating a metaphorical cosmology can function alongside an experientially inductive knowledge of 'self' located within that cosmology.[75]

Whilst for Berkeley, 'to expect that by any multiplication or enlargement of our faculties we may be enabled to know a spirit as we do a triangle, seems as absurd as if we should hope to see a sound', for Dion Fortune, the attainment of such knowledge is merely a matter of evolutionary development.[76] Just as she outlines the development of human consciousness beginning with the simplest of geometrical metaphors, so she describes the continuing evolution of such consciousness as according with the patterns established in that development. Such is the meliorative quality of evolution, reflecting the process of involution and providing a pattern for individual self-development in her psycho-spiritual system.[77] This process is understood to be the key to both involutionary generation and evolutionary regeneration (which is the 'Great Work', the essential purpose of magic); it combines inductive and deductive thought, according to their correlation with the processes of involution and evolution, as a means of training the mind in esoteric philosophy rooted in an understanding of the Hermetic principles of human psychology and foundational to a belief in the effectiveness of magic.[78] The Hermetic understanding of the relationship between the macrocosm and the microcosm as a concrescence of involution and evolution serves, in itself, to consolidate Dion Fortune's methodology of magic. Consideration, by the reader of *The Cosmic Doctrine*, of the conflation of epistemological and ontological reality, of mind and matter, of subject and object, and of force and form, will justify further a foundational identification of the text as magical psycho-cosmology.

In *The Cosmic Doctrine*, it is said that 'although in the Cosmos, the planes are extended in space, being based upon movement, in a universe the atoms of the planes are not extended in space, being the products of an image held in consciousness.'[79] Though not a Berkeleyan idealist, Dion Fortune does posit an exclusively epistemological reality in the universe (as distinct from the Cosmos) because, for her, all things are held in the mind of God. The reciprocal consciousness, which she describes, between the Logos and the universe, expresses how such epistemological reality, or universal matter, may be influenced by human conceptualisation.[80] In a passage from *The Cosmic Doctrine* stated to be revelatory, Cosmic influence in a universe is described as occurring through the Logos, but as being, in itself, an influence which is beyond the 'conditioning Logos'.[81]

For Dion Fortune, then, the Logos is a mediator of Cosmic influence and what may be understood to be the goal of human evolution is 'the development of a consciousness which can unite with the Logoidal consciousness, and pass from the phase of a reflected, or projected existence – a phenomenal existence – to that of a real, actual or noumenal existence in the Cosmic state.'[82] Knowledge of the link between Cosmos and universe is clearly considered to be part of this process of unificatory self-divinisation, for by means of such knowledge humans are said to 'complete the evolution from the human to the Divine in a reflected universe' in order to develop a new universe; thereby, says Dion Fortune, 'they should be as Gods'.[83]

The focal point of magical work, for Dion Fortune, is initiation which – as I have said – she understands to be 'condensed evolution'; this suggests, in the context of systematic initiations according to the pattern of the emanating Sephiroth on the Tree of Life, that the relationship between creative involution and the developing consciousness of evolution can be understood as an exact analogy.[84] The similitude between the 'grades' of initiation and the pattern of Divine emanation shows how magical work is understood as a reflection and a recapitulation of Divine creativity expressing reciprocity between Creator and Creation.[85] In the 'duplicating mirrors' of evolution, says Dion Fortune, 'the consciousness of the Logos projects its own image; becomes aware of, and reacts to, the image thus projected; and the reaction affects the projection, and so the circle is everlastingly revolving.'[86] It is logical, therefore, to assume no essential distinction between human and divine conceptualisation within this revolving circle of creative evolution; in terms of *The Cosmic Doctrine*, when we conceptualise, we create like God does. The concept of 'rising on the planes', as a method of developing superconsciousness, is implicit in a statement from *Machinery of the Mind* when Dion Fortune describes how 'the primitive man lies at the base of our being, but the divine man stands at its apex, and we, in our ascent, are in a transition stage, with subconscious and superconscious not yet correlated in the conscious mind.'[87] Given, in such descriptions of them, the psychological nature of the Cosmos, the cosmological nature of consciousness, and the emanational relationship between the two, the 'potentialities' of human nature may be understood to be divine.[88] The reciprocal possibilities between the fractal emanation of Cosmoi, in *The Cosmic Doctrine*, establish the co-Creative potential of individual human beings (or Divine Sparks). Human 'ascent', in our evolutionary progress, then, is nothing less than a process of self-divinisation wherein conceptualisation may be understood to be a creative, psycho-spiritual practice.

In *The Cosmic Doctrine*, Dion Fortune – referring to her geometrical metaphor – says:

> The concept of the return to the centre might be considered as an extension of the centre, for when return to the centre takes place the centre is thereby extended, and we are taught that the return to the centre is the goal of evolution … the centre is extended to the circumference and all things are as is the centre. This implies the spiritualisation of all the planes.[89]

The 'return to the centre' occurs during evolution, after the passing of the 'nadir', said to mark the turning point between involution and evolution. The turning point is that at which the emanation of spirit has manifested as densest matter, corresponding to the seventh Cosmic plane (abutting the Ring Pass-Not). Return is possible because the emanation of the Spirit of God into Creation and the materialist evolution of the emanated Creation exist along an unbroken line of development and evolve towards perfect reciprocity. The human soul is emanated, but not indwelt, by the nucleus of consciousness (the Divine Spark or 'God within') around which, it is said, 'the individualised being builds up'.[90] The 'building up' or evolution of the individual is, ultimately, the unfolding of 'its realisation of the cosmos'.[91] In this way, the universe and the Cosmos achieve union, which is the stated 'goal of evolution' and which can be understood, therefore, as the overarching purpose of Dion Fortune's magical endeavour (with 'condensed evolution', or initiation, as its focus) as a psycho-spiritual practice.[92]

Conclusion

Dion Fortune posits an idealist, Qabalistic evolution of consciousness as a response to, and (importantly) a continuation of, materialist, emanationist involution. Initiatory experiences recapitulate aspects of this involutionary emanation and, therefore, by magical means, the initiate is capable of 'condensed evolution'.[93] God and humankind develop together, in which process the metaphorical psycho-spiritual system described in *The Mystical Qabalah* and *The Cosmic Doctrine* serves as a methodology of magic. Furthermore, it is – according to textual intention – as a means of training the mind that the magical process presented in *The Cosmic Doctrine* may be understood to function as a performative 'magical methodology'. Simply striving to comprehend *The Cosmic Doctrine*, or contemplating the Tree of Life, may be understood – according to its author's understanding of such – as potentially transformative processes on both a human and a cosmic scale.

Magical cause and effect, or action and reaction, understood as they are in terms of both the universal and Cosmic aspects or 'potentialities' of the individual, form – thereby – an expression of divine being.[94] Dion Fortune says, of her description of the macrocosmic circuit of force manifesting in the microcosm of the individual:

> This is … [a] way of expressing the use of sublimation for the purpose of generating force in the upper planes. The pupil who receives force from his Master on a higher plane for purposes of transmission to the physical plane must be prepared to effect the transmutation of the corresponding amount of force in his own nature from a lower plane to a higher in order to preserve the necessary balance.[95]

This reciprocal generation and reception of force, in the context of building relationships, is a synchronisation of cause and effect which reflects the development of atoms within a universe performing 'the primal act of creation' by means of their logically anachronistic projection of images of themselves which condition the Logoidal projection.[96] According to Dion Fortune, 'at the end of an evolution, a perfect and rhythmical balance of the whole Cosmos has been achieved – a synthesis of action and reaction which maintains stability.'[97] This stability reflects the archetypal origins of manifestation (the 'prime stillness ... the thrust-block') in which the Cosmos is rooted.[98] In perpetual cycles of becoming, it is the prelude to the new fractal development which occurs when stability is overset by the perpetual emanation of the infinite potential of the Unmanifest.[99]

The reciprocity between the Divine will, manifesting ontologically, and human consciousness, developing in accordance with the pattern of that reality, is a key to the meaning and purpose of *The Cosmic Doctrine* as it is to the concept of the Tree of Life described in *The Mystical Qabalah*. Both the Sephirothic presentation of a sequential process by means of the Tree and the geometric metaphor of the Cosmic Rings serve, coherently, to locate the transmutation of values central to Dion Fortune's psycho-spiritual emanationism; in this way, they may both be considered as providing a structure for self-initiation as 'trained' participation in the Great Work.[100] An understanding of conceptualisation as a 'psycho-spiritual' practice gives an insight into the way the images in *The Cosmic Doctrine* can be thought to 'train the mind'. By mentally assimilating the 'new patterns' in the text, images are introduced into the mind of the reader and, being in symbolic form, will incubate before hatching forth.[101] The process of acquiring the 'method of using the mind', which reflects the Logoidal development of consciousness, begins, therefore, by merely reading the text of *The Cosmic Doctrine*. As a text that provides training in this context, *The Cosmic Doctrine* may productively be considered by the reader as much a magical talisman as a metaphysical treatise.[102]

Because the emanation described in both *The Mystical Qabalah* and *The Cosmic Doctrine* is a pattern of both spiritual involution and psychological evolution, human, cognitive 'realisation' expresses the divine, emanationist 'revelation', and is presented according to the same process; it is in this sense that Dion Fortune says all magical operations must be 'earthed', for they reflect the divine 'becoming' of God and Creation as process.[103] It is primarily in this sense that *The Cosmic Doctrine* can be considered performative and the approach of the reader to it as necessarily participative. Requiring the acknowledgment of a link between form and function, such an approach identifies the meaning of the text in terms of the relationship between the text and its context. Dion Fortune's Qabalah, as a conceptual matrix, provides an approach to *The Cosmic Doctrine* in terms of participative epistemology which, in turn, may be said to accord with her definition of magic; her performative symbol-system is, therefore, a 'psycho-spiritual', magical methodology whereby the reader is invited to become both co-author and co-Creator.

1   Dion Fortune, *The Mystical Qabalah* (York Beach, ME: Samuel Weiser, 1998), 32.

2   Dion Fortune, *The Cosmic Doctrine* (York Beach, ME: S. Weiser, 2000), 21-2, 65-6; *Sane Occultism and Practical Occultism in Daily Life*, 68. This coalescing of revelation and realisation demonstrates what Fortune (*The Mystical Qabalah*, 51) understands to be 'illuminated consciousness', a term which may be considered synonymous with 'superconsciousness'.

3   Dion Fortune, *The Mystical Qabalah* (York Beach, ME: Samuel Weiser, 1998) 62.

4   *Ibid* 17.

5   Dion Fortune, *The Cosmic Doctrine*, 19.

6   Dion Fortune, *The Mystical Qabalah*, 28.

7   *Ibid* 34, 254.

8   *Ibid* 41.

9   *Ibid* 135.

10   Giovanni Pico della Mirandola, *Syncretism in the West: Pico's 900 theses (1486): the Evolution of Traditional, Religious, and Philosophical Systems* ed. and trans S.A. Farmer (Tempe, Ariz.: Medieval & Renaissance Texts & Studies, 1998), ix n.2, 29.

11   *Ibid* ix; *Sane Occultism and Practical Occultism in Daily Life*, 34.

12   Dion Fortune, *The Mystical Qabalah*, 86.

13   *Ibid* 52, 214.

14   Dion Fortune, *The Cosmic Doctrine*, 42-8, 101-6. 112-13, 124, 172; *Sane Occultism and Practical Occultism in Daily Life*, 35.

15   Dion Fortune, *The Cosmic Doctrine*, 33-4.

16   *Ibid* 35.

17   Dion Fortune, *The Mystical Qabalah*, 264.

18   *Ibid* 17.

19   *Ibid* 12; Dion Fortune, *The Cosmic Doctrine*, 185.

20   Dion Fortune, *The Cosmic Doctrine*, 124. Philip Clayton (2003, p.206) provides a useful definition of panentheism in his essay 'God and World'.

21   Dion Fortune, *The Mystical Qabalah*, 16, 52.

22   Dion Fortune, *The Cosmic Doctrine*, 152.

23   *Ibid* 159.

24 Dion Fortune, *The Mystical Qabalah*, 27; *The Cosmic Doctrine*, 159.

25 Dion Fortune, *The Mystical Qabalah*, 16, 89; *The Cosmic Doctrine*, 126

26 Dion Fortune, *The Mystical Qabalah*, 73, 142, 269.

27 Dion Fortune, *The Cosmic Doctrine*, 48, 133.

28 Dion Fortune, *The Mystical Qabalah*, 3.

29 *Ibid* 36.

30 *Ibid* 285.

31 *Ibid* 4.

32 Dion Fortune, *The Cosmic Doctrine*, 125-6; *The Mystical Qabalah*, 250.

33 Dion Fortune, *The Cosmic Doctrine*, 136-8; *The Mystical Qabalah*, 80-81, 164.

34 Dion Fortune, *The Cosmic Doctrine*, 19, 141.

35 *Ibid*, 1, 2.

36 *Ibid* 18.

37 Dion Fortune, *Machinery of the Mind* (London: S.I.L. [Trading] Ltd., 1995), 64; *The Mystical Qabalah*, 252.

38 Dion Fortune, *The Mystical Qabalah*, 204, 256; *The Cosmic Doctrine*, 8.

39 Dion Fortune, *The Mystical Qabalah*, 204, 252.

40 Dion Fortune, *The Cosmic Doctrine*, 155.

41 *Ibid* 126.

42 Dion Fortune, *The Mystical Qabalah*, 154; *The Cosmic Doctrine*, 123; *The Training & Work of an Initiate* (York Beach, ME: S. Weiser, 2000), 29-30.

43 Dion Fortune, *The Cosmic Doctrine*, 70.

44 *Ibid* 56.

45 Dion Fortune, *The Mystical Qabalah*, 153, 203.

46 *Ibid* 29.

47 Dion Fortune, *The Cosmic Doctrine*, 20.

48 Dion Fortune, *The Mystical Qabalah*, 30.

49 *Ibid* 29.

50 *Ibid* 86; see also, 16, 29-30, 46, 60, 80, 131, 135, 229.

51 William Shakespeare, *The Tempest* ed. Raffel, B. and Bloom, H. (New Haven: Yale University Press, 2006), IV, 1, 156-7; Dion Fortune, *The Mystical Qabalah*, 16, 59, 86, 131.

52 Dion Fortune, *The Esoteric Philosophy of Love and Marriage* (York Beach, ME: Samuel Weiser, 2000). 30-1; *The Mystical Qabalah*, 8.

53 Dion Fortune, *The Mystical Qabalah*, 195.

54 Dion Fortune, *The Machinery of the Mind*, 68; *The Cosmic Doctrine*, 56.

55 Dion Fortune, *The Mystical Qabalah*, 78.

56 Dion Fortune, *The Cosmic Doctrine*, 146.

57 *Ibid* 22, 64.

58 Dion Fortune, *The Mystical Qabalah*, 80; *The Cosmic Doctrine*, 87, 122.

59 Dion Fortune, *The Cosmic Doctrine*, 122.

60 Dion Fortune, *The Machinery of the Mind*, 26.

61 Dion Fortune, *The Mystical Qabalah*, 9.

62 *Ibid* 90.

63 Dion Fortune, *The Cosmic Doctrine*, 2, 147; *The Mystical Qabalah*, 195.

64 Israel Regardie, *A Garden of Pomegranates; an Outline of the Qabalah.* (Saint Paul, Minn: Llewellyn Publications, 1970), iii; C. R. F Seymour, *The Forgotten*

Mage : The Magical Lectures of Colonel C.R.F. Seymour ed. Ashcroft-Nowicki, D (Loughborough, Leicestershire: Thoth, 1999). 24. Crowley defined magic in terms of causing changes; Fortune defined magic in terms of causing changes in consciousness.

65 Dion Fortune, *The Cosmic Doctrine*, 152.

66 Dion Fortune, *The Mystical Qabalah*, 81, 86, 252.

67 *Ibid* 41, 61, 208.

68 *Ibid* 285.

69 See Dion Fortune, *The Cosmic Doctrine*, ch. 26.

70 *Ibid* 57.

71 *Ibid* 71.

72 Dion Fortune, *The Mystical Qabalah*, 32; *The Cosmic Doctrine*, 181.

73 Dion Fortune, *The Cosmic Doctrine*, 155.

74 Dion Fortune, *The Esoteric Philosophy of Love and Marriage*, 34; *The Mystical Qabalah*, 178.

75 Dion Fortune, *The Mystical Qabalah*, 46, 72.

76 George Berkeley, *A treatise concerning the principles of human knowledge* (Oxford: Oxford University Press, 1998), para. 142; Dion Fortune, *The Mystical Qabalah*, 108.

77 Dion Fortune, *The Mystical Qabalah*, 8.

78 *Ibid* 71-2, 195.

79 Dion Fortune, *The Cosmic Doctrine*, 92.

80 *Ibid* 77. I am using the term 'conceptualisation', here, in its broad sense, without the distinction between analytical conceptualisation and intuitive conceptualisation made by Henri Bergson which may be productively explored in relation to the present context.

81 Dion Fortune, *The Cosmic Doctrine*, 95.

82 *Ibid* 123.

83 *Ibid* 95. In *The Two Sources of Morality and Religion* (Notre Dame, Ind: University of Notre Dame Press, 1935), 317, Henri Bergson describes the Universe as 'a machine for the making of gods'.

84 Dion Fortune, *The Mystical Qabalah*, 68-9.

85 Dion Fortune, *The Cosmic Doctrine*, 126; *The Mystical Qabalah*, 89.

86 Dion Fortune, *The Cosmic Doctrine*, 70.

87 Dion Fortune, *Machinery of the Mind*, 68.

88 Dion Fortune, *The Cosmic Doctrine*, 147.

89 *Ibid* 181.

90 Dion Fortune, *The Mystical Qabalah*, 110, 181; *The Cosmic Doctrine*, 133.

91 *Ibid* 34. The theological process implicit in this sentence undergirds the paradoxical nature of the statement in the preceding sentence.

92 Dion Fortune, *The Cosmic Doctrine*, 123, 126, 133.

93 *Ibid* 126, 146.

94 *Ibid* 147.

95 *Ibid* 150-1. It is clear, at this point, that Fortune's 'transmutation of values' retains both quantitative and ethical significance.

96 *Ibid* 66.

97 *Ibid* 60.

98 *Ibid* 21.
99 Dion Fortune, *The Cosmic Doctrine*, 19, 41, 86, 125; *The Mystical Qabalah*, 31-2.
100 Dion Fortune, *The Mystical Qabalah*, 70.
101 *Dion Fortune, The Cosmic Doctrine, 18; The Mystical Qabalah, 29.*
102 Dion Fortune (in *Sane Occultism and Practical Occultism in Daily Life*, 52) defines a talisman as a symbolic object which enables the mind of the magician 'to go up along a particular line of consciousness' and says that it is through the magician's own nature that the power 'comes down'.
103 Dion Fortune, *The Cosmic Doctrine*, 19; *The Mystical Qabalah*, 256-7.

Bibliography

Henri Bergson, *The Two Sources of Morality and Religion* (Notre Dame, Ind: University of Notre Dame Press, 1935).

George Berkeley, *A treatise concerning the principles of human knowledge* (Oxford: Oxford University Press, 1998).

Philip Clayton, (2003) 'God and world' in *The Cambridge Companion to Postmodern Theology* ed. Vanhoozer, K. J. (Cambridge; New York: Cambridge University Press, 2003) 203 – 218.

Dion Fortune, *The Esoteric Philosophy of Love and Marriage* (York Beach, ME: Samuel Weiser, 2000).

Dion Fortune, *The Training & Work of an Initiate* (York Beach, ME: S. Weiser, 2000).

Dion Fortune, *The Cosmic Doctrine* (York Beach, ME: S. Weiser, 2000).

Dion Fortune, *The Mystical Qabalah* (York Beach, ME: Samuel Weiser, 1998).

Dion Fortune, *Machinery of the Mind* (London: S.I.L. [Trading] Ltd., 1995).

Dion Fortune, *Sane Occultism and Practical Occultism in Daily Life* (Wellingborough: Aquarian, 1987).

Giovanni Pico della Mirandola, *Syncretism in the West: Pico's 900 theses (1486): the Evolution of Traditional, Religious, and Philosophical Systems* ed. and trans S.A. Farmer (Tempe, Ariz.: Medieval & Renaissance Texts & Studies, 1998).

Israel Regardie, *A Garden of Pomegranates; an Outline of the Qabalah.* (Saint Paul, Minn: Llewellyn Publications, 1970).

C. R. F Seymour, *The Forgotten Mage : The Magical Lectures of Colonel C.R.F. Seymour* ed. Ashcroft-Nowicki, D (Loughborough, Leicestershire: Thoth, 1999).

William Shakespeare, *The Tempest* ed. Raffel, B. and Bloom, H. (New Haven: Yale University Press, 2006).

IN A HOLE IN THE GROUND THERE LIVED A HOBBIT

THE COSMIC DOCTRINE AS SEEN BY THE LITTLE PEOPLE, BEING THE MEMOIRS OF BILBO AND FRODO OF THE SHIRE, SUPPLEMENTED BY THE ACCOUNTS OF THEIR FRIENDS AND THE LEARNING OF THE WISE...

J.R. PETRIE

According to its Millennium preface: "The Cosmic Doctrine is a condensed blueprint outline of God's manifestation in this creation."[1] It sets out a series of principles through which we may explore our Cosmos and the nature of our Self. There is a well-known statement at the beginning of the book which tells us that it is intended to train the mind, and not to inform it. This statement strikes a chord with many, who sigh with relief, thinking thank goodness, I'm not actually supposed to understand it! There is no getting away from the fact that this work is not the most accessible. There are several possible ways to read this statement however, not all of which let us 'off the hook' so easily. This material is meant to be worked with on levels other than, or perhaps as well as, the intellectual. We are being asked to experience it. The same preface reflects on *The Cosmic Doctrine* as rather mechanical, and potentially alienating. This present work attempts to address these points.

The Cosmic Doctrine is explicit about our own capacity for creation: "The Cosmos is the framework upon which all is built up. You start where God leaves off; therefore what was in God, is in you, and something of your own which is called free-will, though it is an unsuitable name."[2] Tolkien describes this capacity for what he calls sub-creation in his essay *On Fairy Stories*.[3] For both, our creativity is a result of our divine nature: "...we make...because we are made: and not only made, but made in the image and likeness of a Maker... Man becomes a sub-creator...we already have an enchanter's power..." For Tolkien, creativity is closely linked to an experience of enchantment which opens the door to the 'perilous realm' of Faery. This is about much more than wishful thinking: Tolkien points out that anyone can say 'the green sun' but to make it believable and true is quite another matter altogether. One creates in a believable manner when what is written reveals a glimpse of the underlying truth of the Cosmos.

Tolkien did not approve of attempts to determine or uncover hidden meaning in his stories. His work has, however, undeniably stimulated the public imagination. Quite apart from the popular interest in the books and the films, there is an array of publications from diverse disciplines. Quite an achievement. They cannot be reduced to allegory; rather the legends are more akin to Mythology. Whatever else Tolkien did or did not set out to do, we do know that he set out to write 'a mythology for England.'[4] He believed that he was dipping into the universal 'cauldron of story' and was therefore writing the truth. Mythology illuminates and in its turn influences cosmic reality. The ingredients are already there in the Cosmos; the story-teller or myth-maker selects the ingredients and cooks them in more or less innovative, palatable and believable ways.

I am much indebted to Pia Skogemann's insightful Jungian analysis of *The Lord of the Rings*. She says: "I understand The Lord of the Rings as a symbolic, not allegorical story...it activates the subconscious fantasies of its readers..."[5] As Divine sparks, or 'atoms' (which refer to units of consciousness, including us), *The Cosmic Doctrine* teaches that we are here to experience and develop according to the plane on which we manifest, bringing with us the learning from each preceding plane. This is an iterative process in which the Cosmos is becoming, and we are both explorers in it and co-creators of it. Tolkien begins by portraying this through the Ainulindalë, the Song of Creation, which then becomes EA: let it be, or become, which is the Manifest world.

Tolkien's Mythology is particularly accessible to us, partly because it was written recently, and so speaks to the modern mind, but also because of how he uses the Hobbits, for we can learn about universal principles through their experience. I intend to use the Hobbits to illuminate some of the ideas in *The Cosmic Doctrine,* most particularly around the development of consciousness, and in understanding the nature of the Self. Tolkien uses the Hobbits as a particular aspect of mankind in order to explore the evolution of consciousness undergone during their journey. We identify with them and live the tale through them. Like us they become frightened, and: "...do not know the way."[6] They are in awe of the beings and events that unfold around them, but most of all they are on a journey of discovery, not just of the external world, but of their own inner world. They become, and so illustrate how we may all practise sub-creation of ourselves and of our world. I include here the development of their consciousness stimulated by Faery. It has been pointed out that Faery are not mentioned at all in *The Cosmic Doctrine*; however, my defence is that the Cosmic Doctrine deals with high level principles rather than detail. It does not deal in specifics, but rather it speaks of Divine sparks and atoms and is clear that manifestation is diverse. It would almost certainly see Faery as an aspect of humanity, in accord with Tolkien.

At first, *The Cosmic Doctrine* tells us, there is the Unmanifest. The Unmanifest is pure existence and pure being, the only reality. Everything else, much like EA, is "an appearance and a becoming." If we know it, by definition it is not Unmanifest. However, although it is not Manifest, it is. This is counter-intuitive for us as we tend to think of Manifestation as reality. Everything else we tend to see as somewhat hypothetical, and therefore possibly not real, depending upon our own tendency towards reductionism. However the idea is that Manifestation is rather akin to a painting but is not the inspiration or reality behind the image. Although there is a reality behind the painting, as Artists we have a remit in its translation and expression, and we will also, naturally, have varying degrees of skill. It may be more fruitful to say the Unmanifest and the Manifesting world, as the latter is very much a work in progress. Mythology, and indeed Story, provides a meeting point between us as conscious beings and the framework, or nuts and bolts of the Cosmos. Tolkien's aim was to enchant, to help us glimpse this underlying truth: "...rend(s) indeed the very web of story, and let(s) a gleam come through."[7]

Then at some point, something happens. Out of the Unmanifest, we are told that "space moves" and this is the beginning of Manifestation. Movement can be thought of as the desire of God for the knowledge of God and this necessitates duality: a part of oneself which can know, observe and reflect upon the Self. The Unmanifest on the other hand is unity and being, rather than doing. We are told that the Unmanifest and Manifest will present themselves slightly differently dependent upon the conditions of the particular plane. The prime duality is space and movement, and we might helpfully think of these as the feminine or the unconscious, and the masculine or conscious, respectively. We have then what are described as the simultaneously opposing forces of the desires for both momentum and inertia so that what actually happens is a third thing, the result of this 'push and pull'. Hence a straight line is impossible. It is curved, eventually to become a ring, known as the Ring Cosmos. Its motion over time sets up the formation of a second ring, the Ring Chaos, which pulls against the Ring Cosmos. The Ring Chaos is not evil, but it does upset things, as it pulls in the opposite direction. This mutual 'push and pull' of the first two circles then produces a third ring known as the Ring Pass-Not which results in the creation of a sphere within which things may arise and become.

The on-going spinning motion of all three Rings, and the space within thus securely contained, sets up a series of internalised movements which result in greater and greater complexity of smaller spheres within the first sphere. These descend more deeply into form until they become us, or indeed any other being within that Cosmos. We are thus told that: "Every plane has three Rings – like the Cosmos."[8] And that "…they act and interact among themselves, producing ever greater and greater elaboration of influences."[9] These three Rings are therefore the foundation for our Individuality: "Therefore it is that you, small as you are, have your affinities with these Cosmic Beings…"[10] Forms become more complex and individuated, then eventually they re-integrate, joining each other, driven to unify and reunite with their Source, motivated by Love. We should, then, be able to take these principles and apply them to any situation, finding fresh insight and meaning along the way. However, we might be excused at this point if our head is spinning faster than the Rings and for the spatially challenged such as me it is tempting to go and lie down in a darkened room (which actually would not be a bad place to start). I am very pleased though that I persevered, and I invite you to persevere too: it is worth it. Let us see if we can make sense of our Unmanifest from our Manifest and our: "You cannot pass!" from our Ring Pass-Not.

All humans have available to them all states of consciousness. This is quite remarkable when we consider the range of physical, mental and emotional abilities and disabilities in people, so let us therefore remark upon the obvious. Everyone sleeps, everyone wakes, and everyone who lives dies. This suggests that having available all states of consciousness is a non-negotiable aspect of who we are. Amongst other authors, G. William Farthing confirms this when he says that

"Consciousness is the fundamental fact of human existence."[11] *The Cosmic Doctrine* tells us that sentience is about reacting, and then registering the reaction. Development occurs by the means of experience, memory, and the subsequent processing and integration of these experiences. Consciousness is an integration of reactions, a set of relationships relative to the plane of existence. It will develop dependent both upon where it is and what it does with the experience it encounters.

On each plane then, the Divine Sparks (including us!) acquire a fresh mode of reaction. Therefore we change dependent on the external conditions, our adaptation to them, and our consequent analysis and integration of the experiences. This reaction and subsequent processing occurs in what I shall call the Unmanifest Self as well as the Manifesting Self, and one way we will examine this is through the rather disconcertingly named chapter: 'The Law of the Seven Deaths'. We know from the Ring Pass-Not that Manifestation relies on boundaries and limits and this applies to us too. The limits imposed by the Seven Deaths allow the Unmanifest Self to relate to and utilise the learning from the Manifesting Self, paving the way to the eventual return to Unity. It is a sort of reaping of the harvest of Manifestation which, after a fallow period, then allows a sowing of new seeds from the Unmanifest Self which then grow, and so on. In Tolkien's Mythos this is partly explored through Ilúvatar's Gift of Mortality which is the fate of Men (and Hobbits). Mortality or physical death in *The Cosmic Doctrine* is known as the Third Death. Whilst the Gift of Mortality is described as: "...bitter to receive..." the underlying message is one of hope, as the Fate of Men will eventually take us "...beyond the circles of the world."[12] The similarity in language, as an aside, is striking in the light of our focus here on Rings and on *The Cosmic Doctrine*'s statement that eventually, at the right point of evolution, we will burst through the Ring Pass-Not to seed something altogether new.

It is important to remind ourselves of what an accomplishment, and indeed what a mystery, consciousness is. We tend to take it for granted, finding it instead rather harder to grasp the nature of the unconscious. And we know remarkably little about both states if we only look to exoteric science for an explanation. Marie-Louise Von Franz, a well-known Jungian Analyst, describes how unconsciousness is the primary state and that overcoming it requires great effort: "Consciousness is an accomplishment which requires energy. It can only maintain itself for limited periods, after which a state of unconsciousness – sleep – is again necessary in order to renew the used up energy."[13] Sinking back into unconsciousness is on one hand a sideline of Tolkien's tale, easy to miss; however, the sheer number of times he remarks on the state of consciousness of the Hobbits tells us it is important. It was Skogemann who first alerted me to Tolkien's descriptions of the Hobbits either falling asleep, losing consciousness, or regaining consciousness in the tale. When I checked, the sheer volume is startling.

The Hobbits do not just lose consciousness a lot, they lose consciousness at meaningful points. So for example when they arrive in Rivendell they are told: "It is difficult to stay awake here, until you get used to it." This does not necessarily occur however, at key points of external action. Loss of consciousness often indicates a shift in the direction of higher states of consciousness which may then be brought through to Manifestation. Sometimes this is described directly as an experience, for example when Sam sees the Star of Eärendil in the sky as he and Frodo journey through Mordor; at other times this shift of awareness shows itself in an increased ability to constructively manage the world. In Rivendell it is clear that there is something about just being there which promotes a powerful urge to sleep. It is by no means implied that Rivendell is boring! Likewise, there is no impression that there is a lot of activity which makes you sleepy. Something about the place stimulates a different state of consciousness. This is about being around the Elves.

At the beginning of *The Lord of the Rings* Hobbits are solely concerned with material matters and appear to have no aspirations beyond domestic contentment. At this time, they are at a point of stability having reached a certain level of mastery of the physical plane. They have no apparent wish to move beyond the boundaries of the Shire, or even indeed to wonder what lies beyond them. Maps of the world 'outside' the Shire have become blank and the boundaries are policed. We might helpfully think of the boundaries of the Shire at the beginning of the tale as boundaries of the manifest consciousness for the Hobbits, as Skogemann has proposed. They fear water and the Old Forest, both symbols of the Unconscious that might intrude. They no longer believe in dragons, and mock those, such as Samwise, who do. And we, having already read The Hobbit, know that dragons do in fact exist.

This state is known as denial by Psychologists, which is a state of mind where truth, though known at some level of the psyche, is nevertheless denied by the conscious mind. The motivation for this restricting state is the management of uncomfortable or unbearable states of mind or external realities, but the price is the sacrifice of the truth. Already though, we have a hint that treasure, in this instance the fabled treasure of Bag End, will be found via the unconscious, in tunnels and holes. And this treasure, we know, was not won by sitting at home taking afternoon tea. Indeed the name of Bag End itself conjures up the image of a receptive space, ripe for something to enter into it. This is of course exactly what it is, as Hobbits dwell in holes in the ground, in hollow hills in fact, already telling us that their (our) purpose is to infuse space and matter with consciousness. In Hobbit parlance, the tension between the 'respectable' Baggins and the adventurous Tooks reflects the tension between the conscious, or Manifesting Self, and the unconscious, or Unmanifest Self. The Manifest will seem 'respectable' as part of its purpose is to establish stability, whereas the Unmanifest Self will seem adventurous as it provides new impulses. Bilbo and Frodo, as descendants of both strains, represent the potential for transcendence and growth. Hobbits are also known as Halflings and ostensibly this is about their shortness of stature. I propose that this name conveys their awareness of only the Manifesting part of their being, or the conscious Self. They need to become aware of other aspects of themselves, and their world, including Faery: in other words they are not whole because they are not wholly aware, and nor, by implication, are we.

Growth from this comfortable place will inevitably involve discomfort. Students of the Qabalah know that the task, once the physical plane has been mastered, is to overcome the inertia of the comfort it provides. Indeed, if there was ever a need for an upset, it is now before the Hobbits become irretrievably dull. And as every fledging Psychotherapist knows, denial of the unconscious and of what Jung called the Shadow only makes it stronger, and more likely to encroach in an unhelpful manner. This is exactly what happens as Sauron, representative of the collective shadow of Middle Earth, takes shape and sends his Black Riders out to seek the Shire in search of the Ring. He has now intruded into the Shire, and cannot be fenced out. Frodo and his companions no longer have the option of the false comfort of denial and have to confront a very uncomfortable reality indeed. They are forced to leave behind the safe familiar territory of the Shire into the beyond, or aptly named 'blue', initially in the form of the Old Forest, with all its associations of Arthurian forests. In so doing they step inside themselves.

In order for progression to occur this is of course, exactly what needs to happen. Although everything in the Shire seems well ordered and content, there is a subtle sense of incompleteness, and not only by the given name of Halfling. As we have already seen, Hobbits fear and despise adventure: "We are plain quiet folk and have no use for adventures. Nasty disturbing uncomfortable things! Make you late for dinner! I can't think what anybody sees in them."[14] However, this is not the whole tale, as Tolkien comments: "Now it is a strange thing, but things that are good to have and days that are good to spend are soon told about, and not much to listen to; while things that are uncomfortable, palpitating, and even gruesome, may make a good tale, and take a deal of telling anyway."[15] This is expressed clearly in the description of Bilbo in possession of the Ring as being more than well-preserved: he is actually unchanged. The situation has progressed beyond stability; it has become stagnant, and cannot be allowed to continue. Earthly contentment has its limits for the Hobbits, as from an evolutionary standpoint it is bound to do. It is respectable, but it is tedious!

Frodo and Bilbo have a hint of Faery in their blood already. They are the descendants of Belladonna Took, a Faery name if ever there was one. Tooks live on the borderland between the Shire and the 'Outside', and thus are walkers between the worlds and between states of consciousness. They are famous for their rebelliousness and for having a vast complex of underground tunnels as their dwelling place. We are informed that one of them 'took' a Faery wife long ago. Hobbits (apart from Tooks) avoid water, seeing it as dangerous, which of course it is. We are told that Frodo's parents died by drowning: they literally got in over their heads, and one wonders why. For consciousness to develop there must be a shift in internal equilibrium, and it probably won't be comfortable. It is necessary to step into the unconscious, away from the known, safe and familiar. Frodo, significantly, travels as Mr Underhill.

Some changes of our state of awareness are easier to observe than others, but even here we have scant understanding of them. Let's take sleep for example; which is the Fourth of the Seven Deaths. We can usually observe when someone is asleep, and we usually know when we have slept. Changes in brain activity can confirm or deny whether this has actually occurred. *The Cosmic Doctrine* tells us that we do not understand sleep and this remains true today. Farthing, from a psychological perspective, sees sleep (neatly omitting physical death, presumably because he views death as the end of consciousness) as being the most important of the altered states of consciousness. Sleep is seen as important due to its dramatic changes in behaviour and experience, to the impact on us if sleep is disrupted, and to dream phenomena. The critical defining aspect of sleep is the loss of awareness it entails, and the research frankly gets a little unsure of itself after that.

We know even less about why we need sleep so much. We spend such a large part of our lives asleep, and we are so sensitised to a lack of it (speak to any new parent) that it is quite remarkable that we do not clamour to understand its nature further. Whilst we know that sleep serves a restorative function, we also know that physical rest alone is insufficient, and is no substitute for sleep. The most reliably demonstrable impact of sleep deprivation seems to be on how we feel and think. We are also fairly confident that we process our day-time experiences during sleep. The effects of sleep deprivation are enormously stressful, so much so that people have a rather annoying tendency to drop out of sleep deprivation experiments. Ultimately, we die if there is prolonged deprivation: it seems necessary that we enter a state of unconsciousness at frequent intervals, even if this means death.

We have a similarly incomplete understanding of why we dream. We know that some dreams process the content of our days but this is not an entirely satisfactory explanation. Then there is the phenomenon of lucid dreaming: reflective self-awareness while sleeping. Here is an example of a shade or state of grey where different states of consciousness can co-exist, or more accurately, become something new. Not everyone seems to experience this, unlike the phenomena of sleep, wakefulness and death which are universal, hinting at the possibility that this is a further stage of development. *The Cosmic Doctrine* teaches that sleep is a miniature death, and that by understanding sleep we can begin to understand death; hence my labouring the point here. The message is: "It is death which enables you to utilise experience." Sleep is as vital a part of us as waking conscious. Simply put, it is an important clue as to who we are, letting us know that we are more than our conscious minds. In sleep, the Manifesting part of our Selves is resting, but the Unmanifest part is active.

As we have seen, any aspect of the Self which is Manifesting has, by definition, a dual aspect. Anything else is part of the original Unity of consciousness. So for example, the Unmanifest aspect of the Personality is that which, despite wakefulness, cannot be brought to mind: this would include the so-called Freudian unconscious. There is much, of course, written and debated about the nature of the unconscious mind and Psychology cannot at present agree on its nature or its contents, let alone its implications. It is not too strong to use the word controversy, which surrounds the degree of its influence on waking life, whether its contents have meaning, whether it is full of darkness best left untouched, whether anything positive can emerge from it, or whether it is individual or collective.

One of the aims of initiation and indeed of evolution is to build relationships between the different aspects of the Self as this paves the way for the return to Unity. There is a rather nice illustration of these aspects of the Self coming together in the description of Glorfindel, an Elf-Lord who had lived in Valinor during the paradisal time of the Two Trees. Whilst defending the Hobbits against the Black Riders on their approach to Rivendell he appears as a shining figure of white light and we are told that he "...live(s) at once in both worlds..."[16] This aptly conveys how the different aspects of the Self may visibly and effectively join together in a highly evolved being such as Glorfindel. For those not yet at this point the Self, although whole, will not experience itself as such. Aspects of the Self lose sight of each other during the course of evolution as we experience the planes as separate. It is more helpful to say that the Self is in the process of realising it is whole.

However, just because we may be unaware of all aspects of ourselves, it does not follow that they are inactive. The Hobbits sleep after they first meet Elves following a brush with the Black Riders. Gildor, the leader of the group of Elves they encounter is explicit about what needs to change: "The wide world is all about you: you can fence yourselves in, but you cannot forever fence it out." [17] We already have a clue about a shift in the Hobbits, as Pippin "...recalled little of either food or drink, for his mind was filled with the light upon the elf faces... so beautiful that he felt in a waking dream." Contact with the Elves awakens something other than the usual Hobbit preoccupations with comfort and food. Then: "He fell fast asleep." In this same encounter,

Frodo talks with the Elves while Sam sleeps curled at his feet. At the end of the evening: "Frodo felt sleep coming upon him, even as Gildor finished speaking…he threw himself upon a bed and fell at once into a dreamless slumber." [18]

What is interesting here is that sleep becomes closely entwined with the action, whether it is Sam at Frodo's feet, or Frodo feeling sleep approach even as he speaks with Gildor. We are left with the sense that the two are irrevocably linked in a way that is not about bodily tiredness. There are many sorts of sleep described during the tale, some dreamless as Frodo's above, some restless, and some filled with dreams. Let us also note Pippin's 'waking dream'. It is like a lucid dream turned on its head, where dreams come into wakefulness as opposed to wakefulness coming into dreams. How might we understand this? We might conclude that there is a sense of dream-like unreality in meeting Elves, but this interpretation feels intuitively wrong. Instead we are being given a clue as to how states of consciousness shift and blend in the return to Unity. This is an example of Tolkien revealing the underlying 'gleam' of the Cosmos to us. After their first significant encounter with Faery, the Hobbits slip into their personal equivalent of the Unmanifest. Recall that it is the Unmanifest which is reality, and it is the Manifest which is becoming, and the task is to foster relationship between the two. This is confirmed as the Hobbits then wake refreshed, and more able to deal with the threat of the shadowy Black Riders. The Unmanifest Self helps to process experience; however, one might also reflect on its role in allowing us to 'touch base' with other aspects of ourselves that will have a different perspective on our struggles.

The meeting with the Elves stimulates the Individuality 'filled with light'. Actually, for Frodo this process began much earlier in his meetings with Gandalf, and in being brought up by Bilbo. He had already started to wonder and to reach both inwards and outwards. The activation of the Individuality results in an improved capacity to integrate experience, and manage external reality. Jung too believed that the Self binds together the dualities of the conscious and unconscious parts of our nature and that the search for the (whole) Self is the goal of the psyche. There is a need for balance, and for recognition that light exists in contrast to darkness, much as the conscious mind exists in contrast to the unconscious. Jung said that we realize this through a process called Individuation, which involves recognizing and processing both the shadow and the unconscious, and not suppressing or stifling either of these. The Self thus emerges as an integrated whole (not Half!). Tolkien adds that this occurs through the recognition of and co-operation with Faery. He is not alone, of course, in this view, and I can hardly contribute to a book of Wendy's without acknowledging her own significant contribution.[19]

These matters do not readily lend themselves to exoteric science, and so learning does not progress quickly. Furthermore there is today still some resistance to looking too closely at those aspects of the Self which we are not consciously aware of. This is driven in part by anxiety, lack of knowledge, and the still reductionist and materialist nature of our culture. This in itself is a reflection of our current point in evolution, much the same as that of the Hobbits at the beginning of *The Lord of the Rings*. So we shy away from explanations of psychological distress which acknowledge meaning and an unconscious life, preferring instead to fix so-called irrational thoughts. We see sleep as something of a luxury that can be cut back on, and dreamers are not valued, unless those dreams lead onto the amassing of material wealth. However, Gildor is clearly telling the Hobbits that they cannot ignore the Unmanifest, and by implication he is telling each of us the same.

So, let us return to the Hobbits at the point at which they enter the Old Forest. They have tried to fence it in, by growing a thick and tall boundary known as the High Hay. The sense of danger persists however, and the Forest keeps drawing close to the boundaries. Here they keep their doors locked after dark, which is not usual in other parts of the Shire. Before even entering the Forest Frodo begins to dream. The dreams at first seem to be products of his fear and anxiety, but then become something else, with a striking dream of the sea and a white tower. The sea in Tolkien is no ordinary sea, but is more akin to the astral sea, beyond which lie the higher realms of existence. Towers are usually symbols of initiation and higher states of awareness. The implication is that to achieve higher levels of consciousness, we must first navigate and vanquish the creatures and fears of our shadow and our unconscious mind. And so it proves on entering the Forest.

Tolkien's use of colour is rather sparse, and therefore noticeable when present. There is a strong theme of Silver and Gold running throughout the Mythos, and this can usually be identified with the meanings and consciousness associated with the Two Trees of Valinor.[20] The first Tree is Telperion (meaning great silver wreathed one) the Elder tree, from which fell silver light. Laurelin, the second born (meaning song of gold) has leaves from which fall a golden light. Silver usually denotes an inner journey, the unconscious, receptivity or Unmanifest and Faery. Gold denotes joy, outer expression, positivity, the Manifest, conscious awareness and Humankind.

The light of each Tree waxed and waned over the course of seven hours, and began again an hour before the other ceased to shine. So twice each day, once at dawn and once at dusk, there was an hour where both trees were faint, and their beams were mingled. Where Silver and Gold are seen together, this usually indicates a state of transcendence, which relates to the blending of the light of the Trees. It heralds a shift of consciousness towards transcendence, where the sum of the whole becomes greater than its parts and echoes the Unity of the Unmanifest. The Trees were killed by Morgoth and Ungoliant, their light fortunately having previously been blended and put into the Silmarils. Consequently the Silmarils could leave Valinor and be brought to Middle Earth. This is an illustration of the First Death: where two separate forms are joined together to become a third, with the consequence that they no longer exist in their original form. The gain is that they may exist on another plane, in this case Middle Earth. The Second Death is where a physical form becomes extinct: it is set aside for the purposes of evolution, as new forms will be needed. The closest Tolkien comes to describing this is through the disappearance of the Entwives, with the implication that Ents will eventually become extinct.

As the Hobbits enter the Old Forest the High Hay is netted with silver cobwebs, indicating that an inner journey lies ahead. Straightaway we learn that the laws of the unconscious or Unmanifest are different and it is of no use to try to apply the strategies of the Manifesting world. This is one reason why, incidentally, exoteric science which uses the methods of the Manifesting world fails to shed any light on it. We are told that the consequences of trying to fight the contents of the unconscious are that the trees will attack if provoked, and become unfriendly. What is effective though in managing them is fire, symbolic of the light of consciousness. Inevitably however, the Hobbits soon become disoriented and are forced deeper and deeper into the Forest: "…they seemed unaccountably to have veered eastwards…the trees seemed deeper and darker…they had lost all clear sense of direction…"[21] At the heart of the dark Forest they encounter

Old Man Willow, who entraps them and sings them to sleep, and tries to drown Frodo: "Sleepiness seemed to be creeping out of the ground and up their legs, and falling softly out of the air upon their heads."[22] They are in so deeply now that even fire is not effective and they are almost overwhelmed by the externalised forces of the Unmanifest. Sleep can of course be used to avoid a painful waking reality, which is what almost happens here, and there is a clear warning of the possible consequences of this as Frodo nearly drowns, like his parents before him. It is not desirable for the unconscious to overwhelm the conscious mind or vice versa: we should aim first for balance and then for transcendence.

We learn that the Unmanifest Self can only ever be experienced and allowed rather than actively managed. We know about it by implication, or by its results. The most cursory examination of the language associated with these states is illuminating: thus we 'fall' asleep, or 'drop off,' we 'lose' consciousness, or we become 'spaced out.' Anyone who has had the most passing acquaintance with insomnia knows that you cannot 'make' yourself sleep and it is counter-productive to try; instead you must be able to succumb to it. It is also very difficult to 'make' yourself die, even for those apparently quite determined to do so. How then should one proceed if one desires closer acquaintance with the Unmanifest aspects of the self? Frodo, after contact with Bilbo and Gandalf, began to dream and muse: "... perhaps I shall cross the river one day..." He had begun to feel restless, he looked at maps, and wondered what lay beyond their edges, and why the old paths seemed 'too well-trodden.' If we examine Bilbo's song about the road, there must first be wondering, then intent, made more or less consciously. But then, critically, there should be a willingness to allow ourselves to be swept along by things which we cannot consciously control or know:

"The Road goes ever on and on, Down from the door where it began. Now far ahead the Road has gone, And I must follow, if I can, Pursuing it with eager feet, Until it joins some larger way, Where many paths and errands meet. And whither then? I cannot say."

Paradoxically, if we think we know where we are going, we will not get there. In the words of the verse associated with Aragorn: "Not all those who wander are lost."

The Hobbits then encounter the enigmatic couple of Tom Bombadil and Goldberry. They are rescued from Old Man Willow by Tom who is complete Master of his little country, including its unconscious life. As they make their way to his house they pass water: 'like silver', and as they enter in, golden light streams forth. Goldberry's gown is shot with silver with a golden belt, indicating a being of transcended consciousness. Their journey so far and the shift in their consciousness have had their impact on the Hobbits conveyed by an outburst of flowery language, and they begin, spontaneously, to sing instead of speaking. Frodo demonstrates growth when he then has a psychic dream where he perceives Gandalf as Saruman's prisoner. Merry meanwhile dreams of water, symbolizing a shift of awareness and Sam, who will undergo profound change, sleeps most deeply of all: "like a log."

Neither the unconscious nor the Ring has power over Tom. With him as storyteller and guide they begin to understand and manage the unconscious. Frodo has a further, more intuitive dream as a consequence. Here we see again, silver and gold intertwined: "...a song that seemed to come like a pale light behind a grey rain-curtain, and growing stronger to turn the veil all to glass and silver, until at last it was rolled back, and a far green country opened before him under a swift sunrise... Outside everything was green and a pale gold."[23] This is a premonition of the pulling back of the veil between the worlds, heralding his eventual journey to Valinor and the transcended state that this implies. We begin to see the impact of this change when the Hobbits are captured soon after by a fearsome Barrow Wight on the Barrow downs. Frodo manages to awaken, all by himself, from the Wight's sleeping spell: he is no longer overwhelmed by the unconscious. He finds his courage and resists, calling Tom to the rescue once more. They are rewarded by winning weapons from the Wight's horde in order to help them in their task.

The Hobbits eventually arrive in Rivendell after these adventures. Frodo duly loses consciousness, overcome by the Black Riders. As an aside we might note that the Black Riders were defeated by Glorfindel, but also by fire (conscious) and water (unconscious) together. After his recovery Frodo listens to the Elves singing and we are told that: "The enchantment became more and more dreamlike, until he felt that an endless river of swelling gold and silver was flowing over him, too multitudinous for its pattern to be comprehended; it became part of the throbbing air about him, and it drenched and drowned him.

Swiftly he sank under its shining weight into a deep realm of sleep. There he wandered long in a dream of music that turned into running water, and then suddenly into a voice."[24] Sam had already fallen asleep. So here we see another example of a waking dream, and the enchanting silver and gold. Tolkien, as we know, is explicit in saying that we get into Faery through enchantment. When they leave Rivendell we are told that 'slowly the golden light faded to pale silver': they are off on another inner journey having assimilated their experiences so far. Frodo leaves Rivendell aptly clothed with an undergarment made from Mithril, or 'truesilver'.

By this time we know that the impact of their development is Frodo's offer to take the Ring and to destroy it by putting it into the fires at the heart of Sauron's realm. The Ring is symbolic of the lower self, or Personality, and Frodo's offer to cast it into the fire is not just for his own personal initiation, but is an attempt to deal with the collective shadow of Middle Earth at this point in time. It is one of the most poignant and illuminating moments in the book when he says: "I will take the Ring…though I do not know the way."[25] As we have seen, it is in fact essential that he does not know the way. His motivation is clearly for the greater good, and devoid of ego. Instead we are told: "A great dread fell on him…At last with an effort he spoke, and wondered to hear his own words, as if some other will was using his small voice."[26] This other will is not some mysterious external force to be feared, it is Frodo's own Individuality which speaks and overrides the Personality which desires a holiday in Rivendell, reunited with Bilbo. This is not insignificant and demonstrates the radiant potential of the Individuality, once activated. From a Hobbit who has never left the Shire, he now takes on this Herculean Quest. As we know, he goes on to see it through, for the benefit of all, despite extreme privation to the Personality.

The Fifth Death, which is the Death of the Personality and all its desires, is necessary in order to access the Individuality more reliably. Here the experience of Love becomes less attached to the personal and more to the universal: "…the higher manifestation of love which itself is Love…"[27] It might be more accurate to think of this as the death of the dominance of the Personality. No sense of Self is lost here, which is what one often fears when in the throes of giving up the dominance of the Personality. It is more that the driving seat will be occupied by the Individuality. We might fear that we are handing control to a 'back seat driver' until it happens and we realise that all this time we've been giving control to the learner driver and not the instructor. A sure sign of success is that one feels more rather than less oneself. The Personality actually continues to function, but is enriched rather than diminished by the contact with the Unmanifest Self which shines through the Personality. Significantly at the end of the tale Frodo appears translucent. Returning to our metaphor of the painting, we might say that the painting becomes more alive, more expressive, and closer to the inspiration behind it.

The desire for the Ring, conversely, represents the desire of earthly power for its own end, or to meet the desires of the Personality. This is inevitably limiting. The Ring conveys invisibility which rather neatly illustrates the point; one becomes less visible, and by implication less real and effective, rather than more effective under these circumstances and eventually there is a permanent fading. The Ring does not aid the expansion of consciousness, and the fate of the Ringwraiths rather graphically portrays the consequences of this. It binds one to the Shadow and to the Ego; it does not support growth and expansion. This is succinctly pointed out in the Ring's inscription, only visible when placed in fire:

> "One Ring to rule them all, One Ring to find them, One Ring to bring them all and in the darkness bind them in the Land of Mordor where the Shadows lie."[28]

We might notice as an aside that the One Ring is composed of three within it and so is the antithesis of our three great Cosmic Rings.

The Hobbits' attempt to cross the Misty Mountains by going over ground via Caradhras is then blocked. They are not yet ready and still need to work with their unconscious fears. They are forced to take a dark journey underground through the mines of Moria where they encounter and survive Goblins and other monsters. They are then finally ready to enter the Tiphareth centre of Lothlórien, the realm of the Faery Lady Galadriel: "...the heart of Elvendom on earth." Tiphareth is of course the sphere of the Individuality. Lórien is known as the Golden wood but is also bounded by the river Silverlode, so this is confirmed as a place of transcended consciousness. The point is emphasized by the gold and silver lanterns of Caras Galadhon. Lórien can only be entered by faith and they may attempt this now. They now are able to cross water, and later manage it by leaving Lórien in boats made by the Elves. The Company of the Ring spend their first night sleeping on a platform high in the Mallorn Trees. We are told that Hobbits are usually unable to sleep upstairs, but significantly they do manage to sleep on platforms on this occasion, conveying the shift in their awareness. Most of the Company of the Ring pass the test of Lothlórien, apart from Boromir, who is ensnared by the Ring and is soon overcome by the desires of the Personality.

As a place where the Individuality is accessed, it is implied that the shift in consciousness changes the worlds and brings them together, which Galadriel as mediator is able to do. We are told that "…in Lórien the ancient things lived on in the waking world…on the Land of Lórien no shadow lay." "…Sam was…rubbing his eyes as if he was not sure that he was awake… I feel as if I was inside a song, if you take my meaning".[29] Frodo has grown, demonstrated by his ability to perceive Galadriel's Ring, and his willingness to surrender the One Ring to her if required. There follows a nice description of the Individuality which recalls the earlier portrayal of Glorfindel: "When he had gone and passed again into the outer world, still Frodo the wanderer from the Shire would walk there, upon the grass among elanor and niphredil in fair Lothlórien."[30] As they leave, Galadriel gives them symbolic gifts: for the young Hobbits belts of gold and silver, indicating their shift; and a Mallorn seed for Sam, which will enable him to plant a symbol of Lothlórien in the Malkuth centre of the Shire. To Frodo, she gives a small phial of water from her fountain which contains the reflected light of the Silmaril known as the Star of Eärendil, again confirming a transcendent state of silver and gold.

The Hobbits then are forced to part company and undertake their own development before they meet again when the Quest is fulfilled. For Merry this culminates in the terrifying encounter with the Lord of the Nazgul where the courage of Eowyn rouses his own selfless instinct. Pippin volunteers his service to the unsympathetic Denethor, in payment of the debt he owes his son Boromir for saving his life, and then encounters a Troll at the Battle before Mordor. There follows a description of what Pippin expected to be his physical death. It beautifully conveys mortality and the perspective of different aspects of the Self, with the Manifest giving way to the Unmanifest, of which we hear a faint echo: "Blackness and stench and crushing pain came upon Pippin, and his mind fell away into a great darkness. 'So it ends as I thought it would,' his thought said, even as it fluttered away; and it laughed a little within him ere it fled, almost gay it seemed to be casting off at last all doubt and care and fear... And his thought fled far away and his eyes saw no more."[31]

Frodo and Sam meanwhile, on their way to Mordor, the Land of Shadow, enter the tunnel of Shelob. Shelob is a monstrous spider and, incidentally, is a daughter of Ungoliant, who destroyed the Two Trees. There is rather neat cosmic justice when Shelob is defeated by Hobbits wielding the phial containing the reflected light of the Silmaril. Shelob's tunnel is a dark, fearful place: she retreats but soon returns and stings Frodo who falls unconscious and is thought dead by Sam, who thankfully takes the Ring. This deathlike condition inflicted by the female actually results in Sam and Frodo successfully entering Mordor, as Frodo is captured by Orcs who then almost completely destroy themselves fighting over his Mithril coat (they have not learnt that wisdom can never be gained in this manner). He is then rescued by Sam. This is akin to the Sixth Death, which is trance-like death where the body sleeps but the soul is awake. At this point in the tale Frodo has gone slightly mad and is shouting, running recklessly towards the Orc-den of the Tower of Cirith Ungol, where they would have been killed, or at the least both captured and the Ring taken, spelling the end of the Quest. His loss of consciousness saves the day and it is hard to imagine how he could have consciously chosen this course of action or foreseen the outcome. The Unmanifest Self took control in order to ensure both the success of the Quest and of Frodo's own initiation.

They then undertake the exhausting trek through Mordor, the Land of Shadow. With the exception of the moment when Sam sees the Star of Eärendil, they are cut off from all comfort. Frodo is denied even this, with only Sam as his comfort. They go on when the Personality has no cause for hope, but by now they are functioning at another level. "But even as hope died in Sam, or seemed to die, it was turned to a new strength..."[32] We may also note that the Elven bread, lembas, is more potent when they solely rely on it, rather challenging the warnings of folklore against Faery food (though I do concede that the subsequent change in consciousness is indeed a state of no-return). By now they are drifting almost continually in and out of consciousness. This allows the final Initiation (the Seventh Death) as the Ring is put to the fire. This is the last of many examples where we see that it is the very ordinariness of the Hobbits, their rootedness in this plane that brings success. The shift is revealed after their sleep on the Field of Cormallen when: "...the clear voice of the minstrel rose like silver and gold..."[33]

They return to the Shire to find it in danger, but they have to save it themselves without the aid of any of the other supposedly more powerful beings. The Hobbits are now revealed as great leaders of their own kind, and it is here that we discover the point of it all. The aim of transformation is not to play harps on clouds, nor to rely on discarnate entities to solve our problems, but to function better in the world: "You must settle its affairs yourselves; this is what you have been trained for. Do you not yet understand...you will need no help. You are grown up now. Grown indeed very high..." Merry and Pippin have in fact literally grown following their encounter with the Ents. Saruman too spots this change: "You have grown, Halfling...Yes, you have grown very much."[34] They are indeed no longer Halflings, but are now whole. After their victory in the Shire the summer is "...a marvellous year...an air of richness and growth, and a gleam of beauty beyond that of mortal summers that flicker and pass upon the Middle-earth."[35] Their shift of awareness fully manifests in Malkuth: they are now Initiates, and the freedom of the spirit is brought through to the planes of matter.

Frodo and Bilbo leave the Shire, and are permitted to take the ship to Valinor. Mortals are usually forbidden this passage, so we know that something profound has happened. Now Gandalf can say to Bilbo: "You are not the hobbit you were."[36] Tolkien himself in his letters aptly describes it thus: "Mr. Baggins seems to have exhibited so fully both the Took and Baggins side of their nature."[37] Once they reach the nadir, or furthest, deepest point of complexity and form, the Divine Sparks then gather up everything preceding and begin the return journey to the Logoidal source.

The final touch is the birth of Elanor, the daughter of Sam and Rose. She is named after the little flowers in Lothlórien, the meaning of which is sun-star, indicating that she holds the blended influence of the Two Trees within her as well as both Faery and Human consciousness. It is said that she was often mistaken for an Elf, and served Arwen Evenstar, Faery Queen of Gondor. She subsequently moved to live in the Tower Hills, north of the Shire, from where she could see the Grey Havens which look towards Valinor. Elanor might thus be seen as the Halfling born whole. This heralds the turning of the nadir for the Hobbits alongside the departure of Frodo and Bilbo. Or as Bilbo puts it with characteristic Hobbit understatement: There and Back Again. So, both *The Cosmic Doctrine* and Tolkien concur that once consciousness becomes fully individuated and has reached its limit and potential, it starts to unify as we see in the birth of Elanor and the fate of Bilbo and Frodo: "Man, Sub-creator, the refracted Light, through whom is splintered from a single White, to many hues, and endlessly combined, in living shapes that move from mind to mind."[38]

From the outset, Tolkien expressed the relationship between the Unmanifest and the Manifesting Cosmos. The first line he wrote was: "In a hole in the ground there lived a Hobbit."[39] He was marking an exam paper at the time and did not know why he had written it, where it had come from, or where it would lead. We now have some idea of the significance of this symbolic opening.

1   Dion Fortune, *The Cosmic Doctrine* (York Beach, ME: Red Wheel/Weiser LLC, 2000) Preface
2   *Ibid 52.*
3   J.R.R. Tolkien, *On Fairy Stories* (Oxford: Oxford University Press, 1947)
4   Humphrey Carter, *The Letters of J.R.R. Tolkien* (London: George Allen and Unwin Ltd, 1981)
5   Pia Skogemann, *Where the Shadows Lie* (Wilmette: Chiron Publications, 2009)
6   J.R.R. Tolkien, *The Lord of the Rings,* (Hong Kong: Harper Collins, 1991)
7   J.R.R. Tolkien, *On Fairy Stories,* (Oxford: Oxford University Press, 1947)
8   Dion Fortune, *The Cosmic Doctrine,* 25.
9   *Ibid,* 27.
10 *Ibid,* 48.
11 G. William Farthing, *The Psychology of Consciousness* (Eagelwood Cliffs: Prentice-Hall Inc. 1992)
12 J.R.R. Tolkien, *The Silmarillion,* (London: George Allen and Unwin, 1977)
13 Marie-Louise Von Franz, *Creation Myths* (Boston: Shambhala Publications Inc. 1972)
14 J.R.R. Tolkien, *The Hobbit* (London: Harper Collins, 1991)
15 *Ibid*
16 J.R.R.Tolkien, *The Lord of the Rings* (Hong Kong: Harper Collins, 1991)
17 *Ibid*
18 *Ibid*
19 Wendy Berg, *Red Tree, White Tree* (Cheltenham, Skylight Press, 2010)
20 J.R.R. Tolkien, *The Silmarillion* (London: George Allen and Unwin, 1977
21 J.R.R. Tolkien, *The Lord of the Rings,* (Hong Kong: Harper Collins, 1991)
22 *Ibid*
23 *Ibid*

24 *Ibid*
25 *Ibid*
26 *Ibid*
27 Dion Fortune, *The Cosmic Doctrine,* 163.
28 J.R.R Tolkien, *The Lord of the Rings,* (Hong Kong: Harper Collins, 1991)
29 *Ibid*
30 *Ibid*
31 *Ibid*
32 J.R.R Tolkien, *The Lord of the Rings,* (Hong Kong: Harper Collins, 1991)
33 *Ibid*
34 *Ibid*
35 *Ibid*
36 *Ibid*
37 Humphrey Carter, *The Letters of J.R.R. Tolkien,* (London: George Allen and Unwin Ltd, 1981)
38 J.R.R Tolkien, *On Fairy Stories* (Oxford: Oxford University Press, 1947)
39 J.R.R. Tolkien, *The Hobbit,* (London: Harper Collins, 1991)

7 MAGICAL PRINCIPLES WITHIN THE COSMIC DOCTRINE

DEREK THOMPSON

I first encountered the writings of Dion Fortune as a teenager, in a moment of providence when someone showed me a copy of *Esoteric Orders and Their Work*. I worked my way through her other books – with varied levels of understanding – until only two remained: *The Mystical Qabalah* and *The Cosmic Doctrine*. While *The Mystical Qabalah* (along with Gareth Knight's *A Practical Guide to Qabalistic Symbolism*) has become a well-thumbed reference book, I re-read *The Cosmic Doctrine* sparingly.

Usually I can only take in one or two chapters in a single sitting because it puts me in a particular state of mind that requires effort and focus, which I can best describe as consciously imaginative. When I do make time for *The Cosmic Doctrine* there will always be one theme or aphorism that stands out for me, which naturally has changed over the years. It's a curious book that somehow manages to be simultaneously simple and complex, demanding the reader's full attention yet only meeting it halfway. It is not an easy read, and I think it's all the better for it. Like every good quest the candidate is tested and challenged along the journey, and only the most determined endures to the end!

As a footnote I'd like to add that I always find *The Cosmic Doctrine* to be a great influencer of dreams. Whenever I'm reading it, I find my dreamlife takes on added depth and richer symbolism. I've endeavoured to incorporate that aspect into this chapter. It was inspired by the re-reading and contemplation of *The Cosmic Doctrine*, followed by a good deal of meditation and head-squeezing, to see what came to light. As those familiar with the book will know, its extensive use of metaphor makes it a challenge to speak about any of the contents in concrete terms. Added to that we are dealing with magic here, after all, which itself is a whole other bag of tricks.

"Magic is the art of causing changes to take place in consciousness in accordance with will." – Dion Fortune.

I am aware that there is another school of thought that sees magic as a sort of 'cosmic cash point', where the primary purpose of the Will is to exert influence in order to get you what you want. All I can say is 'horses for courses' and that the ideas in this essay apply equally to both approaches.

The next challenge when encountering *The Cosmic Doctrine* is to put aside the usual expectations of reading a book – even one with such a formidable reputation for being so esoteric. What I hope to do here is to take some of its abstruse ideas down a few planes to show how they are reflected in magical principles that fall somewhere between the occult and psychology. There may also be some meandering along the way, for Nature surely abhors a straight line as much as she does a vacuum.

As Above So Below, but after another fashion

Let's begin at the beginning: *Space moves.* This is arguably the most powerful and, dare I say it, magical statement in the entire book. It reminds us that we are not in a static Universe, and that principle extends to all levels of Being. Reality is fluid, and we are both the influenced and the influencers. Being aware of this cosmic cause and effect, it naturally follows that we are responsible for whatever we put into motion. Hence the magician's caution to develop discrimination and discretion.

Intention (or the Will if you prefer) creates impetus. This, if maintained without constraining factors (or, at least, with those of lesser impact), will create tracks in space. These are likened in the book to conditioned responses or habit – an accretion of stresses and patterns that become self-sustaining.

This helps us to understand why rituals, prayers and hymns that have been worked countless times before are easier to tap into and make use of than something new, (although using existing patterns and formats for new work can also be beneficial). These tried and tested formulae have not only potency but also permanency on their plane of operation. To put it another way, they exist outside of us in a kind of objective subjectivity. An example of this phenomenon is where a group completes a pathworking meditation and discovers afterwards that some people have had similar experiences or encounters that were not in the script.

Exoterically, it may also shed light on the experience of a breakthrough in sport or the sciences by one person that is then swiftly followed – and often exceeded – by others. Once a thing is made possible it is made *more* possible ever after, and each progressive step builds upon the last and those before that.

To get back over to the esoteric side of the fence, *The Cosmic Doctrine* reminds us that: "The Masters as you picture them are all 'imagination.'"[1] The imagery that we use – and can build upon – has endured because it works. Those tracks in space are also clear paths to contact god-forms, other beings and correspondences. These archetypes and established pathways can be used by people with minimal training, to a degree (if you'll pardon the pun), whereas creating or using new pathways and patterns effectively requires a more specialised development of the Will or Consciousness.

Magic is about polarities. The Rings Cosmos and Chaos seem to be mutually exclusive and conflicting influences. However, this dualism is only a limited perspective, made from within the game, so to speak. Our Ring Cosmos and Ring Chaos, exerting influences of formation and dissolution respectively, are as good a definition of the 'right hand' and 'left hand' paths as any when it comes to magic. The one is constructive / progressive and the other is destructive / regressive. There's no moral aspect to that; it is simply a matter of function.

This tug of war is the dynamic polarity that facilitates movement and magic. Whether we're looking at ritual, healing, invocation, banishing, or initiation, something is exchanged or transposed. However, this is only possible within certain bounds.

We can call these conditions a Pass-Not. It also follows that the... let's call them intentions... of the giver and the receiver have to be harmonised into some sort of accord. Susceptibility can be one terminal of the battery, which is why the development of the Will is so important alongside learning magical techniques and attributions.

One of the great Christian conundrums is how God can be all-powerful and yet represent one half of the paradigm of Good versus Evil in the world. Here we are presented with a dualism that can only make sense when reconciled against a more expansive backdrop. Good and Evil exist in the world as two aspects of a larger reality, which also needs to incorporate a third, synthesising / mediating principle that is the Ring Pass-Not.

This is not only the original trinity but also the pattern of stability in growth. In the Qabalah we have the pillars of Mercy and Severity mediated on the Tree by the pillar of Equilibrium – the middle way. Let's not forget that the mediating influence is a direct result of the development of those two polarities – it's not an imposition but a progression and consequence. To borrow from the Egyptian pantheon, Isis and Osiris created Horus.

The Cosmic Doctrine talks a great deal about cycles. The Days and Nights of God, along with the rhythms and dynamics alluded to, are a reminder that magic – of whatever persuasion – is subject to phases that are conducive or antagonistic, depending upon what is being worked and when. This, of course, conflicts with the popular new age idea that 'we can all do/be/have anything we want whenever we want.

By way of an analogy, imagine a blustery day. To the untrained eye there's a wind blowing and that's an end to it. But to the seasoned sailor, the wind is a southwesterly that can bring warmer air than, for example, a northerly wind. Our sailor can make use of that wind if it's heading in a direction she wants to travel, or she can make preparations to tack against it should she decide she needs to travel against it in the opposite direction. Going with the flow is all well and good, as long as you know where you're likely to end up (or if you don't care).

These rhythms and cycles bring us neatly on to one of the great paradoxes of magic and the occult. The more you develop a sensitivity and connection to the reality of magical currents, the more susceptible you can become to them. Individuals and groups working with transpersonal *themes* will be only too aware that *as below so above* can also apply when there is turmoil down here.

The Cosmic Doctrine outlines the evolution of consciousness, starting with simplicity and going through increasingly refined experiences to develop complexity. This 'experienced complexity' then enriches and informs the cosmos by making the experience of those experiences available to the collective (more tracks in space!) What is of note for our purposes is that consciousness is gradually developed through greater specificity. In plain English, if magic is a process for the evolution of consciousness (for individuals and collectively) the secret of magic is limitation or the focus of the Will on a defined objective.

For those familiar with the four worlds of the Qabalah, we could represent this journey like this:

ATZILUTH: Everything – the totality of potential.
BRIAH: Anything – an individualised consciousness.
YETZIRAH: Something – an individualised expression.
ASSIAH: The thing itself – manifestation, definition, and actualised potential.

A more mundane illustration would be someone going into a restaurant, asking for the menu, selecting a dish and finally being served their food (which, due to a number of factors, may not meet the original expectations!)

The cycle of projection and reflection, down through the planes – or out across them – also illustrates how thought forms are built up and stimulated to the point where they develop a form of consciousness and can respond back. This is also analogous to the way in which amulets, talismans and other magical tools can be 'charged.'

The chapters concerning 'The Laws' lend themselves readily to analysis and interpretation from a magical perspective. Here are a few thoughts arising from some of them.

The Law of Limitation reiterates a point made earlier that magic requires a defined goal (which may simply be *contact*). The singularity of purpose is more than just focus – it is a culmination of dedication and discipline. This law is surely evidence of a Universe with a sense of humour, since those who believe and act as if they can have it all, as and when they choose, are correspondingly least likely to achieve anything with that approach. Magic is neither all emotion nor all mind but a blend of the two in some state of equilibrium. Mention is also made of the technique of shifting consciousness beyond the mundane plane in order to resolve issues upon it. This, of course, is a valuable technique – e.g. working something out through ritual and sympathetic magic.

The Law of the Seven Deaths, paradoxically, proposes that despite being in waking incarnation we are well served by learning to function outside of it. Those with experience of astral projection or lucid dreaming will appreciate the reality of this perspective. The Law of Polarity gives a concise overview of both horizontal and vertical polarity, albeit in quite biological terms! This explains, along with other aspects of this essay, how groups and individuals may become *contacted*.

The Law of the Attraction of Outer Space contains a useful depiction of an encounter with the Dweller on the Threshold – an amalgamated reflection of those aspects of ourselves that have not been integrated or negated. The Law of the Attraction of the Centre reminds us that the dualism of Light and Dark is but an aspect of a greater truth, that All is One. Given that both Complexity and Individuality developed from Unity, how could it be otherwise? (Of course, recognising that philosophically and making sense of it in daily life is another matter entirely.)

The second part of *The Cosmic Doctrine*[2] seems to be even more esoteric than the first part (which is something of an achievement!), but it's just as relevant to magical work. It tells us, for example, that we contain the earlier stages of our evolution. Given that the Planetary Being is a collective intelligence or consciousness, of which we are each a contributory expression and part, it follows that we have the capacity to access 'distant memory' in relation to a place, an event or our own past. However, there is significant risk of delusion and confusion in such an endeavour so we need to be on solid ground at the outset. The model of the Individuality and the Personality (and of basing consciousness in the former rather the latter) is the solid ground we require.

The three activities referred to as Movement, Light and Sound, may also be considered as Consciousness, Perception and Expression.

Lastly, the book concludes with the guidance that not only does the Planetary Being guide us, but also that we are able to make contact with it directly and individually. This, to me, brings us to one of the core purposes of magic and takes us full circle, back to Dion Fortune's statement at the beginning of this chapter.

In summary, *The Cosmic Doctrine* contains references to many magical techniques and principles. These include: the use of the Will, raising consciousness, polarity working, the creation and use of thought-forms, contact on the inner planes, and working with the Personality and the Individuality. It is not a light read, but it is an instructive one. I hope this essay has shed some light on its themes and patterns, and that it contributes in some small way to the evolving unity of the Planetary Being.

1   Dion Fortune, *The Cosmic Doctrine*, (London: Aquarian Press, 1957) Introduction: Section 3

2   Part II is headed 'Afterthoughts' in the Red Wheel/Weiser edition of 2000

8 THE COSMIC DOCTRINE: INNER SPACE AND THE CREATIVE IMAGINATION

GWEN BLYTHE

Like many people who have studied *The Cosmic Doctrine*, I have struggled. Initially I had issues with concepts which, while very much of the time in which they were written, seem quaint in the light of subsequent scientific development. I had been told that it was nothing less than an exposition of Cosmology, that it answered all the big questions of how the Universe came into being. I have met scientists and engineers who could discuss at length the nature and relevance of the different planes and sub-planes described in the book as though it was a treatise on physics and higher mathematics. After some serious study I was able to 'see,' that is, visualise the underlying abstract patterns in the processes described, but felt that I was not quite grasping the whole of the meaning, that important concepts were passing me by. That is, until I went back to that phrase "to train the mind, not to inform it."

> *Perhaps I owe my happiest thoughts to the fact that impressions do not strike me at once in their full completion, but first enter my brain in an uncertain and tentative form.*[1] (Novalis.)

I learned a lot from *The Cosmic Doctrine* by meditating on those symbolic images which in Dion Fortune's own words "are designed to train the mind, not to inform it." This phrase goes right to the heart of the issue, which to me lies not in processing the precise details of the twelve Rays or the seven Cosmic Planes and everything that flows from them towards manifestation but rather, through use of the creative imagination, to dwell upon these forms and allow them to sink within the mind, to emerge in time as a cohesive whole. One of the joys of having read *The Cosmic Doctrine* lies in the realisation that different parts of the book stand out for the reader at different times. It is not to my mind a book to read from end to end, but rather to study over time, returning to parts which at first may have made no sense, to find that, as Dion Fortune herself said on the final page: "What is said here, however fanciful the expression may appear, is deeply real and worth the intensest consideration."[2]

In working with *The Cosmic Doctrine*, I learned something invaluable, and it is very simple. If in esoteric studies of any kind you come across things that cannot at first be understood, they will become clear merely by dwelling upon them in meditation over time. At first it may feel as if you are banging your head against a metaphorical brick wall. This is all part of a process, because at first you must explore every possible angle with the mind, diligently and with a sense of childlike curiosity, filled with the desire "to know…" Then, by allowing the mental processes to subside, you can just hold the concept or phrase lightly in mind, leaving it to grow and expand on its own, as it were, until enlightenment (in this narrow sense) occurs. The feeling is unmistakable; suddenly everything becomes clear. There is a breakthrough in understanding. It may well take time and diligent repetition to achieve the breakthrough, but it will come.

This skill, basic though it may be, has had a profound effect on my life, and I cannot speak highly enough of the mind training afforded by this book, although I am unwilling and perhaps unable to use it as though it were a physics textbook. However, having looked at it in greater depth, I now see *The Cosmic Doctrine* in a different light: I see that Dion Fortune has created a work of Art, and that at its heart *The Cosmic Doctrine* is a creation myth.

Every work of art is formed of spirit element. (Novalis)

Viewed as art, the symbolic significance of the ordered progression toward manifestation creates a sense of harmony in an imagined cosmology that links both immanent and transcendent worlds in which we may see ourselves participating in eternal cycles of life, death and rebirth. We may see that in the language of symbol and metaphor, which is the language of myth, that the Rings, Rays, Laws and levels all relate to *inner* states of being that may be accessed by the individual human being who has learned to change consciousness at will. In envisaging these things, we are constructing a mandala, a pattern that speaks clearly to our unconscious minds in a way that transcends thought or word. We are all pattern makers, and the deeper parts of our brains, the 'Inner Eye,' responds directly to patterns and pictures at a pre-verbal level.

> *By its very nature, philosophy is anti-historical. It turns from the future to the practical; it is the science of perception; it explains the past by the future, whereas history takes the reverse process.* (Novalis)

I would differ here from Novalis only to say that "it is the *art* of perception." Yet there is an area within which both science and art are transcended and meet to become one and the same, in a state perhaps only transmissible through the abstract symbology of higher mathematics, or as pure light. One way of seeing the teaching in *The Cosmic Doctrine* is as a mechanical set of explanations, a textbook of engineering which puts abstract ideas into concrete form, but I prefer to think that Dion Fortune is seeking to engage our intuitional and imaginative faculties in striving to understand her cosmogony, while keeping us grounded by her mechanistic approach.

Any creation myth is an attempt to express the indefinable and to answer the big questions: where do we come from? Why are we here? How did things come to be like this? Where are we going? These questions have often been answered in myths linked to a specific geographical area, tribe, god or pantheon of gods; stories that say "our tribe is special, we have a special god or gods, and this land is ours." Any study of comparative mythology will show that although there are many examples of these world views, each different yet strangely similar, there are common strands and themes that cross the ages and the continents and may be found in folk and fairy tales from all over the world. It has been said that the mythic truth is the only truth.

Common images include the separation of light and darkness, a cosmic egg from which all life springs, battles between gods, or a breakage that creates duality from an original unity. Creation myths exist to remind us of the struggles of our ancestors to come to terms with the big questions. How have we come to exist in a world of such transcendent beauty? And as every sense thrills with delight, how is it that we seem to spoil each experience with our very presence? How should we move forward? How did it all begin? Where did we come from?

For some in Ancient Egypt, the Sun rose from an infinite, barren sea, and engendered *Zep Tepi,* the First Morning. The *Kalevala* of

Finnish legend describes how Ilmatar, daughter of the Sky, floated within the primal waters, looking after the cosmic eggs that formed the Sun, Moon and stars, and giving birth to the first man, Väinämöinen, son of the Sea. In fiction, the lion Aslan creates the world through song. The Greeks imagined how the Music of the Spheres kept our solar system in harmonious equilibrium. The People of the Book, Jew, Christian and Muslim, share the familiar Eden myth, with Adam and Eve as the first of humankind. The creator gods are often trickster gods, which may shed an interesting light on the Eden myth!

The idea of a 'Golden Age' long past is common to many cultures too, whether it is the Dreamtime of the first peoples of Australasia or that seen in legends of glorious lost cultures: Atlantis, Eden, Hy-Brasil, Ys. Alongside these stories are those of the spirit worlds, underworlds and otherworlds that lie alongside and interpenetrate our own, worlds of beauty and peril that have given rise to myriad tales of wonder and magic in folklore around the globe. Here are the 'fairy tales' so often dismissed as only suitable for the young, yet full of meaning if approached with an open heart.

When I was reading the first part of *The Cosmic Doctrine* and struggling a bit, someone wiser than me suggested that I should try to express its teaching, briefly, in terms of a different metaphor. I struggled with this for quite a while, and then in a flash I saw the whole thing open up in a short series of mental pictures. I'm including what I saw here as an example, not because it is 'right' but because it shows how a complex theory can be expressed in the language of fairy tale.

"There was nothing. Nothing at all, nothing that seemed like a great empty ocean. King Space arose from the ocean and looked around. He could see nothing for a long time, but then he saw a current in the ocean. From the movement in the waters arose Queen Time. King Space and Queen Time built themselves a sacred space, bounded by a high wall. Within the wall they built a great city with seven tiers and seven canals. Outside the city wall lay the Great Ocean. Twelve fair roads led from the sea-wall to their castle in the centre. Their children arrived, grew and populated the city, travelling from place to place, learning, growing and settling down to create a round table of harmonious living. In the centre of the castle was a deep well that led to the sea. When the city dwellers had evolved to their full potential at that time, the waters rose from the well and flooded the city. Pressure inside and outside the city was equalised. Nothing moved. It seemed that all was lost. But then King Space arose from the waters. He looked at the boundless ocean. In its motion he saw Queen Time, and all began again, but after another manner."

> *The seat of the soul is there, where the outer and the inner worlds meet.*
> (Novalis)

When all the sensory input from our daily lives is taken into the inner world of our imagination, a transformation can happen through the fusion of outer knowledge, emotions and sensations with the inner imagination. Insight is the result, oracular insight that will be revealed from the depths of the self, often in dream, sometimes in waking vision. These are levels and planes of consciousness that can be brought through by meditation on and around mythic forms with which you are familiar. One could say that the physical and psychological aspects of something are being examined in the light of the metaphysical; we begin to see "through a glass, darkly" yet with more light than usual.

We see that in using symbolic language, whether written or in glyph form, ideas can be expressed that are beyond the known, and beyond words. In *The Cosmic Doctrine*, Dion Fortune was writing for the future, and has used abstract metaphor to express a myth of creation and evolution that is not tied to place or time, but rather to a universal, eternal reality. This is both an intelligent and a far-sighted attempt to free us from the local view, and to point us toward a wider vision. We already know that our solar system is not the universe; we know that our Sun is one of countless myriad stars, that our galaxy is one of many. Symbolic imagery representing the eternal realities may perhaps best be expressed in terms of outer space, and so we are led to contemplate the heavens.

However, contemplation of 'the higher worlds' takes us to a place where we are able to contact 'the Universe within,' the microcosm rather than macrocosm. By meditating on these mythic forms and archetypal constructs we may effect changes in consciousness relating to the symbolic representations. We are then able to enter the worlds of Art, the otherworlds and the Dreamtime. What immensities are revealed by dwelling on a phrase such as "space moves."

> Plotinus said, *"Not all who perceive with eyes the sensible products of art are affected alike by the same object, but if they know it for the outward portrayal of an archetype subsisting in intuition, their hearts are shaken and they recapture memory of that Original"*.

Dion Fortune reveals herself in *The Cosmic Doctrine* as an artist and a mystic, even though by using the commonsensical side of her nature she has chosen to express the inexpressible through the lens of the place and the time in which she lived as a hierarchical system and a set of laws. At first glance she is setting forth a Newtonian worldview that seeks to impose order into the apparently chaotic picture that was emerging as a result of discoveries in quantum mechanics taking place at that time. She is seeking to reconcile opposites. She would have been familiar with both Blavatsky's *The Secret Doctrine* and Einstein's General Theory of Relativity. She would have been aware that truth is often best expressed in paradox, and that much may be inferred by considering changes of scale.

She takes us to extremes: to the Unmanifest, to a place before space and time existed. We enter a strange world where a meeting of literary art and higher mathematics melds to show us the creation of a Universe. Then she tempers our flights of fancy by bringing us down to earth, using somewhat mechanistic symbolism so that we are back with our feet firmly on the ground. She has no time for revelation that cannot be made manifest 'in Earth.'

We finish the book and are left with our individual thoughts upon the subjects discussed therein. We may recall that we know nothing. And yet ... and yet, we start to see resonances, half-remembered, that link the stars and the constellations with great archetypal figures. We may relate the tales of distant Atlantis to the Circles and Rays and wave formations we envisaged while engrossed in the descriptions of the rise and fall of worlds. We may see King Arthur and his knights and the Mysteries of the Table Round linked with the Solar deities of ancient Egypt. We may indeed see many things. All this and more emerges from the dream worlds in the light of ideas set forth in the pages of *The Cosmic Doctrine,* as our minds in training develop the ability to perceive the common threads that bind all the worlds one to another in the web of Being.

1   All quotations from Novalis are taken from: ed. and trans. M.J. Hope, *Novalis: His Life, Thoughts and Works* (London: David Stott, 1891)

2   Dion Fortune, *The Cosmic Doctrine* (York Beach, ME: Red Wheel/Weiser LLC, 2000), 212.

9 THE MYTH OF THE COSMIC DOCTRINE

CHRISTIAN GILSON

Since the Nineteenth Century the term 'myth' has been a pejorative one. During that century the triumph of reason relegated myth to the past and there was no longer a role for stories that were of doubtful origin and considered to be untrue. This attitude can still be seen today amongst the general population, where myth is often confined to the fictional. When we talk about myth we imagine those ancient stories of gods and goddesses, impossible tasks and miraculous events. Myth came to be seen as an untrustworthy work of fiction that was deliberately created to be deceptive. As a result it became something for children, a populist canon of stories created as an entertainment, and indeed many films and novels echo the ideas and plots of the ancient myths. These story patterns repeat continually and their appeal is that they are so familiar to us; they explore themes of common concern to all humanity. From this position you may well ask why I describe *The Cosmic Doctrine* as a myth as clearly the style of writing is far removed from traditional myth.

The Cosmic Doctrine does not tell us stories of gods, heroes and monsters, or of impossible challenges. It does not appear to tell a story in the traditional way that we have come to understand as being mythical, but tell a story is exactly what it does; a story about the Universe and our place within it. The story is as otherworldly as you can get; it does not involve fairies or unicorns but rather it creates a whole new cast. This cast may not demonstrate the archetypes identified within classical myths by Carl Jung for example, but the story creates new forms which underlie the text and give meaning to this tale of creation and existence.

It may seem odd to describe this as a work of fantasy but when we consider its origins there can be little doubt that it is so. Dion Fortune tells us from the outset that the text did not come to her in the normal way. It was not the product of her own study and reflection but was given to her from the Inner Planes; that is to say she mediated the text in the belief that non-corporeal entities had dictated it to her. This fantastical origin clearly has no connection with modern reason. A great leap of faith is required to believe it, although no greater leap than that needed to accept the existence of gods and goddesses. The rationalist would exclaim: "This could not have really happened! Where is the evidence?" when referring to the creation of the text and to its very content.

The text of *The Cosmic Doctrine* clearly goes beyond the thinking of its time but it reflects a body of similar thought stemming from Helena Blavatsky's great work *The Secret Doctrine*, which she also claimed was mediated by her from a group of hidden Masters. These texts aimed to achieve a similar end: to re-animate myth and place it back into the heart of a society that had lost touch with the power of this form. Reason, then as now, continues to push out myth, making fun of it. Yet as Roland Barthes argues: "Myth is a pure ideographic system, where the forms are still motivated by the concept which they represent while not yet, by a long way, covering the sum of its possibilities for representation."[1] Barthes is expressing the view that the words which make up any myth create in the reader's mind a series of images that lead them to realise a much wider set of ideas than those being expressed within the text. That is to say the myth stimulates thought and response, leading the reader to construct a greater whole. Reason alone cannot do this; it remains sterile and empty, reducing everything to its basic components. It is this that Nietzsche claims has undermined modern society and left us looking for meaning as the result of our abandonment of the instinctive in favour of the rational. The value of myth, he argued, was its ability to draw people together and ground their culture in a common basis. The precedence of reason results in the fragmentation of that society. Also important is his view that the construction of myth is not in itself a rational process but a surrendering to the creative forces. *The Cosmic Doctrine* is an example of this, being born from an irrational process yet attempting to use a rational, even scientific, form to try to address the society of the time and its obsession with scientific evidence.

A Marxist analysis of this text would begin by identifying it as a source of ideology; a way to reframe the experience of the readers and give them a specific world view that accords with the text. This too is exactly what myth does, although the Marxist would claim that this ideological world view is a false view, a manipulation of reality to subjugate and pacify the populace, a set of false ideas constructed to deceive, and as such clearly a work of fantasy. What Marx seems to overlook is that the cold rationalist world he wishes us to live in lacks purpose and the true sense of community that Nietzsche calls for. It is this reductionist view of life that *The Cosmic Doctrine* seeks to redress, and through the language of Science and Reason hopes to create a new world view that restores meaning and purpose. To this end it is an ideology, but to be given a framework or narrative through which to frame your experience of reality is surely no bad thing; it gives you focus and purpose, it inspires and motivates action. Not only that, but as a printed and distributed text *The Cosmic Doctrine* begins to generate a shared understanding, creating a community of which it is the foundation. It points us to a greater understanding of our being and our existence beyond the biological or economic, rational, reductionist view.

Joseph Campbell also takes this position, and goes further when he says: "We may therefore think of any myth or rite either as a clue to what may be permanent or universal in human nature."[2] The function of myth is to direct both individual and community towards a greater shared understanding of existence. It is directly the opposite of the reductionism of reason that would have us see humanity as a mere machine. The power of *The Cosmic Doctrine* is to rephrase myth within the very language of scientific reason and to occupy the rational mind such that it is led to engage with the spiritual ideas that subtend. Or as Campbell puts it: "Mythology is a rendition of forms through which the formless Form of forms can be known."[3] What he appears to be saying here is that mythology gives substance to the underlying unmanifest conditions of existence or, more simply, that it makes a form of the non-physical, spiritual concepts that give rise to creation. Thus *The Cosmic Doctrine* functions as a modern myth because it uses the scientific/academic form of written expression to explore and explain the unmanifest spiritual ideals that could be said to have given rise to the manifest, or at least suggests that there is such an origin to the manifest world and that to accept this view is not in itself irrational. As Campbell argues: "Mythology is not invented rationally; mythology cannot be rationally understood."[4]

I would now like to turn to the fourfold function of myth given to us by Joseph Campbell in *The Masks of God Volume 3: Occidental*

Mythology in order to demonstrate the ways in which *The Cosmic Doctrine* can be seen to fulfil those functions. "The first and most distinctive – vitalising all – is that of eliciting and supporting a sense of awe before the mystery of being."[5] Surely there can be nothing more awe inspiring than the existence of life within such an immense universe. That this universe has resulted in the existence of life, in particular a form of life that is capable of observing and comprehending its own improbability, is itself astounding. Science tells us that the probability of human existence is so small that it is almost zero, but here we are. In addition, the text of *The Cosmic Doctrine* gives us an elegant image of flowing motion, as of tides that roll in and out, drawing us into a more and more visually complex schema. Yet it is a schema filled with the same beauty that is summarised in sine wave curves that trace the form which artists describe as the line of Grace and Beauty. Each new layer adds another enchantment, forcing the mind to make the pattern more elaborate until the swirling lines take on a form of their own and another image is revealed, leaving the beholder in awe of the beauty of creation. An awe that leads them to conclude that existence cannot be mere chance, there must be a greater source, an unmanifest perfection. In this way the text suggests to us the truth of the aesthetic version of the teleological argument for the existence of God which posits the idea that aesthetic beauty has no functional purpose, so its existence must be the result of the work of a God who wants to express perfection through beauty.

This is not the only way that the text creates awe in the mind of the reader. The very words themselves and the complex construction of the sentences also have a part to play. *The Cosmic Doctrine* is written in a very concise and exacting style, one which renders sentences so complex that the reader is forced to pause and think deeply about what is being said. This creates a sense of respect for the writing as it gives it the appearance of academic text. Certainly within some branches of academia there is a tendency to create a linguistic style that is concise and opaque. In many branches of study, words have evolved and terminology has been created that render the text impenetrable to the lay reader or the uninitiated. *The Cosmic Doctrine* appears to do the same, not so much in its use of terminology but rather in the way that the sentences are constructed. This complexity encourages the reader to see the text as academic and so gives it greater credence than a myth, but it also serves to inspire awe. In the modern world, academia is held in high regard and for many is even held in awe. By using this style *The Cosmic Doctrine* borrows this quality, leaving readers saying to themselves: "It is so hard to read it must be true." It creates an ideology based upon its own form that leads the reader into a state of awe, a feeling that the complex beauty of the cosmos rendered in this philosophically scientific manner can have no earthly source, and so there must therefore be an extraordinary, unmanifest being that subtends everything.

The second function of myth according to Campbell "...is to render a cosmology, an image of the universe that will support and be supported by this sense of awe before the mystery of a presence and the presence of a mystery."[6] As mentioned, this is the prime purpose of *The Cosmic Doctrine*. We begin with nothing, much as scientific theories begin. There is neither space (i.e. the measurement of distance between objects, because without objects there can be no distance) nor time (i.e. the measurement of change, because without objects there can be nothing to change.) All that remains is the potential for the existence of all manifestation, and until it is actualised through the process of the cosmology all there can be is the unmanifest potential. "Of this Unmanifest we can only say IT IS"[7] we are told, and immediately we are thrust into that sense of awe. The word 'Unmanifest' is given status as a proper noun: no longer just an ordinary exclamation of nothingness it now becomes a thing in itself. For the reader it is surprising that nothingness, or mere potential, can itself become 'being,' and here we have our first glimpse of "the mystery of a presence and the presence of a mystery."[8]

The cosmology of *The Cosmic Doctrine* continues by defining the space in which all manifestation will come to be. As the Rings Cosmos and Chaos come into being from pure motion, they oppose in a dualistic interplay which echoes centrifugal and centripetal force, but in this process they are seen to create the Hegelian third, the synthesis of thesis and antithesis. This third ring, the Ring Pass-Not, becomes the defining boundary of the space of manifestation that delineates what belongs to the order within, as opposed to Chaos which is without. In this way *The Cosmic Doctrine* refers to the classic operation of primitive creation myth as described by Joseph Campbell in which each myth creates a central point, a pillar, around which the space is created for the existence of the ordered world.[9] Mircea Eliade draws attention to this same point in his work *The Sacred and the Profane.*

"One of the outstanding characteristics of traditional societies is the opposition that they assume between their inhabited territory and the unknown and indeterminate space that surrounds it."[10] He goes on to report that every cosmogony deliberately focusses upon the centre, from which everything is created. According to this definition *The Cosmic Doctrine* fits perfectly with other creation myths.

Interestingly, the repeated use of groups of three is emphasised in *The Cosmic Doctrine*, and much is made of the importance of three. The underlying idea that duality – or polarity – is the cause of a new, third thing is never far from the surface. This is more than just the Hegelian model of knowledge; it is the very pattern of human life where male and female interact to create new life. This is fundamental to our existence and is never far from the animalistic instincts. Furthermore this focus on Trinity echoes the Christian sentiment that Dion Fortune claims to be her motivational force. The text asserts: "These three movements are the three 'Primaries' of the Cosmos – the first Trinity. That is why the Supreme Being...is always conceived of as a Trinity..."[11] This points readers to the paradox of the presence of a Divine being that is unmanifest yet triune, leaving them with the awe-inspiring mystery of how an unmanifest form can 'be.' The myth deepens when we are told: "Dances of atoms give rise to new Rings Cosmos and the story begins again."[12] The text does not use the term 'atom' in its conventional sense but to describe a unit of life which, although composite, cannot be resolved. A scientific term has been transformed into a mythic one and used to create a layer of meaning that brings with it a new sense of awe; the reader cannot help but conceive of the scientific atom, the basic building block of matter, and then recognise the multitude of atoms in the simplest of objects. We become awe-struck by the magnitude of this cosmology. This is myth par excellence.

The "third function of mythology is to support the current social order, to integrate the individual organically with his group."[13] The second part of *The Cosmic Doctrine* sets out to define the origins and purpose of life and describes some of the 'Laws' that govern these processes. In so doing, it establishes our place in the cosmos and demonstrates that as human beings our manifest form is but one small part of what we truly are. It makes clear that there are many layers subtending the outer physical shell, all ultimately deriving from a "Divine Spark" which itself is part of a greater whole. In this way the social order can be seen as a complex series of layers of deepening interdependence. The sense of relationship between individuals is highlighted by the concept of the Life Swarm. Although individuality is prized as an important point in evolution it is not seen as the end; rather this is the integration of the individual within the greater whole through the development of each individual's understanding of their role within the Life Wave or social group. Irrespective of how complex this seems to be, at the heart of the matter is the reality that however 'individual' we believe ourselves to be, we belong to a social group and have a responsibility towards that group.

Moreover the text gives us a common goal, a sense of purpose, when it tells us: "This is the goal of evolution of a Life swarm, the assimilation of the Group Spirit with the Logoidal Consciousness, whereby the Logos receives the fruits of its evolution."[14] To put it more simply our purpose is to evolve, to become all that we can be in this life. The experiences gained and lessons learned will not only help us to develop individually but the whole underlying spiritual hierarchy will gain from our action. By fulfilling our purpose we bring the Divine itself into the perfection of its own self existence. What could be a greater incentive to work towards our active participation in the social order? When we consider the concept of service, *The Cosmic Doctrine* gives us a structure which allows us to recognise its centrality; to act for the well-being of one is to act for the well-being of the Divine itself. This is the very message of Jesus' parable of The Sheep and the Goats.[15] The Christian term 'atonement' is also important here because it brings to mind the service done by Jesus to all humanity in taking on the cross, and by so doing achieving the possibility of eternal life and union with the Divine. It is this union with the Divine which *The Cosmic Doctrine* is positing as the goal of all manifestation. However, this is not a simple return but an enlightened return, thanks to the work of each Life Swarm.

The text is even more specific about the reader's position in his group, and assuming that he is an initiate of the mysteries it tells us: "The function of initiates on the outgoing arc is to enable their swarms to adapt themselves more speedily to the conditions of a newly achieved plane, because they have acquired some concept of the nature of these conditions."[16] The purpose then is to lead the way, both in the journey into manifestation and back into the Divine source. In other words to serve all creation as a role model, which is no greater challenge than that given to, and by, Jesus. This seems a tall order but in terms of myth it is hardly greater than any of the challenges set for the heroes of the Greeks or Romans for example. The myth of *The Cosmic Doctrine* couches the challenge in a more complex form; it is a challenge to the intellect and the moral standing of the individual. On another level it also places those who have read and actively engaged with the text into a specific role as initiates, regardless of whether or not they have been through a formal initiation. How this person behaves as a member of this group will reflect their commitment to the processes defined by the text. The myth has again created a way of seeing the world and understanding the individual's place within it.

"The fourth function of mythology is to initiate the individual into the order of realities of his own psyche, guiding him toward his own spiritual enrichment and realization."[17] By now we can see that *The Cosmic Doctrine* has fulfilled this final criterion. In its very existence the text guides readers to an awareness of their spiritual potential. Through the complex unfolding of the cosmogony the reader is shown his or her centrality to the whole process. The complexity of the language forces the reader to think deeply about the ideas presented; it stimulates the mind and establishes the principles that lead to spiritual discoveries. The text encourages the reader not just to contemplate but to meditate (in the Western sense of the term) upon the mysteries that it seeks to reveal. In this way it guides readers to an understanding of their place within the world and the purpose of their actions.

The Laws expounded in the text give a framework for this process, helping readers to see how they can move on and where they can gain guidance and support from the spiritual realms. It makes it very clear that progress is not achieved by just treading water, or falling back to an easier place. "To each man his own master. Do not select a master of a lower or a different type of evolution."[18] For those unaware of the spiritual goals implied, the myth makes it clear that every member of this Life Wave is tasked with their own evolution in service to each other.

The modern world is filled with myth, and as Campbell tells us: "...the released creative powers of a great company of towering individuals have broken forth: so that not one, or even two or three, but a galaxy of mythologies – as many, one might say, as the multitude of its geniuses – must be taken into account in any study of the spectacle of our own titanic age."[19] In his final volume of *The*

Masks of God: Creative Mythology, Campbell observes that a huge variety of texts function as mythology, and *The Cosmic Doctrine* is clearly one such. It is apparent that it not only fits within Campbell's four functions of myth but also within a modern definition of myth given by Raymond Williams in *Keywords*: "...myths are held to be fundamental expressions of certain properties of the human mind, and even of basic mental or psychological human organisation."[20]

For me, *The Cosmic Doctrine* is a very clever myth. Concealed within the scientific language of its day is a powerful attempt to define the world and give meaning and purpose to our existence within it. Yet the text also functions as a means of training and adapting the mind of its readers such that they are oriented towards the realisation of the spiritual truths that subtend it. Indeed as Dion Fortune herself tells us at the start of this work, the aim is not to tell us how the world came to be but rather to make our minds work to understand the underlying truths held within the myth. This myth is a grand narrative that gives voice to the power of esoteric study: the power to develop the human psyche and to engage the reader in the process of evolution. It is written in a way which appeals to the modern mind that seeks to use reason to understand the world, while at the same time telling us that the world has not been born of reason and ultimately cannot be understood through reason alone. Like all myths, this is an elaborate "screening allegory coined to hide from exoteric view the facts of an esoteric rite, while suggesting symbolically the rite's spiritual sense."[21]

Bibliography
Barthes, Roland, *Mythologies,* trans: Annette Lavers (Les Lettres Nouvelles 1972: France)
Campbell, Joseph, *The Masks of God Volume 1: Primitive Mythology* (Arkana 1964: London)
Campbell, Joseph, *The Masks of God Volume 3: Occidental Mythology* (Arkana 1964: London)
Campbell, Joseph, *The Masks of God Volume 4: Creative Mythology* (Arkana 1964: London)
Eliade, Mercea, *The Sacred and Profane* (Harper Torch Books 1961: USA)
Fortune, Dion, *The Cosmic Doctrine* (York Beach, ME: Red Wheel/Weiser LLC, 2000)
Mangion, Claude, *Nietzche's Philosophy of Myth,* (Academia.edu)
Williams, Raymond, *Keywords* (Fourth Estate 2014: London)

1   Rolande Barthes, *Mythologies,* trans. Annette Lavers (Les Lettres Nouvelles, France, 1972), 127

2   Joseph Campbell, *The Masks of God Volume 1: Primitive Mythology* (London, Arkana,1964), 461

3   *Ibid,* 55

4   *Ibid,* 42

5   Joseph Campbell, *The Masks of God Volume 3: Occidental Mythology,* (London, Arkana, 1964), 519

6   *Ibid,* 519

7   Dion Fortune, *The Cosmic Doctrine* (York Beach, ME: Red Wheel/Weiser LLC, 2000), 1

8   Joseph Campbell, *The Masks of God Volume 3: Occidental Mythology,* (London, Arkana, 1964), 519

9   Joseph Campbell, *The Masks of God Volume 1: Primitive Mythology,* (London, Arkana, 1964)

10 Mercea Eliade, *The Sacred and Profane: The Nature of Religion,* trans Willard R. Trask, (New York: Harper Torch Books, 1961), 29

11 Dion Fortune, *The Cosmic Doctrine,* 26

12 *Ibid,* 35

13 Joseph Campbell, *The Masks of God Volume 3: Occidental Mythology,* (London, Arkana, 1964), 520

14 Dion Fortune, *The Cosmic Doctrine,* 111

15 *The Gospel According to Saint Matthew,* Chapter 25

16 Dion Fortune, *The Cosmic Doctrine,* 110

17 Joseph Campbell, *The Masks of God Volume 3: Occidental Mythology,* 521

18 Dion Fortune, *The Cosmic Doctrine,* 144

19 Joseph Campbell, *The Masks of God Volume 4: Creative Mythology,* (London, Arkana, 1964), 3

20 Raymond Williams, *Keywords,* (London: Fourth Estate, 2014)

21 Joseph Campbell, *The Masks of God Volume 1: Primitive Mythology*), 96

THE APPLICATION OF ABSTRACT THOUGHT TO EVIL AND THE FEMININE

HOLLY MULHERN

The Cosmic Doctrine is a controversial text, renowned for being obscure and thus difficult to understand. It is stressed by Dion Fortune that its content is designed to train the mind and not inform it, and this is a statement which is at first perplexing and adds to the obscurity of the subject. How is it possible not to be informed by the text as it is read? And what can it mean by training the mind?

However, if we are able to suspend the concrete mind and raise consciousness to think abstractly, we can disregard the linear 'story' of the text and focus upon the principles expounded – the geometrics and their relationships when in movement. As Dion Fortune herself says,

"These images are not descriptive, but symbolic".[1]

The geometrics, numbers and the relationships between them are the symbols of this text: a point, the line, a circle, two circles, a sphere, triangle, square, cube, cross etc, and each of these symbols has a different body of energy. A point may be seen as jagged or precise, a line as thin and sharp, and a circle seems smooth, but no description is finite as the feeling of the geometric symbol is more nebulous than that. It needs to be experienced by meditation upon it, and explored personally. Relationships between the symbols are also described, such as polarity or the movement from the centre to the edge. Besides framing complex ideas through the patterns of movement between symbols, they can also represent different perspectives and create new ways of thinking that can then be applied to a problem, whether it be a philosophical one or a personal one. When meaning is found in these symbols (through meditation), the mind is able to think from different angles, to perceive in different ways, in short to apply a method of thought to all manner of ideas. This is the training of the mind that I believe Dion Fortune was referring to. And it is particularly important with this text to remember that Dion Fortune said 'an ounce of meditation is worth a pound of reading'.

This essay sets out to explain the meaning of geometrical shapes and their movements by looking at a philosophy of numbers rooted in Pythagorean thought. By doing so, we will discover a clear and definitive way of thinking, which we will go on to apply to a subject matter. For our purposes, this will be the relationship between Good and Evil, and Male and Female. Some understanding of Dion Fortune's *Mystical Qabalah* will aid an appreciation of this essay.

PART ONE:
UNDERSTANDING GEOMETRICS AND THEIR MOVEMENT THROUGH THE PHILOSOPHY OF NUMBERS

The first chapter of *The Cosmic Doctrine* is perhaps the most significant as it sets out a philosophy of first principles. I shall endeavour to explain the metaphors which are used, as forces of energy that are applicable to abstract reasoning since geometric symbols are configurations of force that follow the natural laws of creation and thought.

Unity and Duality

To begin with, it is important to understand the significance of Unity, represented by the number one. One is the great unity and two is 'the other'. Two is sometimes said to be the first number, since the number two makes numbers exist, by one and two, and thus makes counting possible. One by itself cannot do this. It is the nature of our everyday consciousness to experience life in terms of two or more, in duality and beyond. Two marks separation and also multiplication. Two is often seen as something sinister because it is 'the other' to the one. Two marks the idea of right and left, good and bad, favourable and unfavourable, of God and the Devil. It marks the idea of opposites, but they are not opposites, simply numbers. They represent tensions, which through the nature of the polarity produce another, known as three. Three is the first odd number, one being neither odd or even but containing all within it. Three marks a process, of beginning, middle and end. Three provides resolution, and consciousness through a journey and completion. Three marks reflection upon the beginning, upon one. For these reasons three is considered perfect as well as uneven.

One is unknowable until it becomes a unit. It becomes a unit when it splits into two, and then it becomes defined by the presence of the other. The one strives to hold the two close to itself. Two strives to separate from the one, because by doing so it has existence.

The resolution of the 'conflict' or 'tension' between one and two comes in the creation of three. Three resolves the tension and thus restores the original unity. It does this because it holds one and two within itself but is different to them, being three. In restoring the original unity three provides perspective, and also a sense of time, because the nature of a journey has occurred. It also makes sense of the idea of the self-revelation of Deity (through the process of consciousness, self-consciousness and reciprocal consciousness), and of the one Godhead being in the three of the Trinity.

In application to *The Cosmic Doctrine* text: firstly, a differentiation is made between Unmanifest and Manifest. The Unmanifest represents Unity. It symbolises One. The Manifest World represents (in the first instance) Duality. It symbolises Two. We cannot study the metaphysics of *The Cosmic Doctrine* without using the concept of duality, for we see more clearly what 'one' is, by beholding it against something else. If we wish to extend our capacity to perceive we extend this to work with a Trinity, Quaternary, and beyond.

On page two of the first chapter, the first duality is given as space and movement. A movement in space is created through a desire for force. Here we have space as inertia and movement as desire for force.

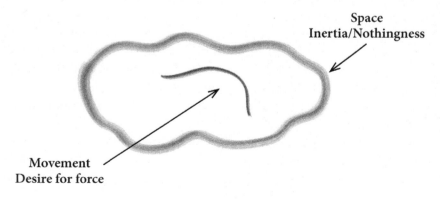

Space
Inertia/Nothingness

Movement
Desire for force

We are then given basic descriptions of force moving and developing further, to eventually become the Ring Cosmos and the Ring Chaos. Important language used in the description of this progression is of the second movement being at *right-angles* to the first. The description of right-angles indicates the forces are opposing and will eventually intersect. At their most basic level of meaning these are metaphors to describe forces of energy that show direction and interaction. E.g:

A force going one way   →

A force going a different way   ←

In the meaning of the above example these forces are not bound or limited. They are free forces. We can look at these as simple formations of thoughts, desires or opinions between two people, or as the working of our own internal thoughts, e.g:

I want this   →
He wants that   ←

I believe in this   →
She doesn't believe in this ←

These forms show differences. Duality enables differentiation and the ability to discriminate is vital in the development of thought processes. When two people disagree over something these two forces can be seen as pulling away from each other, and it is a skill to be able to pause and see the other person's point of view, that is, to understand the force of energy that they are feeling and speaking from. It is to be able to follow a line of imaginary thought processes from a different or directly opposing perspective. Part of the mind training is to attempt to do this, and achieve it. The more you practise the easier it gets – and it is perhaps true to say that to use this tool internally on your own thought processes is more profound in its effects than simply using it to avoid difficult situations.

When two people agree this can be seen as the same force working, and increased in power.

This basic form of polarity can be looked at in greater detail when these same forces are contained, or rather limited, within the confines of a circle. The meaning changes and deepens in complexity because one force takes an inward direction and the other force takes an outward direction – attraction to the centre and circumference. The two forces are now conditioned, one by the idea of a centre represented by the dot, and the other by a limitation that knows no bounds, represented by the outer circle. They are otherwise known as centrifugal and centripetal forces.

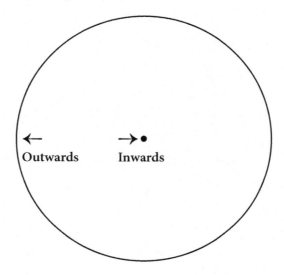

If you imagine yourself to be the force travelling to the centre, perhaps your own centre, then you may feel peace and the expansiveness of your breath. Perhaps you feel this when you meditate or at any quiet moment in the day. If you imagine yourself to be the force travelling to the outer bounds, determined to get out when you cannot, then you may feel anger or despair. You might feel this when in a job you don't like, or when someone just cannot understand your point of view.

Trinity

We have looked at how two forces can oppose each other both in an internal way and externally to ourselves. We can also see how the same force increases. What happens when two forces intersect each other? *The Cosmic Doctrine* goes on to explain how the two rings mutually attract as well as repel each other, and they do this by developing a positive and negative function within themselves that creates a quaternary of force. This quaternary develops, dividing itself again by two and goes on to create spinning discs symbolised by the potency of eight. By this process (which we will look at in more detail later on) the significance of three is born. The spinning discs mark the creation of a third component, the Ring Pass-Not. So, we can see that the forces of the first two Rings together make the First Trinity, or the Prime Trinity, and this initiates the birth of the Cosmos. We can view this as a sphere lined by three rings, or as an equilateral triangle – the geometric expression of the Trinity.

The forces of a Trinity – of any group of three – is a very powerful tool of thought. With the use of a triangle we can extend the practise of trying to see from the perspective of the opposition, to see things from another angle entirely. It's hard, but very useful when a 'stalemate' situation exists. However, when we look at any Trinity, there is potential for realisation in simply searching for the fourth aspect of it – whether we chose to place this on a cross, or a pyramid, or an invisible centre point/apex.

It can help us to explore myriad dualities, and see them differently, and understand the Trinity in question more fully. Chapter 22 of *The Cosmic Doctrine* hints that in order to fully realise the meaning of the First Trinity, we need to bring a fourth component into the equation. It is significant then that the Trinity came into existence because of a somewhat hidden quaternary at work.

Quaternary

The geometric component taking the value of four in its own right is symbolised in *The Cosmic Doctrine* as the Prime Stillness. It is the silent centre point of the three Rings. By its nature, it is often overlooked in significance, yet it is a most powerful symbol representing the Days and Nights of the Gods. Corresponding with the centre of our being, the heart, the Prime Stillness has the potential to act as a direct route to connect with God in the heart of the Cosmos. It also heralds the point of acceptance of limitations. Let us look at the relationship between these four forces, and what they represent by being in polarity with each other.

The Ring Cosmos has its focus towards the centre (the Prime Stillness). The centre is said to be connected to the Unmanifest and thus evil as it refers to the past. But the Unmanifest also symbolises the unknown, unknowable, and thus God. The Ring Cosmos is seen as the force which is positive because it is concerned with the building up of life. Its force is anabolic. The Ring Cosmos seeks to expand the centre, to make known the unknowable. The force is positive, dedicated, determined to manifestation, and thus from a focus comes creation.

The Ring Chaos is seen as a negative force, katabolic, because it breaks up life. Its force relates to dissolution and its tendencies are towards the Unmanifest, but at the outer edge of the circle, not the centre. It diffuses and destroys that which hinders the creative process, until the force is of a point where it is reduced to a component transmutable to the Ring Cosmos. This is like the change in the turning of the wheel, where the force of the Ring Chaos turns from positive to negative, and magnetically attracts the negativity of the Ring Cosmos. Following this the energy is taken into the positivity of the Ring Cosmos and focussed into the centre of the sphere it encompasses.

The Ring Pass-Not seeks to balance the two forces. In this way it partakes of the Qabalistic Pillar of Equilibrium, balancing the swinging forces of Severity and Mercy. Let us look at the three rings in relation to the Qabalah.

The Qabalah is a particularly useful tool that lends itself to work with *The Cosmic Doctrine* because it too possesses geometrical and numerical structures. However, with comparisons of this nature it is important to bear in mind that they are fragmentary, not exact and the purpose of any comparison is merely to extend understanding, not to try and 'box it up'. For example, the Ring Cosmos and Ring Chaos have correspondence with Chokmah and Binah respectively, but the Ring Pass-Not does not fit well with Kether or Daath for that matter. Yet to deny the opportunity of looking at the two rings in relation to Chokmah and Binah would be to miss out on many realisations. But we might say that the three rings have a positive connection to the Three Pillars, and may well shed further light when looked at in terms of the three Mother Letters. The same applies to the Christian Trinity in relation to the three Rings and the Qabalah.

So, the force of the Ring Cosmos pertains to that of Chokmah, and out of it springs Binah, the force of the Ring Chaos, formed in immediate balance to that which caused it to form. Binah, however, is seen as that which creates, shapes force into form, weaving life. This at first glance seems to be in opposition to the teaching that the Ring Cosmos creates through its focus, but on deeper consideration it isn't. This is in part because at the centre of the space into which the Ring Cosmos is focussing lies the Prime Stillness and this takes derivation from the Ring Chaos. Also one can see that the force that emanates from Chokmah goes right the way through Binah passing the abyss into Chesed. The force does not die although it is woven into a different form. It is changed. It develops deeper into manifestation through its will, and this highlights how the formation of the Cosmos is dependent upon both the forces of the Ring Cosmos and the Ring Chaos in order to exist. Binah is the thrust-block that enables Chokmah to develop into Chesed. The Ring Chaos is the thrust-block that enables the focus of the Ring Cosmos to occur. The Ring Chaos could be seen to whisper the words of God to the Ring Cosmos, supporting its desire for evolution, and the Prime Stillness could be seen to call the forces of the Ring Cosmos to it, to dance around it, to become a part of it.

The Ring Chaos takes the numerical significance of three (like Binah) and the Ring Cosmos takes the numerical significance of four (Chesed – manifest universe, though its roots are in two). When we multiply these together the twelve Rays are developed.

The four – the Ring Cosmos, Ring Chaos, Ring Pass-Not, and the Prime Stillness represent four basic compositions of energy. This cosmic quaternary takes many forms, and has done for eternity.

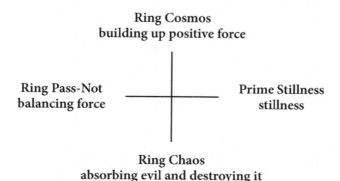

Ring Cosmos
building up positive force

Ring Pass-Not
balancing force

Prime Stillness
stillness

Ring Chaos
absorbing evil and destroying it

It is worth bearing in mind the dynamic of this set of four forces when working with any quaternary.

Quaternaries have been the basis of many scientific and philosophical explorations; Tetragrammaton, four worlds of the Qabalist: Atziluth, Briah, Yetzirah and Assiah, four elements, four directions (that are so important to practical ritual working). There is also Jung's definition of the four functions of the psyche: thinking, feeling, intuition and sensation. Interestingly, he describes three of the functions as being usually conscious and differentiated and one of the four functions as being deficient or hidden, a little like our very quiet Prime Stillness. However, if we were to apply the metaphor of the Cosmos to man, and superimpose Jung's idea of the four functions upon it, this fourth 'inferior' function that is largely unconscious, wild and primitive, uncontrolled and unadapted, could be any of the three Rings or Central Stillness.

The Relationship Between Three and Four

In order for the Ring Cosmos and Ring Chaos to make the First Trinity we saw that the Rings had to intersect each other and that they did this by developing a positive and negative function within themselves, creating a quaternary of force. This progression takes place because the original two lines of force develop a positive + and negative – function within themselves though one remains more dominant than the other.

This is how polarity works, in much the same way as a battery. When it is connected in the right way something happens! So we can see that the two original forces – Ring Cosmos and Ring Chaos – began as a duality, but each one developed two currents of force giving them the capacity to work as a quaternary (see Fig 2 in *The Cosmic Doctrine*). This is where things become slightly more complicated, but also more exciting! Let us look at how this detail affects the mind. We have two lines of force at work, opposing and intersecting (see diagram overleaf).

We can see the horizontal line as the Ring Chaos and the vertical line as the Ring Cosmos. Yet this occurs twice, at the polar ends of the two circles (see Fig 3 in the *Cos Doc*). In the example of *The Cosmic*

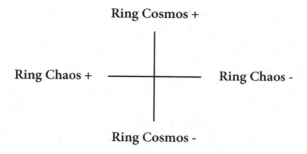

Ring Cosmos +

Ring Chaos +   Ring Chaos -

Ring Cosmos -

Doctrine the interaction of attraction and repulsion (positive and negative force) goes on to create a spinning disc bringing eight factors in to play. This can be symbolised by a figure of eight, also known as the symbol of infinite (see Fig 4 *The Cosmic Doctrine*). Through this progression of two original forces, a third force is born.

In Plato's Timaeus, the numerical significance of one, two & three is discussed in relation to the creation of the body of the universe. He says that the best way to unite two things is by a third, and this unity is most satisfactory if the third follows a geometrical progression *where the proportions between the three remain equal*. A geometrical progression is a sequence of numbers where the quotient remains the same. In algebraic terms this can be written as a, aq, aq^2 ... q being the quotient. (The quotient is the result of the division of one number or quantity by another, e.g. 8 divided by 4 = 2. So the quotient of 8 is 2.) It is as if a natural progression of doubling, or multiplication, occurs from the original desire for movement: 2, 4, 8. We see this occur as a process through watching the intersection of the two original rings.

The important factor about this progression of two into three, is that in order for something to move from a 2-dimensional plane to a 3-dimensional solid there needs to be two means, and thus two pairs of opposites. To apply this psychologically: in order for an abstract thought to become a physical reality (for an idea to be worked through into manifestation) there needs to be two means, and thus two pairs of opposites, as symbolised by a cross. To quote Jung:

"The union of one pair of opposites only produces a two dimensional *triad*: $p^2 + pq + q^2$. This, being a plane figure, is not a reality but a thought. Hence two pairs of opposites, making a *quaternio* ($p^3 + p^2q + pq^2 + q^3$), are needed to represent physical reality."[2]

Understood from a Qabalistic point of view, the progression from plane to solid is represented by the crossing from Binah through the abyss to Chesed. We can at this point also infer that if the union of one pair of opposites creates a triangle, then the union of two pairs of opposites would create two interlaced triangles, and three pairs of opposites would create a three sided pyramid. Here we find a correlation with the Qabalistic symbology of the three triangles: Supernal/Spiritual, Ethical/Evolutionary Personality and Magical/Incarnatory Personality.

Double Quaternary

So it is that we begin working with the symbols of the cross, the square, the cube, and the double cube. We have looked at the metaphor of the creation of the Cosmos and seen how it progresses from Unity to Duality, to a Trinity, and we have seen how within this the forms of the Quaternary exist hidden within it. The relationship between the Trinity and Quaternary, or the three and the four, has been a philosophical debate for centuries. Plato's *Timaeus* opens with the words of Socrates indirectly referring to this issue:

"One, two, three – but where, my dear Timaeus, is the fourth..."[3]

And to quote C.G. Jung again:

"Goethe intuitively grasped the significance of this allusion when he says of the fourth Cabir in Faust: 'He was the right one/Who thought for them all,' and that 'You might ask on Olympus' about the eighth 'whom nobody thought of'."[4]

The reference to the eighth whom nobody thought of is because the quaternary technically has to double before it can become a trinity. Any quaternary can divide itself by two, each hand of a quaternary developing a positive and negative function. This brings us to the doubling of four (the cube) to the number eight (a double cube). Hence the significance of the symbology of Malkuth, the double cube, because it marks the process from unmanifest finally becoming manifest.

The change described from 2D plane to 3D solid, from thought to reality, is how involution takes place, of atoms and man. The force of impactation also follows this process. We see this more clearly through the number eight. To continue with the analogy of the geometrical creation of the cosmos, the figure of eight is arrived at when the spinning discs of the two rings are created (see Fig 4 in *The Cosmic Doctrine*).

Diagrammatically, it would look like this:

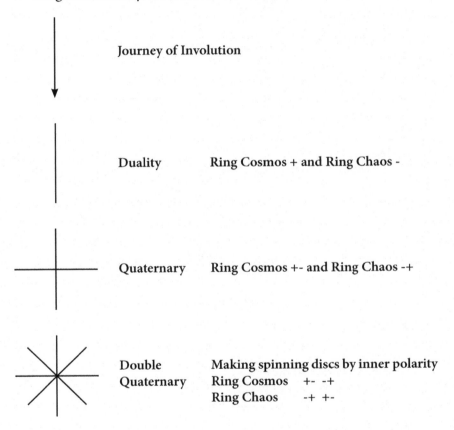

Journey of Involution

Duality   Ring Cosmos + and Ring Chaos -

Quaternary   Ring Cosmos +- and Ring Chaos -+

Double   Making spinning discs by inner polarity
Quaternary   Ring Cosmos   +- -+
                         Ring Chaos   -+ +-

Creates Trinity – the unity of a duality

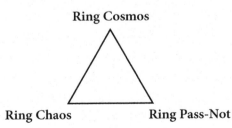

Ring Cosmos

Ring Chaos   Ring Pass-Not

This is the geometrical structure of the creation of the Cosmos as given in *The Cosmic Doctrine*. This is also the course impactation follows, or for want of a better word, initiation. Here the 'cross bar' is the vertical line of the quaternary, the spiritual force that impacts down on the initiate's head. Interestingly enough, the double quaternary is also the fullest symbol of the self – a clock of the equinoxes.

Now we have studied the geometrical shapes in *The Cosmic Doctrine* in relation to their numerical significance, we can see that there is a structure of thought which can be used to apply to a discussion or exploration of thought.

1st	Delineate (circumscribe) the problem	Circle	One
2nd	Place on Duality	Line	Two
3rd	Find Quaternary	Cross	Four
4th	Create Double Quaternary	8 pointed star	Eight
5th	Resolution of original duality in Trinity (Unity)	Triangle	Three

By following this process we will see that the final point, resolution of original duality, marks the birth of something new: Trinity. That which is Unmanifest becomes Manifest. Let us now see this entire process at work when applied to a subject.

PART TWO:
APPLIED PHILOSOPHY – EVIL AND THE FEMININE

"For I am the first and the last.
I am the honoured one and the scorned one.
I am the whore and the holy one.
I am the wife and the virgin..."[5]

There is a crystal-like clarity to the geometric depiction of creation given by *The Cosmic Doctrine,* and because of this it provides an ideal base for philosophical discussions to take place. To begin with we will circumscribe our attention as suggested in the Law of Limitation so that we work within the bounds of the Ring Pass-Not. We will place our subject matter to be explored within the centre of the three Rings, and then use the geometric structures to create the patterns and shapes to perceive relationships and meaning. The subject matter

I have chosen is to look at Male and Female in light of the ethical principles designated to the Ring Cosmos and Chaos: Good and Evil. For our discussion, we will start with the structure of a duality and look at what is meant by the reference of Prime Duality to good and evil. Secondly, we shall look at the consequences of this reference when the duality of male and female is added to make a quaternary. We will then go deeper using a trinity and double quaternary, bearing in mind the various dynamics of these numbers.

Good And Evil

After explaining the basic creation of the three Rings and Prime Stillness, *The Cosmic Doctrine* text goes on to develop the idea of the first two Rings by designating ethical principles to them.

> "Now these 2 Rings we will call Good and Evil; Life and Death; Light and Darkness; Spirit and Matter; Being and Not-Being; God and Devil; because each of these potencies has its root in its respective Ring."[6]

But we are told…

> "Let it be clearly conceived that the Ring 'Good' and the Ring 'Evil' are not good and evil as you understand them."[7]

The Ring Chaos is the Prime Evil, and the Ring Cosmos is the Prime Good. The Ring Chaos, made from the body of inertia, is larger than the Ring Cosmos, and contains it like a vessel. Evil contains Light. Inertia contains desire.

It is the prime dualities that are described and so designated because they are from the original sources at root. We can add our own to the above list:

Male	Female
Positive	Negative
Manifest	Unmanifest
Active	Passive
Peace	War

We are told that good and evil is not meant in terms of them being opposites, simply that they are relative to each other. In the same way, dark is not evil, it is simply relative to light. Therefore we can see that our perspective of good and evil, right and wrong, can change depending on our standpoint. And any moral philosophy will not always be right in all situations. It must be flexible enough to take account of each situation because each person is different. For example, a child steals food. This is wrong – but not in light of the fact that the child is starving. With this information revealed the child becomes innocent. This is where it is wise to understand that the truth is sometimes not the whole truth, and can be veiled, or at least dependent upon perception. Sometimes, we may even be blind to our own truth. Yet we still need to have a strong sense of right and wrong – good and evil – that prevails under most circumstances so that common laws are adhered to.

There are different kinds of evil and darkness: figures from stories or histories; evil spirits which are earthbound and bent on destruction (those who have lived before us, and were deprived of life for whatever reason); the collective shadow, where the darkness of nations is played out; the personal shadow, where our own darkness affects us either unconsciously or is rising to consciousness; cold evil and hot evil. In this way we can see clearly that evil is that which prevents involution (what is coming into matter for the first time) and opposes evolution (return journey and inherent development). The text goes on to state just this: 'evil' is that which is 'not good' because it opposes evolution. Yet we can also see, with irony, the prime duality is vital to evolution itself.

The various kinds of evil need to be dealt with differently, and two ways are discussed in *The Cosmic Doctrine*. The first is to oppose the evil with its opposite, love, and defeat it that way. To my mind this conjures up images of Christ and the Buddha. The text says that when evil is successfully opposed with love, it brings creativity. This is the positive way and corresponds to the Ring Cosmos. This way of dealing with evil is right when it occurs on the involutionary arc. If evil were allowed to reign on this arc, it would cause a disintegration of creative force.

The second way of dealing with evil is to face it. For this I hold a metaphorical image of warriors on horses about to do battle, hating the enemy – but key to this is to move beyond the battle itself to then 'hate the hate' and by giving full expression it is rendered inert. When the hate/evil is destroyed, then love can prevail. So when this kind of evil is unopposed and allowed to be, it actually destroys itself. The armies destroy each other. Evil burns to its own destruction. This is the negative way, of natural dissolution, where the Prime Evil exists in perfect harmony to the Prime Good. When the evil reaches a state of dissolution it is as if a wheel has suddenly changed direction so that good emerges from the Prime Evil, the Ring Chaos. Then the force becomes constellated as the Prime Stillness. This is the sublimation of a force and occurs on the evolutionary arc. If evil were allowed to reign on this arc, it would be a degradation of force. It is the Ring Pass-Not that enables this balance to exist.

Good and Evil is a strong theme throughout Christian teachings, beginning with the stories in Genesis of Adam and Eve, and their eventual expulsion from Eden. According to Christian tradition if you are not good and you disobey God you will go to Hell, the place of the devil. "Love thy neighbour" is the command, alongside the recommendation to be meek and mild, which is fine if you are a feisty hot-headed warrior starved of battle, but not if you are on the receiving end of such a character. Then, it becomes important to stand up for yourself, or the weak and wronged, and confront such a person with your heart and mind. Archangel Michael is a good ally in these situations. Here we can see that the way evil is dealt with is important to ensure that it isn't perpetuated. One way is through love, the other through facing it and fighting.

We know that the creation of the cosmos in geometric terms is pure and good, and requires the dual forces of Ring Cosmos – Prime Good, and Ring Chaos – Prime Evil. An interesting shift occurs when we add into this equation the principle of male and female. Then we have the Prime Evil and the Feminine, and the Prime Good with the Masculine. This addition opens our understanding to see that the second way of dealing with evil comes under the domain of the Feminine. In attributing the Ring Chaos to Binah whose Titles are Ama, the dark sterile mother and Marah, the Great Sea (amongst others), the force of the Ring Chaos can be seen as falling back into the arms of the Great Mother to be reborn anew. The Ring Chaos then becomes a way of renunciation and sacrifice, which is a positive use of destruction – is evil in the sense of being relative to good, not evil in itself.

Likewise, the first suggested way of dealing with evil can therefore be seen to fall under the domain of the Ring Cosmos and the

Masculine principles. When creation is occurring then love can be strong enough to hold the evil inert, and so then can be opposed. But otherwise, to resist evil is futile, as it only serves to lock up the forces of good as well. As Jesus said: "Resist Not Evil."

This diagram seeks to show the different ways of dealing with evil subject to its appearance on involutionary or evolutionary arcs.

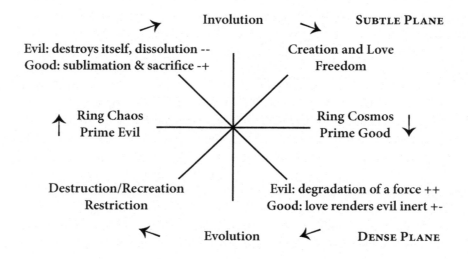

Woman and Evil

It doesn't seem a particularly fair statement (particularly from the eyes of a woman) to equate evil with the feminine. But yet the analogy is there on many levels.

We can assume that since *The Cosmic Doctrine* tells us that Evil is not evil as such, but that which is relative, then woman also is not evil! The Ring Chaos and the Ring Cosmos are both a part of creation and together they create life. They cannot create without each other, and it doesn't make sense that one half of the power to create is evil. Yet when we bear in mind the Prime Dualities, and the basic functions that we have seen them to have, there is something that resonates and rings true. This leads us to question, what is the truth about this connection between woman and evil?

The association between evil and women has been a part of our religious heritage and history for thousands of years, and it feels like a wrong accusation upon the feminine. You may recall the stories of Lilith, found within the Old Testament, the Zohar and the Talmud amongst others. Lilith is perhaps known most widely as being Adam's first wife, and then the devil Samael's wife, but she began her life in Sumer, 3000 B.C., as a storm or wind spirit. In Mesopotamia she became a night demon and by the 8th Century B.C. she was succubus as well as child-killing witch. B.B. Koltuv in her book about Lilith describes Lilith's origins beautifully in line with the creation of Ring Cosmos and Ring Chaos.

> "Lilith's origins are shrouded in the time before time. She arose from the chaos. Although there are many myths of her beginnings, all make clear that she is a counter force, a balancing factor, an opposite but equal weight to God's goodness and maleness."[8]

Besides having macrocosmic significance, Lilith has also had a major personal impact upon man throughout history. Her resonance with man accounts for her long-standing mythical status. This time the evil is directly related to sexuality, and Lilith's ability to seduce a man against his will. The Zohar, which first appeared in Spain in the 13th Century (although it is said to have its origins in 2nd or 3rd Century) is considered to be a meditation upon the Torah, and it warns men about Lilith, She-demon, who visits men that sleep alone at night.

> "She roams at night, and goes all about the worlds and makes sport with men and causes them to emit seed. In every place where a man sleeps alone in a house, she visits him and grabs him and attaches herself to him and has her desire from him and bears from him. And she also afflicts him with sickness, and he knows it not, and all this takes place when the moon is on the wane."[9]

Lilith is clearly an example of the Dark Feminine, associated with the night, the moon, the devil and through her sexuality becomes demonised. Lilith is also inextricably connected with Eve, Adam's second wife. By comparison, Eve is the good and obedient wife, also naive and innocent. However, even Eve disobeyed God's command by listening to the serpent's tempting words and eating from the Tree of Knowledge of good and evil. Whilst the myth in Genesis does not overtly state this as being a sexual matter, it has sexual overtones because the first thing Adam and Eve realised was their own nakedness and of this they were ashamed. The evil serpent quickly becomes associated with the feminine and sexuality.

> "Shameful nakedness soon became sinful sexuality, especially when the phallic serpent entered theological speculation. Sometimes the serpent and Lilith were equated, and the serpent was drawn with a woman's body, which would have been understood as Lilith. At other times the serpent had a face like Eve's. For this reason, sexuality, or rather a view of sexuality as 'ungodly', pervades legends about Lilith as the darker aspect of Eve, and also subtly underpins the character of Eve herself." [10]

The association between sexuality and evil continues into the stories of the New Testament with the figure of Mary Magdalene. She was a prostitute and considered too lowly to be one of the twelve disciples. The Gospel of Mark and the Gospel of Luke both tell how Mary had seven devils removed from her.

Menstruation also receives a dark perception, being viewed across different cultures as magical, dangerous, powerful and evil. Some Christian denominations forbid sexual intercourse, and advise against taking Holy Communion whilst menstruating. Understandable then why historically, women were separated from the men during their menstrual time. Seemingly just to be a woman was to be evil, and a part of the devil! It is perhaps not surprising that the witch-hunts followed over a thousand years later.

On the one hand, our religious heritage shows the feminine to be wholly evil, and on the other it shows us the ideal feminine figure through the Virgin Mother Mary, who was so pure she could conceive without having sex. Naturally no woman can aspire to her purity or godliness, because it is impossible, and therefore we are relegated to the realms of the evil and sexual feminine. We might therefore deduce that the Christian Religion, heavy with its doctrine of good and evil, does not depict woman in a positive or balanced light, and sadly sees her as a hindrance to man's spiritual development, because of her sexual allure.

But this isn't good for man either, for the male in polarity to these configurations of feminine force (Lilith, Mary Magdalene, Eve or Virgin Mary) is limited in his expression and capacity for relationship because the face of the feminine is neither wholly real or whole.

This may well be an echo of the fact that Christ is not depicted with a woman and therefore is not often seen as being able to polarise. Though there are many saints and nuns who speak of spiritually loving embraces with Him, this is not the same as having a wife and experiencing the nature of a long and deep relationship. The ideal of Christ being alone (with God) is upheld in the figure of the Catholic Priest who is required to be celibate, and this is followed through in the catholic doctrine of 'no sex before marriage,' alongside an anti-contraceptive attitude. Little more than 100 years ago the damnation of a woman pregnant out of wedlock was severe. But yet we know and understand today, so clearly, the physical expression of love between a man and a woman not to be evil. It is amongst the most holy of acts, being that which brings new life into the world, and with it light. So we can see that for both men and women it is important not to be cut off from the dark feminine and our sexuality lest we inadvertently and unconsciously arouse another or lest we feel evil or impure. Rather it's important to become conscious of it: both sexuality and the dark feminine.

The Christian attitudes towards spirituality, sex and women that have permeated the collective consciousness for two thousand years have taken many changes, particularly in the last century. They are no longer considered to be balanced or indeed healthy attitudes to live by. In Dion Fortune's day she recognised the damaging effect that the Christian viewpoint was having on modern men and women and she worked for many years trying to cause an effect on the racial psyche. Her novels *The Sea Priestess* and *Moon Magic* were, among other things, an attempt at this, aiming to bring understanding to this dark side of the feminine and point out its positive qualities, also to extend consciousness upon the idea of sex and polarity. Her work on *The Esoteric Philosophy of Love and Marriage* and *The Circuit of Force* also develop this, the latter by making an acquaintance to Yoga and the Eastern esoteric teachings on sexuality. This work was continued by others in the 1960s with the very well known principle of 'free love' that this era brought. Coincidently, there was also a collection of esoteric texts that came to light in Egypt in 1945, first published in 1977 under the title of *The Nag Hammadi Library*. They include the Gospel of Thomas, the Gospel of Philip, the Gospel of Mary (Magdalene) and a script spoken by a feminine figure called The Thunder, Perfect Mind. These documents cast a different perspective on the idea of sexuality and the role of women in Christianity. Gnostic Christianity broadens the perspective of the feminine, taking its roots from other esoteric and mystical sources. It provides an antidote to the Dark Feminine through the figures of the Sophia, Goddess of Wisdom, and the Shekinah of later Qabalistic mythology, both of whom symbolise Light.

Even though there have been these successful attempts to break down the Christian hold on men and women in relation to sex throughout the 20th Century, the Christian attitude towards woman and sex has residual remains deep and hidden within the psyche of modern men and women, and for some this still wields a profound effect in their lives. For how a woman sees herself, presents herself, and expects to be seen and treated also affects how the man responds to her – not withstanding his own inbred attitudes as to how a woman 'should be' or how he wants her to be. It's the psychological mechanism of projection at work, and it can be seen working clearly in some of Dion Fortune's novels such as *Moon Magic* (chapter four), where the character Miss Le Fay Morgan tells how she creates a magical persona with which to do her work. With awareness, we have the power to manipulate, change, destroy and recreate our personas, not for magic, but by taking responsibility for our spiritual growth. So, how might we achieve this, and change or come to better understand woman's dark side, that in Christianity appears to be primarily sexual and evil? First we must ask – what is woman, the feminine, in all its fullness? Who is She? What is She made up of? And how does the feminine polarise with man?

To start simply, if we take the basic polarity set up by the Ring Cosmos and the Ring Chaos and follow it, we might end up with a list like this:

Ring Cosmos	Ring Chaos
Good	Evil
Male	Female
Masculine	Feminine
Man	Woman
God	Devil
Adam	Lilith
Christ	Mary Magdalene
Holy	Sexual
Spiritual	Sensual

Clothed	Naked
Sky	Earth
Heaven	Nature
Light	Dark
Creation	Destruction
Life	Death
Chokmah	Binah

The words listed in the column headed by the Ring Chaos certainly conjure up a powerful sense of woman, and whilst they only represent the dark side of woman we nevertheless must remember it is still Divine – a part wholly essential to life and creation. And so it is important to embrace this part of the feminine that is dark, earthly and sensual, comely even. Here we may think of the strange passage in the Old Testament known as the Song of Solomon, before we even come to the Greek and Pagan realms of Pan, Orpheus, Dionysus and their successors.

The Qabalah is also a useful tool in developing an understanding of the dark feminine because the Sephirah Binah is very strong in female energy. Here, the feminine is depicted as the Matron, the mature woman, and of a goddess force who has the ability to weave men's fates, to give life, or call death to a person. The forces of Binah are very well depicted in *The Sea Priestess* through the character Miss Morgan, in the Rites of Isis. Binah, then, is a Sephirah that shows the dark feminine in her destructive element, which we can see is a vital component to ensuring life, even if it can be a difficult aspect with which to deal in reality. The ability to 'weave men's fates' is represented in Greek Lore by the three Fates, and in Norse myths by the Norns, and so we know it as an ancient power with roots steeped in mystery. It is perhaps less understood that this power to weave life on a psychic level concerns our waking dreams. For example, all pregnant women are blessed with the power to dream a beautiful future for their baby, and it is an important, powerful function of the imagination.

Within the dark feminine, we also find that the number three frequently surfaces. Binah is Sephirah number three; there are three Fates or Norns, and there are three muses (although this multiplies itself into nine further down in history). We also find the number three in the Greek Kore, known to us in the feminine archetypes as Maiden, Mother and Crone. The Crone force we associate with Binah.

The Maiden force we associate with Netzach, home to the Goddess Venus and Aphrodite and sphere of romantic love. This is a much more positive and light side of the feminine, and in this sphere is the skill of being able to polarise from a passive position. It marks the beginnings of being able to be passive, to receive and to hold and contain all energies, symbolised by the image of the vessel. The Mother force we associate with Malkuth, and the fertilising earth Goddesses such as Demeter and Ceres. We have seen how the Feminine takes the attribution of the number three, and as any Trinity benefits deeper understanding when viewed in terms of a Quaternary, so we can apply this to the Divine Feminine. Here, it is interesting to find that Socrates said that there are four phases of the feminine, not three. Socrates thought of them as Maiden, Mother, Queen and Goddess. A happy thought for women passing into middle stages of life! It is possible to see that each of these four phases of the feminine have a dark and light side to them.

This very quickly brings us out of looking at the dark side of the feminine, to embrace a more whole perception of the Divine Feminine. I believe we are meant to be women embracing dark and light, living the full potential of the force of the Feminine. The light side of the Feminine in Christianity is found in the assumption of the Virgin Mary, who is crowned with stars. This mirrors other images of the Heavenly Goddess such as Isis, Aphrodite-Urania, the Qabalistic Shekinah and the Gnostic Sophia.

Thus, we can see that the pure light of geometry enables the connection to be made between women and evil, but also gives an understanding of why evil is misinterpreted in connection with the feminine. This is because of the duality being seen only in terms of opposition and negating the inherent relativity to each part as mentioned above. Now we can clearly distinguish between a woman being identified with evil, and a woman being dark, passive, receptive, with the power to destroy – remembering that deeply hidden in the darkest depths of her, there is light. We have gone some way to explore this by looking at the positive and negative aspects of Good and Evil in relation to ethical principles – and now we come to the next geometrical point, where we must remember that a duality contains forces that not only oppose, but intersect!

How can we move from seeing the Prime Evil/Feminine and Prime Good/Masculine as a duality, to seeing the forces intersect? We can see from the diagram below that in order to more fully understand the feminine, having looked at its relationship with Evil and Good, we can now go on to look at it in relation to its true opposite – the male.

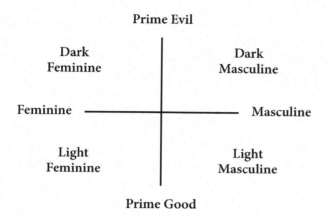

Prime Evil

Dark
Feminine

Dark
Masculine

Feminine ———————————— Masculine

Light
Feminine

Light
Masculine

Prime Good

Woman and Man

It must not be forgotten that the Christian attitude towards women has not (as we might first think) been that way since the beginning of time. Before Christianity became a world religion, before even the world was ruled by men, it was dominated by the Matriarchal forces because creation was seen to be a process emerging from the feminine and this was the spiritual focus of the people of its time. The Bronze Age marked the evolutionary shift from a Matriarchal spirituality to a Patriarchal one, a process which was completed at the start of the Iron Age (approximately 1250 B.C.). Anne Baring and Jules Cashford write in their book *The Myth of the Goddess* that:

> "The Enuma Elish is the first story of the replacing of a Mother Goddess who generates creation as part of herself by a god who 'makes' creation as something separate from himself. All myths of the Iron Age in which a sky or sun god or hero conquers a great serpent or dragon can be traced to this Babylonian epic, in which humanity was created from the blood of a sacrificed god and no longer from the womb of a primordial goddess."[11]

Baring and Cashford go on to state that this change marked the separation between creator and creation, bringing the dualism of spirit and nature which has continued for 3000 years, to date. The overthrowing of the matriarchal powers was also a period in history that has unconsciously contributed to woman being viewed negatively and also has residual power in the unconscious. The serpent or dragon that the god or hero overthrows is symbolic of the feminine matriarchal powers that were once dominant. The serpent and dragon are animals that remind us of Lilith and Eve too, whose darkness becomes under the control of the Iron Age hero. In the myths that follow across Western Religious cultures, creation becomes

"the result of a divine act that brings order out of chaos." [12]

However, as in the nature of a duality – one or two – neither the Matriarchal or the Patriarchal forces have the power to be dominant eternally. Woman's journey through comparatively recent history (last 100 years) has been one of rising to equality with man. The only problem with this is that a re-evaluation is then required of the feminine and her qualities, so that we become women on our own terms and not simply second rate men in a paternally dominated world. Change occurs naturally as geometrical progressions take place, so that eventually the two will become unified in a third way. It takes age after age, because it is an evolutionary shift, and the journey towards that shift can firstly be seen geometrically as a quaternary of male and female. So, instead of looking at a duality, of Male and Female,

| One | | Two | |
| Male | • | • | Female |

we are now looking at a Quaternary.

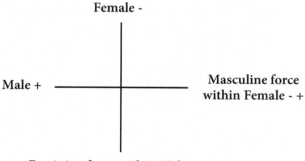

Female -

Male + ———————————— Masculine force within Female - +

Feminine force within Male + -

Within the female are masculine forces, just as within the male, there are feminine forces. Carl Jung defined these inner forces of the psyche as animus and anima, and much can be read about these forces from his life-work and that of his successors. Looking at the inner masculine qualities within a woman (the animus), and the inner feminine qualities within a man (the anima) we are able to see the very real forces that flow from noumenal existence though the psyche and soul that go towards making up whole men and women.

So, we can say male and female each contain the other within themselves. In the male is a female aspect, and within the female, a male aspect. There is a lot of growth in exploring this aspect of one's being which will positively affect relationships with others.

If we refer back to the earlier text under the heading of quaternary, we can see how the two feminine forces (of light and dark) equate with the Ring Chaos and the two masculine forces (again of light and dark qualities) equate with the Ring Cosmos. As we have seen the geometric nature of the quaternary doubles itself. For our purposes it would then look like this:

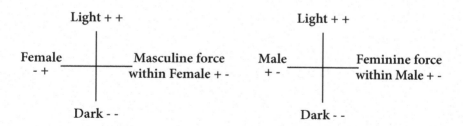

Polarity occurs horizontally within, and also vertically spiritually, and there is cross polarity on the outer plane with others. One may be able to see or impose all manner of relationships into this diagram to see different aspects at work. For example, a man may experience the anima consciously or otherwise in the psyche as muse, fairy being, swan maiden, or other ethereal being and these are very positive feminine forces of the male psyche. A man may also experience the dark anima forces, such as Lilith or an old witch figure. Whilst the tendency may be to suppress this dark inner presence, it is a force which, as we have seen, is not evil in itself, but has spiritual significance if it can be worked with as a shadow force and integrated. Its danger is when the figure is loaded with the projection of all of one's personal negative force, and projected externally onto another. Women too, may also have to wrestle with the shadow force of Lilith, but again, as we have seen, within her figure is the potential for a huge amount of creativity, wisdom and eventual light. Koltuv reckons Lilith to be such a key part of woman that has to be integrated, as it is one half of woman. She says of men and women in connection to the Lilith force:

> "Men experience her as the seductive witch, the death dealing succubus, and the strangling mother. For women she is the dark shadow of the Self that is married to the devil. It is through knowing Lilith and her consort that one becomes conscious of one's Self." [13]

This means that man, through his anima, can face the dark feminine, explore the evil associated with sexuality within himself, so that the evil that he perceives is not projected, but seen as a part of himself. Then, a spirituality can be found through sexuality and a change in the patterns of religious parts of the psyche take place. It is in some respects an initiation given at the hands of the Great Mother – not to return to the Palaeolithic tribal consciousness, but to re-discover and re-create it on a higher arc.

Equally, for the woman, there are male figures in the psyche to contend with: well known dark animus figures are the burglar, intruder, even torturer. More positive animus figures may be a king, sage, judge, or what in esoteric circles are known as the IPA – Inner Plane Adepti – such as Socrates and Thomas Erskine. This point serves to remind us that the forces of the psyche, anima, animus and beyond, have independent existence in the psyche. We are able to observe the forces of the psyche and our responses to them, and also distinguish between fantasy and reality, refining our understanding of the power of imagination.

The development of a man and woman both making steps on the path of individuation or integration of their higher self (which is not limited to the Priest and Priestess of the temple) follows the geometrical structures which have been outlined. The double quaternary signifies the possibility of impactation, and therefore extension of consciousness and recreation. The process can also be likened to the seven deaths (following which is rebirth), and associated to Mary Magdalene who had 'seven devils' exorcised from her. When men and women are able to embrace the dark feminine, they are on their way to finding and understanding the inner and divine power of the Feminine. Without this darker side of woman, with only the light bright side, a wealth of earthliness, creativity, spirituality, depth and wisdom is lost. For within the darkness there is light, and the creative spark, just as the dark womb holds the egg that is brought to life. From this journey of man and woman looking at their light and dark selves, male and female selves, comes the potential for a new union between men and women, which we could see as being symbolised as a Trinity. This is to evolve in the ages to come, where men and women can live in a balanced, whole and harmonious way, with neither dominating the other, but both living to their own personal fullness, supporting each other's creativity and life-force, in much the same way as the Ring Cosmos and Ring Chaos work together in harmony to create the Universe.

When the Two Become One

It is hopefully clear from the above that good and evil are a part of both male and female, and that our understanding of evil is one that no longer separates us from each other, or from an inner part of ourselves. Sexuality is related to our spirituality, not least because sex has been associated with evil for so long, and evil needs integrating because it is one half of our being – as dark is to light.

The journey to inner wholeness is achieved through a process that at first separates and defines. It is the understanding of duality that enables us to exercise our capacity for discrimination, and for self-consciousness. It also allows for conscious relationship between two parts and this applies to human beings as well as subject matters. But to remain observing and experiencing life from a perspective of duality, always seeing things in terms of separation or opposition, is limiting and damaging. The development from this viewpoint is to engage in reciprocal consciousness, where we realise that we cannot separate ourselves from the thing we behold and that we are completely interconnected by the experience of *participation*. This development of consciousness provides a tool for evolution.

> "Relationship is again the fundamental reality within which the two terms – observer and observed, subject and object – are brought into being together."[14]

If we are able to behold our inner self as well as truly behold another, seeing them in their fullness, then we have potential to enter into a transcendent experience with each other and with all life. Geometrically expressed, this would see each person symbolised initially as a cross (quaternary) and together as a double quaternary, before emerging as a Trinity in new experience. Poetically expressed, this would be experienced as the union of two, out of which emerges a third, new component that we may call divine love.

We may end with a quote from the Gospel of Thomas:

'They said to Him, "Shall we then, as children,
Enter the Kingdom?" Jesus said to them,
"When you make the two one, and
when you make the inside like the outside
and the outside like the inside, and the above
like the below, and when
you make the male and female one and the same,
so that the male not be male nor
the female female…
then you will enter the kingdom." [15]

CONCLUSION

Deeper Into the Mysteries

We have looked at the geometrical shapes used to describe the process of creation in *The Cosmic Doctrine*, seeing how they progress in terms of their relationship to numbers. We have then seen how to apply the geometrical structures to a subject matter, taking into account the philosophy behind numerological significance. This has enabled us to deepen our understanding of a subject matter and given guidelines as to how we might pursue our own inner growth.

The process of using geometrical shapes, both alone, in relationship to one another, and in progression so that they depict a journey of movement, can be applied to a number of different subject matters. It is a way which is indicative of a certain type of thinking and supports the initial notion laid out in *The Cosmic Doctrine* that the text is designed to train the mind and not inform it. The idea of being able to see how something manifests from the Unmanifest, shifting from 2D to 3D, has profound implications. As we have seen with the issue of good–evil and male–female, it is possible to transcend the dualities and develop new ways of being and experiencing the world.

As a last thought, I would like to apply the findings of our geometrical structures and our exploration of good and evil with male and female – to the mystery of the Holy Grail.

The Mystery of the Holy Grail

In the Arthurian Legends the Holy Grail was witnessed by several of the knights, Lancelot, Perceval, Galahad and Bors, but none of them were able to bring back the Holy Grail to Arthur and the Round Table. It remains on a mystical level, and has not yet reached the permanence of physical manifestation. Metaphysically, the Holy Grail exists in the realm of thought, and it needs to make the transition from 2D to 3D, plane to solid, in order to become manifest at the Round Table. This requires that we follow the geometric formation of duality and quaternary, finding two pairs of opposites and then two means. Invariably, the attainment of such a task would require an indepth inner process of growth, and would also need to be applied in terms of an evolutionary age. The first part is to experience a personal vision, the second part is to make it available to others by (metaphorically speaking) bringing it to the Round Table.

The Holy Grail itself constellates the very issue between the three and the four because the Trinity is said to be contained within the vessel. It is said to contain a vision of the Holy Spirit and the doctrine of the Holy Spirit is that the three persons of the Godhead are all one and the Holy Spirit is the love that passes between Christ and God the Father. So we can see, part of the problem in looking at the mystery of the Holy Grail is in relation to the Trinity, and in order to understand a trinity more deeply we need to look at it firstly as a quaternary. Many scholars think of the fourth aspect of the Trinity as the devil, or evil, which we might now be able to equate without judgement to the feminine. Robert De Boron departs from this, writing of the fourth aspect of the Trinity as the Holy Grail itself. However, Emma Jung in her book *The Grail Legend* gives us the following quaternary, making the Grail synonymous with Mary, and thus the feminine.

"The Grail really forms a quaternity in which the blood contained within it signifies the Three Persons of the One Godhead, and the vessel can be compared to the Mother of God"[16]

We can see there is a strong association between evil and the feminine within the Holy Grail and the Trinity, and it is therefore essential that consciousness develops a capacity to be able to discriminate between good and evil. In Robert De Boron's version of the Arthurian legends, *Merlin and the Grail*, when Joseph of Arimathea meditated with the Grail he heard the voice of the Holy Spirit talking to him. Without the Grail he cannot do this, due to a lack of judgement. The fact that the Holy Grail was 'withdrawn' (or concealed) suggests that our contact with the Holy Spirit may also be diminished or obscured and we must raise consciousness high enough to be able to differentiate between things. Discrimination might therefore be said to be the voice of the Holy Spirit in one's heart. It is being able to distinguish the difference between good and evil, even though the nature of what is good and evil has evolved over the last 2000 years, and will change again in the future. In Wolfram's version of the Arthurian legends the two knives in the Grail procession are a positive indicator, representing discrimination and a new level of thought. We have to go through this level of applied intellectual consciousness, before going onto experience synthesis with all things.

Another significant factor in this process of discrimination is that the Siege Perilous at the Round Table, which is the seat of the Grail Bearer Perceval, is said to represent evil, because it has fatal consequences if sat in by the wrong person. It is said that the stone would break in two and the earth swallow up the unfortunate victim. The Empty Seat represents the primeval unconscious, and its dark nature is reminiscent of the dark side of the feminine because it represents the seat of matter, and metaphorically the mouth of the Great Mother. To bring the Grail to the Round Table means that 'Perceval' has to sit in the Empty Seat. When he doesn't do this, heaven and earth are separated by the disappearance of the Grail. This relates to men and women's own connection with matter and spirit, which as we have seen above relates to the need for development of consciousness so that we experience ourselves as an interconnected part of life, not separate and of a consciousness that experiences separation. It also requires that men and women are not victims of their own shadowy darkness.

This implies again that the Grail Bearer must be able to differentiate between good and evil and have walked the path of integration of dark and light, for in order not to be caught out by evil, one has to have mastered it.

When we have understood good and evil and are able to embrace dark and light aspects of the feminine and masculine forces within our own being, and are able to be at one with both spirit and matter – then the Holy Grail has a chance of becoming manifest at the Round Table. It would bring not only a vision of love and the interconnectedness of us all, but the continuing presence of it. This will bring us to a new evolutionary age, where matriarchal and patriarchal aeons are recreated in a poetical New Age that is able to transcend the limitations of dualities through its reconciliation of opposites – an Age yet to be imagined…

*   *   *

The cosmos is the macrocosm, and man the microcosm, and so our metaphor of the three cosmic rings, and their fourth component – the central stillness – can be applied to man. If we look at ourselves on an inner level, we can imagine two rings at right-angles around us. They represent the forces set by the idea of duality: feminine and masculine, shadow and light, negative and positive, passive and active. There is also the Ring Pass-Not which sets the bounds of limitation of our capacities and abilities, and the Central Stillness, which is the place of the heart, or 'the inner sanctuary' of our being. The Ring Pass-Not represents the limitation that serves to focus our attention to the centre of our being, from which flows the well-spring of authentic action. Within this metaphor are our primordial beginnings and the journey to the Self.

The Central Stillness of ourselves is the way through which we can come to understand God, or Spirit, not through the penetration of the surface. It is by accepting our limitations and coming to a still point within our selves that we come closest to this spiritual essence. In the vast stillness of our inner being we can imagine ourselves as the vast space in which a movement took place – and know there that male and female, dark and light, spirit and matter are one.

1   Dion Fortune, *The Cosmic Doctrine* (York Beach, ME: Red Wheel/Weiser LLC, 2000), 19

2   C.G.Jung, *Psychology and Western Religion* (East Sussex: Ark Paperbacks, 1988), 17

3   Plato, *Timaeus and Critias* (London: Penguin Books Ltd, 2008), 7

4   C.G.Jung, *Psychology and Western Religion* (East Sussex: Ark Paperbacks, 1988), 17

5   James M. Robinson, General Editor, *The Nag Hammadi Library* (USA: HarperSanFrancisco, 1990), 297

6   Dion Fortune, *The Cosmic Doctrine* (York Beach, ME: Red Wheel/Weiser LLC, 2000), 23

7   Dion Fortune, *The Cosmic Doctrine* (York Beach, ME: Red Wheel/Weiser LLC, 2000), 23

8   B.B. Koltuv, *The Book of Lilith* (York Beach, ME: Nicolas-Hays, Inc, 1986), 1

9   Trans. by H. Sperling and M. Simon, *Zohar, vol 1, 19b* (London: The Soncino Press, 1984).

10 Baring and Cashford, *The Myth of the Goddess* (England: Arkana, Penguin Books, 1993), 512

11 Baring and Cashford, *The Myth of the Goddess* (England: Arkana, Penguin Books, 1993), 273 – 274

12 Baring and Cashford, *The Myth of the Goddess* (England: Arkana, Penguin Books, 1993), 274

13 B.B. Koltuv, *The Book of Lilith* (York Beach, ME: Nicolas-Hays, Inc, 1986), 6-7

14 Baring and Cashford, *The Myth of the Goddess* (England: Arkana, Penguin Books, 1993), 663

15 James M. Robinson, General Editor, *The Nag Hammadi Library* (USA: HarperSanFrancisco, 1990), 129

16 E. Jung and M.L. Von Franz, *The Grail Legend* (New Jersey: Princeton University Press, 1998), 339

THE COSMIC DOCTRINE AND THE COSMOLOGY OF THE PHYSICIST

STUART DELACEY

"I made no special study of that branch of esoteric science which is herein dealt with, and have only the most elementary knowledge of physics and none whatever of mathematics."[1]
Dion Fortune – in her introduction to *The Cosmic Doctrine*

The Cosmic Doctrine was 'received' by Dion Fortune in humble circumstances in 1924. It stepped through the door of manifestation in a series of spontaneous dictation sessions and "...no other work whatsoever went to its production..."[2] whether preparatory work in relation to the subject or subsequent modification and embellishment. All that was done to change the original, spontaneously dictated script was to add punctuation. She describes the circumstances of its conception and leaves it to the reader to decide how the work came into being: whether it was derived from an 'external' revelatory source or from subjective emanations originating from her own nascent knowledge and experience. We are left in a quandary which Dion Fortune recognizes: there is no way to prove the source and we must therefore make up our own minds as to where this or any other profound, poetic or inspired writing comes from. Even in areas more susceptible to research, such as the origin of some aspects of Shakespeare's plays, for example, there is still debate, and fiction-writers still imagine possible scenarios. We even have Dr. Who assisting the Bard from time to time! Dion Fortune however does not wish us to be distracted by this dilemma and advises us to suspend or maintain our preconceptions and beliefs, as we choose, by asserting that even if *The Cosmic Doctrine* had originated solely from her own conscious or sub-conscious resources, this does not in the least detract from its significance. In the words of the dead Professor Dumbledore to a Harry Potter temporarily held in a limbo-like Kings Cross Station:

"Of course it is happening inside your head, Harry, but why on earth should that mean that it is not real?"[3]

Dion Fortune's method of approach seems, at first glance, to be a very different method of working to that of the Physicist-Cosmologist who trains for years, learning to work with complex relationships of algebraic symbols until she or he is fluent in that language and mode of conception. (If you don't believe me, and are serious about understanding contemporary postulations concerning the nature of the Universe, space, time, origins and endings but are commencing your study from baseline zero, try reading – and maintaining clarity of understanding – more than half way through Stephen Hawking's *A Brief History of Time*[4] without a grasp of the essential mathematical language.)

Once a theory is derived from this foundation of learning, the mandate is to corroborate[5] it through precisely defined experiments that are rigorously refereed by contemporary experts. Those experiments can entail highly expensive and significantly intensive efforts such as, for example, surround the £3.74 billion, 17-mile long CERN Hadron Collider designed to test a number of extant – but at the time of writing merely theoretical – propositions of contemporary Physicists. Other propositions have been corroborated by even greater experiments which have been generated by ulterior motives or by nature itself. For example, atomic explosions and the bending of the light from a distant star around the sun observed during an eclipse have both been used to support core postulations within Albert Einstein's general and specific theories of relativity. The former has demonstrated how much energy can be generated by matter in direct corroboration of the most famous equation in the world: $E=mc^2$; and the latter to demonstrate, through the observed alteration in the position of stars within the penumbra of the eclipsed sun, that gravity is capable of bending space-time.

But at the root of their conception of the universe, do scientists really work in a different way to the so-called 'occultists' in the tradition followed by Dion Fortune?

The methods of the Mysteries and the methods of Science

The Cosmic Doctrine derives from an ancient tradition of cosmological investigation. The origin of cosmology is grounded in that tradition. It seeks to explore the depths of the mystery that our being and our totality derive from the Unmanifest or *noumenal* which is the source of all that is within the manifest world or the *phenomenal*. The training prescribed by this ancient tradition is rigorous and the route to knowledge is tortuous – and this knowledge is not merely fire in the head but a knowledge that can be experiential or even deeper: *soul-iential* or even *spirit-iential*. Such occult enquiry is the antecedent of current scientific enquiry and they share a deep, perhaps unquenchable desire to know. This fundamental relationship is nevertheless easily forgotten.

A few years ago an English university was faced with a proposal for a new degree examining traditional approaches to cosmological enquiry. Ironically, the University refused the use of the word 'cosmology' in the degree title because, I am informed, the Physicists within the University argued that the word 'cosmology' lay solely within the domain of physical science and there should be no confusion between science and mumbo jumbo. There is significant irony surrounding this decision since the concerns of the scientists are based on incorrect *a priori* assumptions that contradict their own methodological approach as it should be applied to historical knowledge. The roots of cosmology derive from ancient traditions and the idea that those who investigate the Mysteries should have permission to use the word is absurd. What is more remarkable is the manner in which contemporary scientists so quickly forget that they are carrying on the work of traditional cosmologists; they appear to have selective amnesia when it comes to recalling the explorations of some of their greatest founding fathers and intellectuals. These include Isaac Newton (described by John Maynard Keynes as the 'last of the magicians') and John Dee, a founding fellow of Trinity College Cambridge, one of their greatest intellectuals and a notorious explorer of the magical and the numinous.

Moreover, in their cosmological work many scientists limit their enquiries to propositions that can be proven only through the methodologies of science and, for the most part, they examine only the nature of matter and form rather than enquiring into the vastness of the Unmanifest which lies beyond the manifest world. This failure to explore the apparently inexplicable occurs because the contemporary scientist will only acknowledge that which can be known through scientific method as having grounds for existence. This is a dangerous denial of what may be unequivocally real and indeed so pressingly significant that all of manifestation might be eclipsed thereby. Indeed, in the view of some of those who dedicate themselves to the quest into the Mysteries such as the Qabalist-Cosmologist, scientists examine what is probably less than one tenth of the manifest world (if it were capable of being proportionally measured) by restricting their enquiries to the final stage of manifestation represented by the 10th Sephirah of Malkuth on the Tree of Life. They neglect to enquire into the Mysteries of Being embodied in the nine preceding Sephiroth or forms of manifestation and that which lies beyond, within the vastness of the Unmanifest or, in the language of the Qabalist, the Ain Soph Aur.

However, some contemporary Physicists are finding the need to move into the first foothills of the numinous. For example, Stephen Hawking and others have difficulty in applying the existing laws and theories of Cosmo-Physics to the phenomenon of a singularity (of the sort that is said to be located at the centre of a black hole, the greatest of all singularities that preceded the Big Bang expansion). Instead they rely on postulation and describe in an abstract manner how particles, forces and laws cease to act in predictable ways; they use abstraction and symbols to describe what cannot be experienced or described in a direct manner. In other instances Physicists talk about the universe 'expanding' although beyond mathematical postulation it is very difficult to answer the question 'expansion into what?' This is especially so when we consider that there was no-thing before the explosion of Big Bang. The concept of the material into which space is continuing to expand can only be abstracted, so it must be concluded that space entered the infinite no-thing, or Unmanifest, in which there is infinite capacity for manifestation to expand. However even this statement cannot communicate a great deal because it is beyond our capacity to understand such a description without the use of symbols.

A third example of the manner in which Physicists are moving into inner realms of manifestation, although not necessarily into the numinous, is found in the context of *string theory* in which one of the hypotheses is that there are numerous parallel universes all close to each other, indeed overlapping, but which are currently separated by dimensional gulfs that make travelling between them impossible, at least for now. This mirrors the occultists' concept of the Inner worlds, for example the seven worlds described by the traditional Qabalist, and takes physical theory beyond the realm of Malkuth into the more subtle levels of manifestation.

A key difference between the ancient cosmological approach and the contemporary scientific approach is, therefore, that scientific methodology as yet only permits an examination of the tangible manifest universe. Beyond that, theories may be intelligent and promising but they can have no greater credence than the cosmological conjectures – or mumbo jumbo – of the ancients, which have grown out of many lives of remarkable discipline, self-sacrifice and dedication to the quest for knowledge.

Delving into the nature of our being and exploring the vastness of the universe is of course an extensive enough ground to facilitate a near-eternal quest into the nature of material reality which may, when all is said and done, be merely an illusion. Even to the scientist, what was once thought of as solid matter is now perceived within quantum theory as a field of energy, or by the string theorists as vibrational nodes on strings of energy, like musical overtones on a single guitar string. Nevertheless, in terms of scientific method the tangible universe is technically knowable; it can yield its secrets to those who seek to corroborate hypotheses through the application of experimental enquiry. Unfortunately the method severely limits the enquiry.

According to *The Cosmic Doctrine* and those who are said to have brought its wisdom to Dion Fortune, the only reality is within the Unmanifest, although it can only be described obliquely. (As far as scientific method goes the Unmanifest or noumenal is entirely unknowable.) The Unmanifest can be 'known' and 'experienced' through methods entirely different to those of scientific enquiry, such as the use of symbols and analogy. It can also be transmitted through a process that might be called 'initiation' to those who are appropriately trained and can subjectively access the experience of that knowledge for themselves. One other factor that ought to be mentioned is that the Unmanifest is limitless: many lifetimes are needed even to climb the foothills of its vast mountain range yet it is this which draws traditional cosmologists to persist in their work. To avoid persecution, their quest for knowledge – which ultimately is aimed at regeneration of the self – is carried out within a rigorous programme of self-discipline, their work taking place within a secret or 'hidden' environment. This literal meaning of the word 'occult' still applies to such work and is, according to Dion Fortune and her successors, the source of *The Cosmic Doctrine*.

It is perhaps not surprising that some scientists can be scornful of the occult examination of cosmological issues. First, they are not likely to admit that some aspects of the cosmos cannot be penetrated either by experiments or even abstract calculus. Second, many of the old propositions such as those put forward by Newton for example, have been disproved or modified, finessed or elucidated more clearly with the advent of new hypotheses and more subtle experiments to corroborate them. Thus new science eclipses the old, and perhaps unwittingly belittles the old in the light of contemporary technological cleverness. Also, as we have seen, occult work rarely uses contemporary scientific methods and thus cannot be seen to possess any basis of truth within a scientific context. Because of this, the work of the occultist might even challenge the scientist's sensitivity in a fundamental way, either causing an honest self-examination or a superficial response manifesting in defensive mockery or even arrogance. In the light of this the proponents of a degree in traditional cosmology who lose the right to use the word 'cosmology' might well have been pleased that they drew such a strong reaction. This is reminiscent of the comedian's plea (I think it may have been Dave Allen) when he lamented that: "they laughed at Newton, they laughed at Galileo, they laughed at Einstein – why the hell won't they laugh at me?"... or words to that effect!

We have therefore an apparently deep epistemological gulf between the occultist and the scientist, irrespective of their often shared quest to discover a unified theory of everything. That gulf is widened by the scientist who restricts knowledge to that which can be proven by scientific method, but equally can be widened by occultists who feel that a knowledge of the laws that support the tangible world in which we live is not material to their quest. Should we not acknowledge that neither can move on without acknowledging the achievements of the other? And perhaps the result of a fusion of the two approaches to knowledge will promise to greatly exceed the sum of the disparate parts.

Contemporary physical cosmology has reached the borders of manifestation: playing at the outer reaches of time and space, both at the extremes of alpha and omega and at the minutest of levels of particle physics where, as if travelling through a fictitious wormhole, the voyager may find that the 'inside' is even greater than the 'outside' of infinite space. The Physicist is dwelling at the edge of practical experimentation: the next generation Hadron-type collider might be so prohibitively large in order to deal with future propositions that it would have to be as big as the Earth itself. After that we may need to deploy a field of experimentation in a tube greater than the perimeter of the solar system! Consequently, the Physicist, more than ever, is forced to progress new theories at a conceptual level by expressing 'proofs' in the form of symbols – an esoteric approach to conveying information to the few who possess the ability to decode the symbols and appreciate the information that derives from their combination. Those who cannot decipher that language have little hope of participating in the Physicist's cosmological journey.

But this use of symbols, and the necessary training for their interpretation and understanding, is not far at all from the occult training methods of the Mysteries that led to Dion Fortune's own work. Indeed, *The Cosmic Doctrine* is prefaced by a crucial postulation, a key to the door of its secrets. Thus the information within it is designed "…to train the mind, not to inform it."[6] *The Cosmic Doctrine's* mission is for us to *become knowledge and witness and experience it with the totality of ourselves.* Does that proposition separate the occultist from the Physicist? It might seem to do so if we assume that scientists only think logically and proceed step by step to prove or logically deduce concepts. But we know that they do not. In many cases they retrospectively show their working to 'justify' in scientific terms revelations that have been experienced in a *Eureka* moment or in a '*Eureka*' slower phase of realization.

The well-known example of Archimedes having a bath and discovering how to measure the volume of a complex solid by displacement is a good example, but we can come closer to home. The 19th century chemist August Kekulé acknowledged that he had dreamed of a snake eating its tail, and that this experience facilitated his discovery of the nature of the crucial carbon ring that is a fundamental component of life. Einstein acknowledged that after he had become saturated by scientific conceptual thinking he finally dreamed – and thus experienced in an imaginal context – what it would be like to travel on a photon of light. He was thereby equipped to postulate aspects of his legacy of theories relating to relativity. When Hawking challenged himself to discover what could have 'existed' just before Big Bang he had to ask what would it be like to be present before time and space 'is'? He did not solve this question by scribbling esoteric calculus on a blackboard into the early hours of the morning until visitors walked into his private study to see a tired young man with tangled hair and a room full of crossed-out symbols – that is the Hollywood depiction of the process! The question necessitated a 'thought experiment' which allowed the idea to pervade his totality. He had to perceive the experience of 'being' before or beyond time and space. Indeed you could try the same thing now and resume reading later. Sustained, earnest and sincere meditation on a subject of this nature might yield staggering results, although you may not receive a Nobel Prize in recompense as you will probably find yourself utterly unable to communicate what you have learnt!

From out of this experiment Hawking saw the mother of all black holes. *The* singularity. To communicate what he had seen to the outside world he corroborated his findings by applying scientific theoretical method, and this can be followed through in an article written in collaboration with the mathematician Roger Penrose.[7] However, unless the reader has a considerable knowledge of the appropriate scientific language the article may not easily yield its secrets.

There are other ways in which we can understand the differences between the cosmologists who proposed *The Cosmic Doctrine* and the Physicists who propose the current hypotheses, rules and laws that make up contemporary physics. Dion Fortune's work seeks to discover our place in the universe, to unravel the mysteries of Being and to try to understand how we may evolve, develop and regenerate. The latter part of this sentence highlights a general distinguishing factor. Whereas the Physicist seeks to understand the nature of matter, to go behind matter in order to find the laws that govern the universe and to discover the particles that provide the foundation for operations within our universe, the occultist seeks to embody the knowledge in a subjective way: literally to journey on that knowledge. There is a similar desire behind both quests which in scientific terms can be described as the desire to find a unified theory that explains everything: to discover the so-called 'God' particle which glues everything together and makes sense of all things and operations within the material universe.

The problem with searching for the God particle within matter is that this is simply an operation bound within the phenomenal – the manifest – whereas the ultimate source is in what *The Cosmic Doctrine* describes as the only reality: the Unmanifest. If God is anywhere 'It' is Unmanifest – beyond the concepts of good and bad, justice or lack of justice, unfair behaviour and fair behaviour. This 'God' is not even describable by the use of the verb 'to be.' And this creates another divergence. Thus if the occultist uses the word 'God' at all it is the verb 'to be' reflected back into pure being and thereby bereft of both its inherent dynamic, dimensional movement in time or space and any manifestation of polarity. In consequence the word 'God' is removed beyond any possibility of self-reflection; the term evades linguistic description absolutely since language presupposes a speaker and a listener. We cannot begin to understand this or even begin to climb the mountains that are the foothills of understanding the Unmanifest; we can only embody that knowledge and follow it. That is why the occult approach to understanding is by symbols and analogies, training the mind and not informing it. The Physicist does not penetrate that far if he or she wishes to remain in a comfortable zone, although theorists examining string theory may be moving towards the Unmanifest when they postulate a number of parallel universes which are impossible to perceive from our position in the 'multi-verse.' In order to exist, these parallel universes must in some way be 'manifest' but they are nevertheless theoretical possibilities that are far beyond the zone of manifestation in which we exist as humans. And thus theoreticians are beginning to concede that there is some sort of no-thing behind the 'something' in which we live and have our being and which we call the universe, even though we are not capable of an intellectual conception of its increasing boundaries as it expands into no-thing.

Carlos Castaneda was a lone occult writer using (whether as an instructive device or otherwise) a vehicle of scientific anthropology – ethnography – to express his ideas. In his book *Tales of Power*,[8] his teacher Don Juan seeks to explain to him the nature of being by reference to objects on a table. He explains that everything on the table is within manifestation which, deploying the Mexican *Nahuatl* language, he calls the "tonal." He even includes our concepts of God in all that is within the tonal or manifest universe. He then explains that everything beyond the table is unknowable and he uses the Nahuatl word *'nagual'* to describe this. He goes on to say that everything in the nagual is utterly unknowable and indescribable but nevertheless exists. It is a place that our totality can enter and a place in which the vehicle of the self can perceive, although we can never tell anybody about it except through analogous stories and symbols. These images that Castaneda uses to depict the Mysteries are extremely helpful in giving some idea of the vastness of the inexplicable reality that is beyond us and yet is ever present. This inexplicable reality is not the Physicist's dark matter (although the term provides a useful image to depict the unknowable) because that is on the table even though it can never be tested or described.

Castaneda himself secured a Ph.D. in anthropology in a very respected university. This University subsequently removed the Ph.D. because it was not sure that the work had been based on fact, but has since reinstated it. I suspect that at least some – perhaps Californian – academics dealing in frontier ideas and concepts within contemporary physics, including string theory, have read some of Castaneda's 'tales' and may well have been influenced by his analogies. Thus a work that describes the occult may have entered their thinking and perhaps begun a process of cross-fertilization between the ideas of the Physicists and the propositions of the occultists.

Nothing that I have said should be interpreted as a dogmatic assertion that there is a cast-iron difference between the occultist and the scientist. Scientists, in their day jobs, seek to prove hypotheses. But of course in their private world they can dream, just as Einstein's dream generated his theories long before they were proved by the application of scientific method. We are all mysterious beings capable of much more than we may believe and at root there can be no real difference (beyond the cloak of profession that we all wear) between a scientist and an occultist: both are enquiring into aspects of the Mysteries of the universe.

Nevertheless it helps to polarise differences in order to understand the relative values of different approaches, and to alternate between these opposing views. To reiterate: the approach to knowledge taken by the Physicist differs dramatically from that of the occultist in that the Physicist focuses ultimately on the objective (with some meanders and diversions on the way which constitute intermediate conceptual phases) while the occultist emphasizes the subjective, with objectivity playing its part from time to time but not crucial to the journey. This is all due to a fundamentally different emphasis and approach which for the most part creates an epistemological chasm – a chasm which will not easily be bridged even where scientific proofs might corroborate significant contentions of the occultist about the nature of the universe. This fundamental distinction derives from that which can be externally measured and fixed in space-time for all to observe in a similar and consistent manner, as opposed to that which is subjectively known and cannot be transmitted by word, thought or even deed but can only be known experientially. The distinction becomes more apparent when we examine what the Physicist does and what the occultist seeks to do.

The Physicist-cosmologist has a wide and increasing range of work: the observable universe is an inconceivably extensive 'space' and is currently, and increasingly, expanding. This expansion is occurring not only in real terms but in terms of our capacity to observe it as technology develops. Developing technology increases our ability to process information and to detect the outer reaches of our visible and invisible universe at both the macrocossmic and microcosmic levels, perceived through the Hubble Telescopes, better radio-astronomy techniques and bigger and better particle colliders.

Nevertheless there are plenty of examples within this burgeoning field which will demonstrate the objective nature of the scientific enquiry. One fundamental example that might appear to be crucial to both the Physicist and the occultist is the search for a general unified theory of everything whereby the entire Universe can not only be explained by a group of natural laws but whose future can also be predicted by those laws. At present no single theory stands up to the scrutiny of the experts. There is a plethora of theories which need to be tested through observation before any of them can qualify; some theories work in some contexts but not in others, so they need an intermediate linking theory in order to meet the requirements of a theory of everything. The hunt for a Nobel prize in this aspect of research is intense and may well be one of the driving goals, a very different prize to that which is sought by the occult seeker! The problem arises because the postulations of Newtonian physics, through the application of subsequent modifications deriving mainly from Einstein's two theories of relativity, work well at the macrocosmic level but break down at the minuscule level and let us down completely if we travel through the event horizon of a black hole and on into a singularity. This not only causes difficulties but also requires leaps of logic in all directions; thus the scientist is left feeling both vulnerable and insecure, if not downright incorrect. Of course to date no one who has had the misfortune to fall into a black hole has returned to describe their observations and provide us with appropriate data.

In *A Brief History of Time*, Stephen Hawking takes us through many of the attempts to get round these problems. Luckily for the reader the journey is made lighter by his approachable style and the inclusion of aspects of his personal history in the story of his search. The description of the many bets made between Hawking and his competitors and collaborators alone makes the book a good read. He details the attempts to link the two separate theories of quantum physics (which work well in the microcosmic world) and relativity (which works well at the macrocosmic level) into a single and unified thread of enquiry. In so doing he points out how most attempts to glue these theories together can go terribly wrong when they are applied to the pre-origin state of the universe, or indeed to its post 'end' state. Science, for the moment, has real trouble in dealing with the Unmanifest and the concept of there being both an end and a beginning to time. Hawking describes all sorts of virtual – and sometimes rather contrived but nonetheless highly imaginative – schemes to get round this problem when dealing with the mode of inflation from the initial Big Bang and the ultimate contraction (or otherwise) of the universe. In one attempt to get round the difficulties he uses a purely mathematical concept of 'imaginary time' which in effect sits on the 'y' axis of a graph while space sits on the 'x' axis. When time is determined in this way, the 'arrow of time' as he calls it can move in both directions in a symmetrical fashion rather than travelling in the traditional route from the past to the future only.

In this way the idea of an end or beginning of time is no longer essential and the rise and fall to and from the absolute decline of space-time in what we call the universe can take place within a closed-loop system. Now this idea cannot be experienced; it can be expressed only through mathematics, so it cannot get off the ground until some data is gleaned or observed which will allow us to move a little closer towards seeing how it might explain the way in which things work. Only then would it provide a means to reliably predict the course of the universe both back and forwards in time. Until that happens this imaginative and purely abstract mathematical idea is just one of many theories to explain why the universe is where it is now and why it appears to be doing what it appears to have done since its inception. Unlike the occultist, Hawking and others would not see this theory as a means to personal development, regeneration or evolution but merely as an attempt at an objective definition of the course of the universe which, if ever proved, would allow us to gain more knowledge in a pragmatic sense of the manifest world around us. Indeed in many cases the scientist develops his or her knowledge as part of a career strategy, their goal being to have a successful career with the concomitant personal satisfaction and accolades that derive therefrom, whether these accolades are tangible – such as the winning of a Royal Society Fellowship or Nobel Prize – or something much more abstract, just as the mountain climber may ascend a peak 'just because it is there.'

However, it would be wrong to suggest that the scientist has a more career driven and mundane goal than the occultist who is sincerely seeking knowledge because selfless service is required from him or her by a greater power or a greater self. Only a theoretical distinction, with exceptions on both sides of the fence, can truly be said to exist. The motives of scientists are also capable of being utterly selfless and sacrificed to abstract goals: driven almost spiritually, for want of a better descriptor.

So in contrast – and maintaining a generalized enquiry – what is the occult seeker engaged in, or looking for? Well, for the most part they may not be seeking the accolades of their fellows and will be as likely to win a Nobel Prize as win the Lottery two weeks in a row. Some write books, give lectures and workshops and attain the status (whether correctly or inappropriately) of a western guru, although if this happens to be their personal target they are unlikely to hit the mark. But it is equally likely that the true occult seeker may be heading in the opposite direction which is characterized by increasing obscurity and the complete abandonment of any sense of 'self' capable of experiencing any sense of achievement from receiving a prize or the praise of co-travellers.

In a sense the occult seeker is attempting to become one with the knowledge she or he seeks: to merge the subject with the object. But some of the greatest Physicists may also share these qualities. It takes total immersion in a subject to incubate a dream in which you float on a photon of light and derive from that experience the information that builds space-time and even creates the foundation for weapons of mass destruction. It similarly takes incredible dedication to the quest and a dynamic volition to keep body and soul together while entering the space of a singularity and floating freely in an imaginary event horizon. This might result in Hollywood acclamation or a Nobel Prize, but the dedication and sacrifice was not made for that purpose and the originator of the ideas may not have even conceived of that result. Once you see the face of God you are changed forever. You might not walk with God as did Enoch but you will never quite come home again.

Ultimately it may be said that all seekers have a similar thirst for a unified theory of everything. And for that theory to be achieved, there may have to be a joint effort which absorbs the knowledge and methods of both the Unmanifest and the manifest. The type of dedication that is witnessed on both sides of the epistemological gulf may be an absolute necessity, because to seize knowledge will require the embodying of that knowledge in a manner which may obliterate the self. Thus the links between *The Cosmic Doctrine* and contemporary cosmological physics are likely to be present but they may be latent rather than patent. *The Cosmic Doctrine* evinces experiential knowledge which does not sit well with the type of knowledge that will enable you to achieve an 'A' level or higher qualification in physics, but that journey may well from time to time coincide with the journey of the theoretical Physicist.

We cannot expect to find equations and postulations that can be understood by the epistemic community of scientists within *The Cosmic Doctrine*. It is not particularly concerned with the level of tangible manifestation that we can perceive by physical means. As has been said, Physicists restrict their work to the manifest world. Even in the far reaches of string theory where multiple parallel universes are conceived, all that is in those universes remains within the realm of the manifest, although the laws of physics may differ so much from one universe to another that only those beings derived from the substance of each individual universe may perceive, move and have their being therein. *The Cosmic Doctrine* tells us about the noumenal or Unmanifest and its commands, emanations, transformations and metamorphoses into the phenomenal. It witnesses (but does not pin down or describe) the 'Mind of God' that Hawking seeks to know and goes on to tell – by analogy – how it is imprinted in the guise of a thought-form which builds the universe. One might say that *The Cosmic Doctrine* begins with the Mind of God and ends with the Earth. Whereas the Physicist begins with the Earth and seeks the Mind of God.

Shared Reflections in Physics and the Mysteries

If my suggestion that *The Cosmic Doctrine* and the Physicists are on the same path but travelling from opposite directions is correct, we might hope to find some clear landmarks or at least some hints that would indicate that the road is indeed the same. We do in fact see some potential signs of these landmarks – some reflections of contemporary theories – throughout the text, often as images that are intended (to repeat the key to *The Cosmic Doctrine*) to train the mind rather than to inform it. Thus we find, after the immediate first transmutation towards manifestation which creates the Ring Pass-Not, how within that phenomenon there is a parallel image to the physical constant that is the speed of light within Einstein's relative universe. Both the Ring Pass-Not and the speed of light are unbreakable barriers to those participating in and limited to our manifest universe. In the terminology of *The Cosmic Doctrine* we read that: "The Cosmos is bounded by that movement which is called the Ring Pass-Not. But besides the Ring Pass-Not there are movements in two directions."[9] On the other hand, in terms of the current understanding of the laws of physics, the speed of light according to Einstein's Special Theory of Relativity is perceived by an observer occupying any position in the universe as always the same speed, while the dimensions of space and time can curve, bend, change and be measured in different ways depending on the observer's position. By following the logic of Einstein's famous equation, the constant that is the speed of light forms a keystone within the structure of space-time that cannot be broken – within manifestation – and in terms of the structure of the universe, that keystone is by analogy a type of barrier (or, in the words of *The Cosmic Doctrine*, a 'Ring Pass-Not') which creates a boundary for the Cosmos.[10]

The early parts of *The Cosmic Doctrine* come much closer to contemporary theories, particularly when we examine the nature of the singularity in which Einstein's postulations begin to break down and string theory comes into its own. The text opens with the 'presence' only of no-thing and a symbolic description of pressure building up which instigates a phenomenon described as space 'moving.' Is this the reversal of the imploding of the pre-Big Bang singularity and the beginning of the universe that is then governed by, *inter alia*, Einstein's postulations? There may be something to go on here but we are stretching possibilities. Not all contemporary theories would follow this route of entry into manifestation: there are, for example, a number of theories of how the Big Bang occurred which do not necessarily coincide with the idea of 'pressure' described at the beginning of *The Cosmic Doctrine*. As an example of one conceptual approach, string theory proposes that our universe began as a result of the collision of multiple universes. Contemporary Einstein-based physics as proposed by Hawking and Penrose also take us away from the origins of the universe as described by *The Cosmic Doctrine*, suggesting that when we observe the death of a singularity the result is an explosion that leaves nothing behind rather than providing the genesis of the universe. However, the images within the text can enable us to experience the descent of the noumenal into the phenomenal and thus, to mirror Einstein's experiential and imaginal ride, we too can ride on a fragment of the Unmanifest in order to understand the ascent or descent of Being into manifestation. Many great discoveries began with nothing less than pure inspiration which derives from the 'breath of God.'[11]

It might be argued that *The Cosmic Doctrine* reveals Dion Fortune's own level of understanding of particle physics and that this may militate against the validity of the text. The opening chapters build images that resemble the physical world but are depicted at a comparatively elementary level in which atoms comprise a central gravitational pull and revolving electrons are individuals following multiple spherical and elliptical paths. It disregards the conceptual and factual developments in quantum mechanics that were taking place in her time, in which fields of energy replaced revolving particles and complex calculations designed to indicate the points of emphasis within orbits replaced the idea of fixed electron positions. Therefore at one level the alleged supernatural source of the knowledge within the text appears not only to be lacking in vision but does not even keep up with contemporary advances in human knowledge. But we must fall back on the advice given by Dion Fortune herself that the text does not provide information but a means of training the mind. If an image is used – whether of school-level physics or of quantum physics – it forms an analogy which encourages the reader to confront the Unmanifest and to penetrate some aspect of the Mind of God directly, subjectively and personally.

The desire to discover the 'Theory of Everything' relates to the manifest, not the Unmanifest, and is necessarily concerned with discovering data that is objective and communicable, not imaginal and experiential. Nevertheless it may indicate the location of a door that all can use, whether such a door is found inside a wardrobe, down a rabbit hole or within a tumulus that leads into the world of Faery. While the Physicist may focus on the 'outerworld' entrance of the door, it is what lies beyond the door that is relevant to those who study *The Cosmic Doctrine.*

At the end of *A Brief History of Time* Hawking reiterates his belief that through the application of scientific method we will ultimately discover the Mind of God. I believe that he is mistaken and that through this approach alone we can only discover the whisperings and hints of the mind of God in the world of Malkuth or of physical manifestation. However, there are wonderful analogies to be found in the concepts, theories and propositions of the current pantheon of cosmological science which derive from the work of those such as Einstein, Penrose and Hawking. We can appropriate these concepts and use them as symbols, metaphors and vehicles to train the mind.

We might for instance begin with the concept of light – something which through our biological inheritance we all seek and lean towards. Light operates in the manifest universe as a 'Ring Pass-Not' with a fixed velocity that uniquely does not alter according to the observer's speed or position. It is thus an immovable keystone in the structure of space-time in which we live. But this description of the properties of manifest light can only be an analogy, a shadow of the true light which is the light that *inspires* the soul or (to translate the root of 'inspire' from the ancient Greek) the light that 'God-breathes' into the soul. The properties of light and its relationship with space-time may nevertheless be used as a symbol to train us to find 'soul' and help us to understand the nature of the 'light' that guides and inspires soul. As we move into the noumenal we have no eyes to see and no senses to feel, and so what we encounter cannot be constructed or limited by photons. The light at the foot of the rainbow bridge between the manifest and the Unmanifest is constant and can be utterly depended upon not only to lead us truthfully to the crown of our journey but also to witness the breath of command emanating from the creator which is the template for the descent of creation into manifestation.

But there is much more, because when we seek the light it provides the key to who we are. In our search we will find that words fall away and no longer have meaning. They become as coracles tossed on a wild ocean, but it is on this very ocean that we may experience our first true encounter with the Mind of God.

1   Dion Fortune, *The Cosmic Doctrine* (York Beach, ME: Red Wheel/Weiser 2000) 1

2   Dion Fortune, *The Cosmic Doctrine*, 1

3   J. K. Rowling, *Harry Potter and the Deathly Hallows*, (London: Bloomsbury Publishing, 2007) 579

4   Stephen Hawking, *A Brief History of Time: From Big Bang to Black Holes*, (London: Bantam Press, 1988)

5   Note that I say 'corroborate' rather than 'prove'. The latter word is too permanent and not many laws of science survive, and thus corroborate is a safer term in that it connotes evidence rather than eternal proof.

6   Dion Fortune, *The Cosmic Doctrine*, 19

7   Stephen Hawking and Roger Penrose, *The Singularities of Gravitational Collapse and Cosmology*, (Proceedings of the Royal Society, 1970, Volume A 314 Issue 1519) pages 529-548.
    Note, however, that in *A Brief History of Time* Hawking later questioned the idea that the universe emanated from a singularity and proposed that by combining "quantum mechanics with general relativity, there seems to be a new possibility that did not arise before: that space and time together might form a finite, four dimensional space without singularities or boundaries..."(Supra note iii). Thus the boundaries move, and the uncertainty that persists at the edge of scientific cosmology perhaps reflects the inevitable excursions into the numinous.

8   Carlos Castaneda, *Tales of Power*, (New York, Simon and Schuster, 1974)

9   Dion Fortune, *The Cosmic Doctrine*, 26

10 Note that this example is only a possible shared perspective between physical science and *The Cosmic Doctrine*. The idea of the 'Ring Pass-Not' could also be applied to the limits of the universe although in this example the Ring Pass-Not is obviously a more flexible term since the current universe is expanding even as you read these words.

11 The word *inspiration* is used to describe the origin of the word of God in the King James version of 2 Timothy 3:16 in the New Testament . The use of the verb is a translation of the NT Greek *theopneustos* which literally signifies: "God-breathed" (See: Vine W.E. (1979) *Expository Dictionary of Bible Words* (London: Marshall, Morgan & Scott), 263.

12 THE SEVEN PLANES OF CONSCIOUSNESS

ALAN ROBINSON

The object of this essay is to develop some of the teaching in *The Cosmic Doctrine* concerning primarily the seven planes of consciousness, their relationship to man, to the aura and to the evolution of consciousness. It is assumed that the reader will have a basic working knowledge of the Mysteries and a reasonable amount of practical experience of occult practices such as meditation. The main structure referred to in this teaching is derived from the three Rings of Space revealed in *The Cosmic Doctrine* but apart from the concept of the three Rings very little else will be used. Although the text is a very useful tool when used with contemplation and discretion, the communication of such matters from the Inner Plane Adepti to the outer plane receiver can give rise to considerable problems when something of this magnitude is undertaken, not least in that some of what is written is not quite as it was intended and is inevitably coloured (as are most of these types of work) with Dion Fortune's consciousness itself, which in its turn is coloured by the consciousness of that age.

Taking into account the problems that can occur with direct communication of extended pieces of work, the Inner Plane Adepti chose to communicate the following material to me in a series of images and experiences, so that those who read what is written and use the exercises described herein may then use their own discretion in its evaluation rather than accept all that is written as Divine truth! Where necessary some of the writer's personal experiences are described to help explain or emphasise a point, but the aim is for readers to contemplate what is written and then use what they perceive in order to gain their own insights. For this reason, much of what has been written is left at a basic level of interpretation so that any realisations that you form are yours alone. Your own realisations will always benefit you more than someone else's. Some of the suggestions and implications in the following pages may come as a surprise to the more seasoned occultist, so it is hoped that you approach this work with an open mind. Listen to your heart, for if what is written here is true, Light will find a way to confirm its validity to you.

The Meaning of Life

The Cosmic Doctrine is about life, above all else. It is about 'being' and 'consciousness.' Many times people ask 'what is the meaning of life,' but as is so often the case they are asking the wrong question. What we should ask ourselves is not 'what is the meaning of life,' for life is its own meaning. What we should ask is 'what is life,' and the answer that will come roaring back to us with the full force of nature is the simple fact that life is experience, nothing more or less. And so from this we can deduce that the meaning of life is experience, and this must be kept in mind for it is the lynch pin on which all that follows is secured. Indeed, it is the sole basis for creation. But first we must consider what there was before creation took place!

The Unmanifest

Many of the great Mystery traditions tell of the Unmanifest as 'that from which all springs'; the place from which arises all subsequent manifestation into creation, whether creation on the Inner planes or in the outer world. But the most that can be said about the Unmanifest is that it is Nothing or no-thing. It can be imagined as an absolute absence of anything, but its true nature is almost unfathomable and impossible for the conscious mind to comprehend. Therefore we can think of the Unmanifest as absolute Nothing or no-thing – a complete vacuum without beginning or end.

Imagine that we had a flask, hermetically sealed, which was completely empty of anything, not even containing a single atom, neutrino or anything else that science recognises (in other words full of no-thing; a complete vacuum in its ultimate sense) and that we passed this flask of nothing amongst ourselves, each of us contemplating it as we did so. If we were asked "What can Nothing do?" the first answer we would probably give is "nothing." However, in passing the flask between us we would have done something with Nothing – the only thing that no-thing can do – we would have made it move!

And so we now know that Nothing can move.

At the level of the Unmanifest, if Nothing moves, the only way that it will move is in a straight line. The reason for this is that since all is Nothing, if Nothing moves, there is no resistance to cause it to deviate from its course. Therefore we can conceive of Nothing moving in a straight line. Now, Nothing has gained a potential: the potential to move, and we can visualise this as a straight line moving in space. We can represent it, if we are so inclined, with a minus sign (-) to indicate Nothing and a plus sign (+) to indicate the potential to move.

If Nothing has the potential to move, it necessarily follows that it also has the potential to stop. We can represent this as a minus sign (-) representing Nothing, and as another minus sign (-) representing the potential to stop or to not move. Therefore if we visualise our line moving through space, we can assign (- +) to one side, and (- -) to the other side.

Knowing that a minus multiplied by a positive cancel themselves out leaving us with Nothing, we also know that a minus multiplied by a minus creates a positive. Therefore, our Nothing now has a positive potential acting on it: the power to stop. From Nothing, something has arisen! We must still consider all of this as potential, for if it was an actuality it would no longer be Unmanifest but Manifest, a part of creation. We shall discuss this point later, but for now let us return to the image of a line moving through space, and visualise it in our imagination.

As we contemplate it moving through space, we can envisage to one side of the line a minus multiplied by a positive which makes a negative, and to the other side a minus multiplied by a minus which makes a positive. So we can now see that the influence acting upon one side of this line of movement will not have any effect; the result will be Nothing and therefore it is at one with all that surrounds it. However, the influence acting upon the other side, being positive, will act upon the line. What now happens is that the positive influence (which is the potential to stop) will bend the line so that eventually it will form a curve until it reaches the place where it started, forming a vast circle.

The first movement creates the potential for one dimension but when the circle has completed its journey there is the potential for two dimensions: inside the circle and outside the circle. What happens when the circle arrives back where it started is that Nothing moving has gained the potential in the course of its journey to become Something by acquiring the positive influence achieved when minus is multiplied by minus. When the end and the beginning of the circle meet and the circle is completed, just as when two objects of equal mass collide, the energy of the moving object is transferred into the object it collides with.

The beginning of the circle will only absorb half the energy inherent in the end of the circle, the energy of Nothing moving ($- \times + =$ nothing) since in terms of mass they are both the same. But as the moving circle or current of energy also contains the power of Nothing to come to a stop, this being the other half of its potential, this part of its energy ($- \times - = +$) will be deflected. As this potential is exactly half of the energy inherent in the circle or Ring, it deflects at a right angle and therefore causes a second Ring to emerge which curves round at right-angles to the first. It deflects at an angle of 90° and not at any other angle because exactly half of its energy is deflected: the energy of the potential to stop.

We can call this first ring the Ring of Space, and as the second ring intersects the first in two places and therefore creates the concept of position, we can call the second ring the Ring of Time. However, what now occurs is that as soon as the second ring has completed its cycle it transmits its potential to the first ring, and likewise the first ring to the second ring, so that the Ring of Space becomes the Ring of Time and the Ring of Time takes on the attributes of the Ring of Space.

We can now visualise these two rings turning in space.

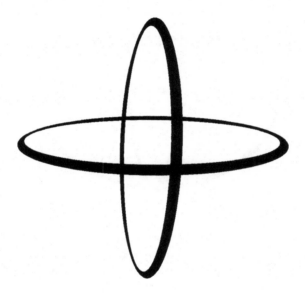

In mathematical terms both rings now have the same equations acting upon them, therefore the positive potential of one ring will attract the negative potential of the other, while at the same time the positive potentials of both rings will push them apart. We can therefore envisage the second ring moving in a sideways motion to the first, and this causes the creation of a third movement in space which creates another circle. This third ring we will call the Ring of Event, and meditating on these three names will reveal much.

So now in Nothing, or no-thing, we have the potential for Time, Space and Event, and also the basis for dimensional space. If we wished to use Qabalistic terms we could think of these three principles as Ain, Ain Soph and Ain Soph Aur, or the three veils of negative existence.

What we have achieved is a way to conceive the unconceivable in our three interlocking Rings and therefore a way to approach them with the concrete mind.

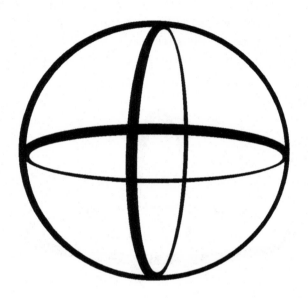

Before we go any further, this may be a good point to stop and consider what we have before us, which is three interlocking Rings revolving in a great Sea of no-thing. As we look, we can perceive a central point within the three Rings around which all revolves. Therefore we have three things: a structure, that which is outside the structure, and a central point within the structure. The central point by its very nature partakes of the great outside even though it is stationary. Although it will experience all that happens within the three Rings it remains a central point of stillness around which all revolves, and is relatively immutable in its nature. That it partakes of the nature of that which is outside the three Ring structure is an important point to understand, for if this is not comprehended correctly many misconceptions can arise. Humanity likes to limit things so that it can understand more easily, but the great Sea of non-being in its most natural state is so far above and beyond the highest human comprehension that it is almost impossible to explain. Perhaps the most we can say about it is that it is not only the potential for everything but also the achievement of everything. Here, not only is everything possible but it has already been accomplished. This is purity of being in its highest sense, partaking of the beginning, middle and conclusion of any event simultaneously while also maintaining stability and remaining essentially unchanging. From a religious point of view we can consider the central point within the structure of the three Rings as the great *I Am who I Am*, the Sun behind the Sun, God in the highest; the concept on which all monotheistic religions are based. However, to understand this correctly we must set aside the solar concepts and return to a consideration of the ancient cults of the Sea. Although at our present stage of development the monotheistic solar cults are quite rightly the highest viewpoint of God to which we can aspire, we must not believe that we can limit God's greatness, for as humanity evolves and undertakes the great journey from involution to evolution, it is to a higher understanding of the Sea cults to which we must return.

With this in mind, we shall return to the formation of the Rings of Time, Space and Event, all revolving around a central point, all held within the great Sea of non-all-being, and begin to approach these concepts on a practical level.

PRACTICAL WORK

These exercises needs to be built and worked with over a period of time to get any real benefit from them. The practitioner should set a certain period each day for meditation on each exercise, taking a period of about three weeks to complete each one before moving onto the next exercise.[1]

Exercise 1 – The Ring of Time
Sitting quietly in meditation, visualise a Ring of light which begins in front of you and then moves clockwise around your body until it completes a great circle of light about your being. Realise that there are four distinct points around this circle or Ring. One is before you at the start of the circle, another to your right, one behind you and another to your left. You can also equate these directions with the cardinal directions of East, South, West and North. Contemplate this Ring as the progress of a day, and see morning before you, midday to your right, sunset behind you and night time to your left. Try to feel the

rising sun and the freshness of the air before you. The warmth and heat of the midday sun to your right. The cool evening breeze and the time of dusk behind you and finally the calm, peaceful time of night to your left.

Next contemplate this Ring as the great circle of the seasons with Spring before you, Summer to your right, Autumn behind you and Winter to your left. See each season in your mind's eye as your focus of attention moves around the circle. Try to see how this natural law progresses throughout all nature and contemplate the starting point and potential of each created thing. See how this potential grows to development as the circle moves round to your right, until the initial potential is achieved at the point behind you in its first, active phase. Next see how everything that has been achieved, slowly breaks down as the circle progresses round to your left, where all the lessons that can be learned are gleaned in this reflective phase before setting the seeds for a new cycle.

Finally, contemplate this circle as representing the cycle of human life with birth in the East, a person growing into maturity in the South, reaching middle age in the West before moving into old age in the North.

It will help greatly if you write a summary of your realisations after each meditation.

Exercise 2 – The Ring of Space

First, build the Ring of Time as described in Exercise One. Now visualise a second Ring appearing, this time starting above your head and moving down your right-hand side where it intersects the Ring of Time. Then see it continue around your feet and returning around your left side where it intersects the Ring of Time before its completion above your head. Contemplate it as the lifeline of your personal life, with the moment of your birth above your head and your present position in life below your feet. To your right, be aware of experiences you have gained which are superimposed at various points on this Ring, and to your left see the possibilities of things that are yet to come.

Next, contemplate this great Ring as the movement of the human spirit down through the course of involution until it reaches our present phase of human development at the base of the circle, then see it moving back up the planes in the course of evolution. Contemplate how the Ring of Space interacts with the Ring of Time and try to feel your being expand to fill this Ring so that you can touch the circumference at any place with your hands or feet. Again, try to record any realisation or experiences after each meditation.

Exercise 3 – The Ring of Event

Finally, see a third Ring emerge, created by the actions of the other two Rings. See it start above your head, this time moving down in front of you until it intersects the Ring of Time. Now see it continuing down under your feet, then moving upwards behind you to intersect the Ring of Time before rejoining itself above your head. Contemplate this as the Ring of Event. See how any event has a relationship in Time and Space and realise that this is also a ring of Personal Will. See how the idea for an action comes into being above your head, developing into fruition at the point before you. Beneath your feet you can see the action being forgotten, while its final assimilation into your being takes place behind you, before the impetus moves on to stimulate another action above you.

Realise that the part of the Ring of Event before you represents those events of which you are consciously aware, and the part of the Ring behind you represents those things of which you are unconscious. Feel how both parts contribute to your being and realise the control that you have over them. Contemplate the themes of internal and external events and see how they are related.

These exercises should firmly build the Rings of Time, Space and Event in your consciousness and can be expanded upon in time.

The basis of the human spirit

Through the practice of regular meditation we can build these three Rings, all moving around a central point, as if we ourselves form the central point. We can thus build them on a personal scale and experience how they affect us individually in our earthly life. But we must also consider them on a universal scale, particularly in relation to the Unmanifest. If we consider the three Rings in relation to Unmanifest existence, we will see that any point anywhere within the boundary of the complete sphere formed by the three Rings will have a position in relation to the Rings and also to the central point. Focusing on any point within this sphere, we can begin to perceive a pinprick of light.

The fact that no matter where we focus our attention we find that each point of light is identical need not concern us for the moment even though it reveals a great truth, for what is important is that each point is situated in a different position in relation to the Rings of Time, Space and Event and also to the central point. Therefore, each point of light will have different stresses or influences acting upon it depending upon its position, and this is the start of individualisation.

Each point of light within the sphere can be considered as a point of consciousness in potential and can be equated with the highest aspect of an individual human being in potential (that which God would have us be) or with the highest aspect of the spirit that will eventually become individualised. But we must remember that in their most basic nature these points of light still partake of the great Sea of the Unmanifest that lies outside this sphere, even though they are now partaking of the influences within. These sparks of light will eventually start to move in orbit around the central point although this will not occur until each Ring has completed its evolution and has gained stability. It is from these points of light that human consciousness will eventually be projected forth into manifest existence.

THE SEVEN PLANES OF CONSCIOUSNESS

The First Plane

Returning to our considerations of the three Rings and the structure of the sphere itself, the next thing that we perceive in the Rings' progression is an attraction between one point where two of the Rings intersect and the corresponding point of intersection on the opposite side of the sphere. What happens now is that, according to the law of attraction, a current is initiated across the Rings from one point to another. If we build an image of the three Rings in meditation and then relate to this initial movement across the sphere, what we will perceive is a state of pure being. It is not yet self awareness, but a state more akin to just 'being'. It is awareness in its most simple state and to describe this state is difficult because our attempt to describe it is more complicated than the state itself. The only thing I can suggest is that you build this system in your consciousness and experience it for yourself, and actually all you will be doing is remembering something that is so ingrained in the basis of your being that you have never really forgotten it; it can be recovered. Perhaps the best explanation I can give is that it is individual consciousness without an awareness of the individual, for if it was anything else it would partake of the great consciousness that lies outside this three ring system and which is part of the great Sea of non-being. But it is this movement that creates the basis for the first plane of consciousness.

If we return to an overview of what is happening within this three Ring system we will perceive that once this current is initiated, and as the Rings revolve, so the current will pass through every point within the sphere which means that this pure consciousness is imparted to each and every point. These currents are initiated between each opposing point across the sphere and they always pass through the central point. If they moved diagonally from one point to another without passing through the central point they would not achieve stability and so would cease to exist, exerting no influence, for stability is an underlying law inherent in the three Rings. If we count these initial movements we will find that they are six in number, and the implications of this will be present in each of the seven planes of consciousness that later develop. That there are six movements and seven planes of consciousness is important, for the seventh plane is always created by the influence of the central point, and this is the key to much. Therefore if, for example, we consider the fifth plane we can see that it will contain the influences of the preceding four, but the preceding four planes will not have the influence of the fifth until involution is completed and consciousness is returned to the first plane, bearing with it all that it has learned.

Exercise 4

Build up the three Rings in meditation. Feel the vastness of the structure about you, and then from the point before you where the Ring of Time meets the Ring of Event see a brighter point of light detach and move directly across the sphere, forming a straight line of light. Feel it moving and try to relate your being to any point along this line. Become aware of the movement inherent within it. Feel how it draws you along as it moves from one side to the other, and feel the oneness of all about you. If you do come to any realisations while completing this task, write them down, but at this point it is unlikely that you will because what we are aiming for is more akin to the nature of a 'feeling' or impression. Once you have an understanding of this state of pure being, the exercise will have been accomplished.

The Second Plane

When this initial cycle of movement has been completed, the next stage is that the line of light, having passed across the sphere from one point at which two Rings interlock to the equivalent point on the opposite side, then starts its passage of return along the same path. Now if we build this image in meditation and relate to it, we perceive that at any point along its path of return where the current passes its position on the original path, self awareness is imparted to the original state of consciousness. This differs from the relatively simple consciousness or state of being that existed in one plane only, in that in plane one where it could be said 'it is,' it can now be said 'I am,' although without any knowledge of the self. Here, consciousness of what is without is identical to consciousness of what is within. However, we must remember that all this is still only in potential. We can think of it as laying down the principles on which manifestation will subsequently be based.

Exercise 5

Again, building the three Rings in meditation, see the current of light described in Exercise Four reach its destination on the opposite side of the sphere (where the Ring of Time intersects the Ring of Event) and then see it turning back upon itself and retracing its course. Relating to these currents of movement in your meditation, feel yourself being drawn into the first current, but this time also feel the presence of the returning current of light. Feel the point where the returning current of light meets you and contemplate how although it is the same, it feels different. Be aware also of how the return journey gives position to the first movement.

The Third Plane

Having witnessed the potential for development of self-awareness we can now consider the next movement that occurs within the complete sphere which is between three points of intersection, thus forming a triangle. It is a law of this system that any movement will eventually arrive back where it began. These laws are laid out by the nature of the Rings, and this is a very important point in the evolution of consciousness for now we have the basis not only for self awareness but also for realising subsequent action and reaction, as well as having the basis for the creation of form. In terms of consciousness, however, all is still one as before. This is perhaps why a group of three is such an important feature in many religions and philosophies, for where we have previously observed 'it is' in plane one and 'I am' in plane two, we can now consider the potential of 'it will be' in plane three. Possibly it could also be said that it is at this stage that the notion of separation first comes into consciousness, although this is more in the nature of an awareness of something being separate from the self even though that 'something' *is* the self. It is the notion of action and reaction, of viewing the self from a different point of view, and this is caused by the influence of the principles behind the Rings of Time and Event.

Exercise 6

Having built the three Ring system in meditation, again see the point of light moving out from where the Ring of Time meets the Ring of Event in front of you, travelling straight across the sphere and passing through the centre. But now when it reaches the other side, instead of returning along its initial path, see this line of light move upwards to where the Ring of Space meets the Ring of Event above your head. Then, it travels down to where it started, forming a triangle. Feel yourself being drawn into this movement and contemplate the other two lines that make up the triangle. Contemplate the principle of action and reaction, and also the principles of freedom and limitation. Write down any thoughts that may occur to you, no matter how trivial they may at first appear.

Before we move on to the fourth plane, this is an appropriate moment to consider other types of consciousness than that which will eventually become human. If we reach up high enough in our own consciousness whilst we are manifestation we can touch the level of abstract thought, and from this level we can perceive two types of movement. The first movement consists of currents of force which, if we could step back far enough, we would realise were circular in nature. The other movement we would perceive is a line of force intersected by another line of force, and we would be aware that where two lines of force intersect is always the basis for consciousness. From this level of abstract thought, if we looked down we might perceive one line of force above another, and another, each at a lower level, but wherever these lines intersect and join, there we will always find consciousness present. As light passes through each line of force it is coloured by the vibration inherent in each line, so that any entity subject to the influence of this light will be subject to the factors imparted by these lines and vibrations. The more lines that intersect the more variations are available for consciousness to develop, although not necessarily human consciousness.

As in the manifest world, so also to a strange extent in the Unmanifest, and what we find is that in the intersection of the three Rings of Time, Space and Event other conscious entities are present in potential, and these we refer to as the Lords of Flame, Form and Mind. Each of these takes its nature from whichever Ring it was initially created in. Their consciousness differs from human consciousness in that we are of the Great Unmanifest which lies without the Rings and we enjoy the freedom inherent in such, but they are of the structure of the Rings themselves and so are limited in their development by the potential which is present in the Rings' structure. Those limitations produce beings that are very great indeed, and their controlling influence behind the whole of creation must be kept in mind, but nevertheless they have limitations. The reason they are mentioned here will become apparent when we consider the fourth plane in potential – and we must stress 'in potential' for we must not forget that we are still only referring to patterns being laid down in the Unmanifest.

The Fourth Plane

Returning to the next development in the sequence, we can now consider the current of energy moving through four points of the interconnecting Rings, and here we can now see the basis for what will later become form. Remembering the need for stability (and if this is not achieved all will amount to nothing and will exert no influence) it is possible for a square to be created within the three Rings which does not pass through the central point. In this square we have the potential for a new form of consciousness to arise. Although this consciousness may be aware of the existence of the central point it is not directly in contact with it, and it is here that the basis for those creations we refer to as the Planetary Beings takes place. (Another possibility is created when the moving current passes through the central point, across to the other side and then up to the top, but from here it moves to the base of the sphere and then back to the beginning, creating two triangles.)

Many consider the Planetary Beings each to have a different plane of existence to the others, but this is incorrect. The basis for all of them is created within the Rings when the first four-sided movement occurs. There can sometimes be confusion between what is meant by a Planetary Being and a Planetary Spirit, but the difference is that the latter is a construct of a sphere of evolution within the influence of the Planetary Being. Thus the Earth's Planetary Being is a fourth plane construct, and this plane is also where are created those forces that we know as the four elements in their purest sense: the elements of Air, Fire, Water and Earth.

Now as the three Rings each create a consciousness that we have referred to as the Lords of Flame, Form and Mind, so does our Planetary Being create four regents of its own structure. Therefore the four elemental kings are to the Planetary Being of our Earth what the Lords of Flame, Form and Mind are to the three Rings of this system. This is the key to much and is well worth pondering. An important point to consider is that while the currents of movement bring possibilities to the sparks of light within the sphere that partake of the Unmanifest without and give them a means of development, the Planetary Beings do not partake of the Unmanifest without but, like the Lords of Flame, Form and Mind are creations of the structure itself and so are also subject to the restrictions imposed by it. It is for this reason that human beings are referred to as 'the children of God' and other forms of creation as 'the created of God.' There is an important distinction here for if these other forms of consciousness are to survive the completion of this great adventure into manifestation and beyond, they have to rely upon humanity to impart to them the spiritual vibration of the great Unmanifest. Thus is humanity truly a priesthood and we have an enormous responsibility upon our shoulders.

Exercise 7

Building the three Rings in meditation, first contemplate the line or current of light passing from in front of you to behind you (passing through the centre) then up to the top of the sphere where the Rings meet before travelling straight down to the base of the sphere and back to the start, forming two triangles. Feel yourself being drawn along this line of light and contemplate each triangle. See the triangle opposite you and consider it, then consider the central point that joins the two triangles, and finally consider the central point's relationship with all that is outside this system. Contemplate how the two triangles are the same and yet different.

Then, see a current of light begin from the point of intersection in front of you and move straight across to the point where the circles intersect on your right, before travelling to the point behind you and then across to your left, before travelling back to its starting point, forming a square. Contemplate how this sequence does not move through the central point and instead feel its relationship with the Rings of Time, Space and Event. Record any realisations that may occur during this sequence of meditation.

The Fifth Plane

Returning to the Rings of Time, Space and Event, we shall consider the current of light moving through five points, and now something happens that appears slightly strange the first time we see it. The only way that the current can achieve stability in five movements is by flowing across the sphere and through the centre to the opposite side, then up to the top, then diagonally down through the centre to the point below, then to another of the side points before returning to the start. Yet the only way stability can be achieved is through the balance of misplaced opposites, and this causes the revolving of this five-pointed structure in a strange orbit as it tries to achieve stability. It is at this point in the sequence that the notion of separateness fully emerges.

Various mythologies talk of humanity's fall from grace; a separation from the Spirit through some misdemeanour initiated by humanity and for which we have been paying ever since. Although there is a small grain of truth in the concept of original sin (for example whenever we think that it is Spirit which serves us rather than we who serve Spirit) the reality is that the concept of separation is a natural result of the creation of the planes as they come into manifestation. The fifth plane in particular, when it became manifest, is remembered by humanity and recalled in such legends as the story of Adam and Eve. It is known in esoteric terminology as the Lemurian period. The fact that what took place is still remembered by us today on the seventh plane, if somewhat distortedly, is a testament to the power of the fifth plane and its importance in the development of mind. It is as if we dress this memory in our seventh plane consciousness, so that we see it as if it had occurred on this plane. But these events belong to plane five, and when this is correctly realised and the reason behind it is understood, the mental blocks that we put in place against the realisation of Spirit through genuine ignorance and forgetfulness will lift, and all will become clearer as we remember. Then shall we see our common heritage as sparks of the Divine, travelling forth from the first to the seventh plane, and will realise that each spark is charged with the task of gaining experience in accordance with the different factors that play upon it from the influence of its initial position in regard to the three Rings. We will then see that one of our greatest tasks is to help each other complete the experiences set forth for each spirit, for it is in the completion of the all that we shall all become complete.

The fifth plane is also the first stage at which we can consider the principles of male and female, although at this level there is no sexual nature as we understand it for that does not come into existence until seventh plane manifestation. However, when we are able to see the development of experience from the first through to the seventh plane and adjust our perceptions to account for the fifth plane, then we shall truly be aware of God whilst on earth. But we shall say more about the fifth plane when we consider how these potentials become actualities in manifestation.

Exercise 8

After building the three Rings in meditation, once more see the current of light or movement that passes directly across the complete sphere. But this time, instead of following a pattern which has been described to you, try for yourself to make the current move in five straight lines, passing through the central point at least once and completing its journey where it began. Do not attempt at first to gain any insights or realisations for this is an exercise that teaches the soul and intuition as opposed to the concrete mind. Finally, after some periods of meditation have been spent on this, follow the description of the flow of energy described in the section headed The Fifth Plane, and contemplate its movement.

The Sixth Plane

The motion that creates plane six takes place when the current of light passes across the centre of the sphere to the far side, then up to the top, before travelling straight down through the centre to the point at the base of the sphere. From here it travels diagonally up to the left, then straight across the centre again to the opposite side, before travelling back to its point of origin, thus creating three triangles. This is perhaps the most difficult plane to describe for it concerns the principles of attraction and rejection occurring between three points. The reason that it is so difficult to describe is that the word 'rejection' is unsatisfactory, but a better word to describe it does not yet exist in the English language. We can think of it as a drawing together and pushing apart at the same moment in a three way motion. The result could be described as a type of perpetual motion, and it is a forerunner to manifest time. It is discrimination in its highest and most abstract sense. When the sixth plane manifests, memory of it comes down to us as our recollection of the period that is called Atlantean. Here are three triangles each occupying a different plane of existence: one triangle under the influence of the Rings of Event and Space, one under the influence of the Rings of Space and Time and one under the influence of the Rings of Time and Event. We can consider it as the influence of past, present and future and it is what lies immediately behind the physical universe as we know it. At the level of the Unmanifest it imparts to consciousness the understanding of 'I was', 'I am', and 'I will be.'

Exercise 9

Build the three Ring system and then visualise the current of light moving exactly as described above, to create the three triangles. Centre your attention in the triangle influenced by the Rings of Space and Event. See in your mind's eye how the attraction which draws one triangle to another and the opposite effect of the third triangle pushing them apart, causes the structure to spin. Contemplate the concept of attraction and rejection.

Now move your viewpoint from the first triangle to one of the others. View the structure as if this was the dominant triangle and contemplate the other two from this position, observing how although the forces acting upon it are the same as before, they may appear or 'feel' different. Finally, consider how you react to situations arising in your daily life which may reflect this particular formation occurring within the three Rings. Record any realisations.

The Seventh Plane

We have now come to the crux of the matter. We have utilised all the points around our Three Ring system. So far, there are (in potential) six planes because there are six intersections in the three Rings, yet there are seven planes of consciousness. So where do we look for the basis of the seventh plane? The answer is that it is the addition of the central point to the previous six that creates the seventh plane, and the concept behind this is really quite profound. So often we think of the planes as higher and lower, more spiritual or more earthly, but each is as holy as the other, for all of them can absorb the influence of the central point. If you experience these planes correctly you will find that the reason plane three feels more spiritual than plane seven or six for example, is that plane three is less complicated in form, so consciousness feels more liberated and more expansive when operating on this plane. This does not mean that plane three is more spiritual, and this is an important point to understand.

Also, you will find that exactly the same amount of energy is made available to each plane but as more structure is utilised by the energy the less 'free' energy there appears to be. For example, when we operate on the fourth plane we are aware of a feeling of enormous energy that seems to be lacking on the seventh, yet the amount of energy available on each plane is the same. We are presently manifest on the seventh plane yet this plane is no less holy than any of the preceding planes, even if it seems so when we contact them. The seventh plane has more complexities present and through these complexities consciousness can experience all that is available for expression. Therefore we can just as easily enter into a relationship with God on the seventh plane as on any other, for true unity with God will only be found in the Unmanifest and beyond. When this is truly understood then we are ready to converse with angels and the other beings of creation without awe or fear but as from one consciousness in the great sea of creation to another.

It is the correct understanding of the relationship of the planes that is so important. So many times humanity has glimpsed things and misunderstood what they see. One example for instance can be seen in the beliefs of the Cathars, who glimpsed the relative freedom of the sixth plane (or perhaps their initiates taught it to followers, who in time misunderstood) and deemed the seventh plane to be the work of an anti-god who enslaved its inhabitants. Considering the relative freedom of the sixth plane it is easy to see how one could make this mistake. They even forsook sex in an attempt to regain the sixth plane, which is interesting as sexual energy is not available on the sixth plane but is one of the results of the seventh plane. This seems to suggest that this area of Europe with its long traditions of faery is particularly close to the sixth plane, just as are the British Isles. But all of this is the result of the structures that are inherent within the Planetary Being. Each succeeding plane will have more complexities available for the development of consciousness and these complexities should not be avoided. For humanity, the way back to the sixth plane is found by following the path of the Ring of Time from involution down the planes to evolution and back up. We should neither attempt to turn back without passing the nadir as the Cathars did, nor see the complexities of the seventh plane as an obstacle to spiritual awareness, but gaining all experience available to us without harming others, join the dance round this circle of life with joy and expectation.

Before we move on to the next section of this work, there is one more thing to consider in regard to the circuits of force around the Rings of Time, Space and Event that create the basis for the planes. Once these patterns of force have achieved stability, it is possible for parts of them to move backwards through the Ring of Time, twisting these structures into multidimensional shapes. Linear time as we know it does not exist in the Unmanifest and it may be that past, present and future happen simultaneously. Therefore if we consider the divine sparks that fill the sphere and represent humanity in its highest potential, not only are they the beginning of us, but also the middle and end. Therefore we should strive to make a link with our individual point in the great Unmanifest at all times, for great guidance and adjustment can come from such.

Exercise 10
This is perhaps the most important exercise of all, for it is one that is not carried out in meditation but in everyday life. As you move about in the world, from time to time contemplate all that you have come to understand from the exercises you have accomplished and see the physical world about you from this viewpoint. Realise that you are now situated on the seventh plane as a result of this process and do not be surprised if the Spirit now starts to shine through into everyday life. At first it may be seldom and take you by surprise but the more you open yourself up to the inner principles behind the seven planes of existence in everyday life, the more it will happen. Reflect upon the preceding planes and try to gauge their influence in the world about you, for it is possible to see their actions in nature and in the events that occur in the physical world. However, be sure to perform the allotted tasks of everyday life and be ever mindful of the genuine needs of others, be it family friends or acquaintances, for we do not seek to withdraw from the world to within ourselves but to fully immerse ourselves in the outside world. Only thus will we reap the rewards of experience.

THE SEVEN PLANES WITHIN THE AURA

It is now time to work with the seven planes made manifest and specifically as they manifest within the aura. Again, we must create a structure from which we can approach our subject. If you have completed the previous exercises described you will have your own method of meditation, but I will describe the method that I personally find most helpful in this type of work.

In a room or place that you can set aside for daily meditation, preferably for a period in the morning and again in the evening, stand and take note of your surroundings, including the clothes that you have on at the time. Then, closing your eyes, visualise your surroundings, including the clothes you are wearing. (It helps if you keep the room uncluttered!) Raise your arm above your head and visualise a sphere of light about your raised hand. Slowly bring your hand down before you until it is in front of your brow about a foot from your body, imagining as you do so that a current of light is emanating from this sphere and is traced by the passage of your hand down before you. Next, touch your brow, and as all our work must be dedicated to the Most High, silently voice the words: "In thy hands." Return your hand to its position a foot or so before your brow and continue down in a circular motion to your navel about 18–24 inches from your body. Now touch your navel and silently voice: "is the Kingdom." Once this is done, return your hand to about 18–24 inches before your navel and continue to move it downwards, visualising the light continuing in its circular motion until it is beneath your feet where you should visualise another sphere of light. If you have trouble getting the energy to your feet once it has left the tip of your hand, feel your aura move upwards from the bottom of the feet to the groin and you should find that this makes the passage of the light easier.

Now visualise this current of light travelling back up behind you in a circular manner until it rejoins the sphere of light at the top of your head. Next, starting from this first circle of light before you, move your hand round to touch your right shoulder, visualising as you do so that a second line of light emerges from the first, travelling in a horizontal direction about you. As this circle of light passes about your right shoulder, voice the words: 'and the power.' Return your hand to its position before you and see how this second line of light passes behind you in a circular manner, passing around your left shoulder. Touch your left shoulder, silently voicing the words: 'and the glory.' You now stand at the centre of two circles of white light.

Cross your hands over your heart and think: 'for ever and ever,' visualising a small sphere of light at your heart centre. Placing your hands together as if in prayer before your throat centre, think: 'Amen,' and as you do so feel these four small spheres of light (one above the head, one below the feet, one at the right shoulder and another at the left shoulder) expand, opening the aura slightly as they do so.

Now you are almost ready to begin. Sit quietly and clear your mind for meditation. As this work is mainly concerned with the aura it is important that we take care of the basic things, and the first of these is to choose a seat or chair that is not made of metal, for metal interacts with the aura in a restrictive way. Therefore a seat made of wood is preferable. So, sitting in a relaxed posture, begin by feeling your aura, moving your awareness of it from the top of your head and down around the *back* of the body until you have traced it all the way down behind you, to below your feet, sensing your aura radiating out from the physical body as an enveloping sphere of light.

You may be aware that your aura is slightly restricted by the chair you are sitting on, so it is important that you slow down and give the light of your aura time to penetrate the seat until it is balanced with the light radiating out in front of you. The next step is to concentrate on your breathing and, on your in-breath, feel the energy of your aura simultaneously flowing up through the bottom of your feet and down through the top of your head until these energies meet at the navel. It usually takes about three in-breaths to accomplish this, and if you find that the energy retreats to its original position as you exhale, pause for about three seconds between inhaling and exhaling and you will find that the energy you are directing becomes stabilised. Once the energy travelling up meets the energy travelling down and they have intermingled at your navel, concentrate on your out-breath and see a line of silvery-black light emerge from your navel. On each out-breath extend this line until it is about four feet in front of you. At this point relax, concentrating on your breathing, and visualise a point of silver light at the end of this silvery-black cord. Holding the point of light steady in your mind's eye, be aware of the silvery-black cord shrinking back into your body, and your aura re-absorbing it.

Returning your awareness to the point of light, imagine it moving around your body in a clockwise motion until it rejoins itself before you, forming a circle about you. (I prefer at this point to feel my consciousness in another body which is created with the mind, in which I move around my physical body, taking the light with me in one hand, until I have completed the circuit around my physical body. It was found to be easiest at first if I put the other hand of this visualised body on top of my own physical head while making the circuit, and although this option is not necessary you may find it a good exercise for loosening the strings between your consciousness and your physical body.)

Once the circle of light is complete, see it with your mind's eye expanding outwards until a large circular sphere of light has been created about you. Then relax your conscious mind for a short while and briefly contemplate the space between the atoms that make up both yourself and the room you are seated in.

The next stage is to visualise a clear glass chalice at your heart centre. See that the bowl of the chalice is formed of six sides of equal diameter, with a curved stem leading to a glass base. When the image seems stable, begin to expand it until the base is level with your feet, the base of the cup where it joins the stem is level with your navel, and the rim of the chalice is level with your shoulders. Be aware of the stem curving inwards around your groin and down then back outwards to meet the base at your feet, and again pause until all feels stable. Now expand the chalice so that it moves outwards and upwards, and let your consciousness expand upwards as it does so until you feel as if you are floating in the centre of this great glass chalice suspended in space. Looking down, take your attention to the circular base and here visualise a Round Table. Realise that this is the Round Table of the Elementals.

Drawing your attention up the stem of the chalice, be aware that at the base of its six-sided cup is another Round Table. This is the Round Table of all those initiates of the Mysteries who are incarnate in the world, and of all those who seek to serve the Mysteries and have yet to become initiates. You can visualise the sides of the chalice becoming milky white at this point, with the Round Table situated within it. Taking your seat at this table, you may find that others who are not incarnate are also present here. This is a good place to sit at times around the table and talk with them, noting what they have to say. At first the conversation may seem not to impart much but as the contact with these beings grows, you will find that they can both help and guide you if you so desire it, for just as you are building this level in your consciousness, so are the Inner Plane Adepti also building this structure in order to contact you.

But for now we shall draw our consciousness upwards until we reach the top of the chalice. Here, beneath an indigo sky (although this will change in time as the contact here strengthens) you should visualise a third round table. This is the Round Table of the Masters. Contact here will not necessarily take the form of any verbal communication, although this may occur. The Masters of the Great White Lodge (as they are known) are often thought of as some sort of super human beings, but this is unhelpful. They are beings just as we are, albeit rather more experienced, and never to be underestimated, but if you approach them as a type of superhero you will find that it makes contact with them harder than it needs to be, and something of a hindrance to them as well. You may see them as men and women sitting at this Round Table, in different coloured robes or as spheres of light. The image does not really matter, for at this level we are beginning to reach to the extreme limits of form.

Far away, around this table, you may also be aware of the twelve positions of the Zodiac, and these arise from the division of the three Rings when these powers become manifest. If you visualise any of the three Rings you will notice that it is intersected by the other two Rings at four points to create four segments, which makes twelve in all. These twelve segments manifest as that which we know as the Zodiacal powers. However it must be borne in mind that the manifestation of these segments as the Zodiac are formed after the interaction of the consciousnesses with those Beings that we call the Lords of Flame, Form and Mind. We can contemplate this in terms of the Lords of Flame undergoing their evolution within one Ring, the Lords of Form within another and the Lords of Mind within the third Ring. Each interacts with the others during their evolution and it is only after this interaction has taken place that the twelve segments are imbued with the ability to impress the Zodiacal forces upon creation.

The next step is an act of faith. You may become aware of a vortex of force spiralling down from above, and if you move to the centre of the Round Table of the Great White Lodge you will feel this vortex draw you up. All might appear darkness at first, for you are approaching the level of what is known in Qabalistic terms as the sphere of Daath. Pass through the darkness until you become aware of a pinkish grey light that grows brighter as you ascend. This is a high level indeed, and looking down you may become aware of great circular lines of energy and of the angles created where the lines intersect. This however is more the concern of the Masters who interpret what they see emerging from the sphere of Daath and make account of it, so that these forces may become manifest without too much disruption to humanity. For this is the principle work of the Masters, who are much concerned with the smooth passage of consciousness from involution to evolution, and also, to a certain extent, with tidying up some of the results of past cycles that are completed so that they do not impact on future cycles of events.

Now become aware of an opening above your head, for here we are standing beneath the Unmanifest. Feel and be aware that somewhere above you, beyond this opening, is a point of light revolving around the central point of the three great Rings of Time, Space and Event in the Unmanifest, and identify with it. Do not try to bring the point of light itself down, for you will be unable to, and to attempt to do so could prove harmful. Instead see a ray of light emerge from this small point of light and realise that it is coming from the highest point of your spirit within the Unmanifest, that which God would have you be. Now feel it pass through you and speed downwards, passing through the Round Table of the Masters, down through the centre of the Round Table of the initiates, down through the stem and into the centre of the base, energising all three tables as it does so.

Here at this point I relate the lowest table to the sphere of physical manifestation, so that this table serves two purposes. Seeing my body there, I am aware of this white light passing through the top of my physical head and down beneath my feet. Alternatively, you may at this point find that you have been drawn down by the light so that you are situated at the centre of the chalice again.

Next, as if in reply, see a ray of black light pass swiftly up through the centre of the ray of white light until it reaches the point from whence this white light emerged. Be aware that the white light represents the impulse of involution and the black light that of evolution. Once this circuit has completed you may find that the two lights merge and change into gold and silver. When this happens you may feel a great force coming down the sides of the chalice and into the earth from above, and as if in reply another force will rise from the earth and ascend through the six sides of the chalice. You may now perceive points of light within the sides of the chalice, and these are points of different consciousness present in the six planes that the sides of the chalice represent. You will find, in time, that they can be contacted, but concentrate on the main visualisation first.

Now feel yourself sinking downwards until you join your physical body. See the chalice shrink until the Round Table of the Elementals is once more at your feet, the table of the initiates is at your waist and the table of the masters at your shoulders. Finally watch this structure shrink and as it does so draw it into your heart centre and become aware of your physical surroundings. Open your eyes and look at your surroundings. If it is dark, or there is a dim light, look at your feet and then your hands and examine what you see. Move your feet apart and you may find that in a dim light you can now see your aura around your hands and feet, and also the energy that you have indeed brought through may be visible as specks of different coloured lights around the room, so sit for a short while and take note. Then make a physical gesture like clapping your hands gently three times to return to complete waking consciousness. This ends the first part of this work of readjustment.

During this exercise, we mentioned the sphere of Daath which seems to form a transition between the first three and the fourth planes. Working within the aura we can feel the base of plane one just above the head, plane two to the right of the head and plane three to the left. We can envisage Daath at the throat centre and plane four circulating the shoulders. Plane five is situated in the aura circulating the heart centre but whereas plane four seems to have an attraction in its circuit between one shoulder and the other, plane five has an attraction in its current between the front and the back, with its focus situated in the heart. Plane six is level with the navel just above the top of the hips, and as with the shoulders there is an attraction in the current from one side of the body to the other. Finally, plane seven extends from the groin to below the feet and moves in a vertical circular motion as opposed to the horizontal circuits of planes four, five and six. Remember that these planes are not literally situated at these points, but it is the flow of energy within the aura at these points that is stimulated by the seven planes. There are also points within these circuits of force about the body, both before and behind you, that have specific qualities when stimulated.

When you are able to see the physical body with more of the inner senses, you become aware of the body of light that seems to be connected with the electrical field generated by the body and that which we call the aura, but if you look deeper you will be aware of a network of grid-like lines that make up what is called the etheric body. It is these subtle bodies that are affected by the seven planes of existence. The Qabalist places Chesed and Geburah one at each shoulder but in reality they are part of the same force that circulates the body. Likewise the Qabalist places Netzach and Hod at the hips, but again they are one and the same force. Similarly, Yesod is usually placed at the groin and Malkuth at the feet, but if you learn to feel the aura correctly you will experience how these are part of the same current of energy that flows in the aura from the groin down to the feet and up again in a circular fashion. The Qabalist's custom of dividing them into separate masculine and feminine forces is a symptom of the seventh plane in which we exist, for from any of the other planes these forces would be viewed as inseparable. The same way of thinking means that we often attempt to divide 'god' into male and female.

This is an important point, so by way of example I will pause here to discuss one of the many myths that illustrate what I mean, that of Andromeda and Perseus. The myth makes little sense until you look at the part played by Medusa who is one of the principle characters. The story goes that while she was worshipping in the temple of the divine female she was ravished by Poseidon, a male god. But if we look at this story from a higher level instead of looking upwards to it from below, we will see that Medusa was not at this point able to accept the initiation into the full powers of Godhood that were being offered, or in other words accept the concept of God that lies beyond the division into male and female which is the result of the limitation of human consciousness. As a consequence, she was turned into a serpent-headed creature. Or to put it another way, her nature had become distorted and unbalanced and cut off from the divine in its totality. There is much here that is similar to the story of Adam and Eve. Just as Jesus took Adam's place we find in the myth of Perseus and Andromeda that Andromeda eventually takes Medusa's place. The great forces of the Sea have been invoked and become unbalanced, and she sends Perseus on a series of adventures, travelling even to places or planes of earlier development, until eventually he confronts Medusa and forces her to see her own reflection, or in other words what she has become. Medusa then stops projecting her twisted inner aspect outwards upon creation by turning it into stone and directing it back into herself. When this has been accomplished, Perseus strikes off her head. The winged horse Pegasus, and the warrior Chrysaor who carried a golden falchion or sword, then rise up fully grown from her body as a result of her impregnation by Poseidon.

This sequence is symbolic of the forces of the natural world once more being able to take wing and fly upwards to join with the divine, and of the inspiration and the spiritual will being redirected upwards to become one with divine will. It is a highly symbolic initiatory action which re-balances the great Sea forces that were brought into action when Medusa was unable to accept the totality of god beyond male and female. When you truly understand this sequence you will have taken a huge step in reconciling the seventh plane with the preceding six and will be able to view seventh plane existence in a different light.

Returning to the influences of the seven planes within the aura, you may have noticed that the fifth plane mainly affects the heart centre. Now as we have stated, the fifth plane concerns the principle of separateness and the heart centre traditionally represents Tiphareth, the Sephirah of unification. There might at first appear to be something of a contradiction in this statement, but without separateness there can be no unifying principle. As the heart centre is associated with the sphere of Christ you will find that here is another great Mystery concerning the central point in the Unmanifest and how its influence is expressed in manifest creation. Much will also be gained by meditation upon this.

The final part of the aura which we shall discuss is the throat centre. This does not represent any of the seven planes but rather the transition point from the first three planes to the remaining four, and corresponds to what Qabalists traditionally call the sphere of Daath. There are many occultists (some of whom I respect greatly) who will explain Daath as nothing more than a place of change and leave the subject at that. However, this is unhelpful – and so on this occasion I will recount my own experience of this sphere so that it may be of help to those who have not experienced or understood it fully.

Some years back during a 'routine' pathworking up the central pillar to Tiphareth, I entered a temple structure situated in the Sun and therein found the figure of Christ seated upon a throne and bleeding from his wounds which flowed down into the earth below. I spent some time contemplating the principles of sacrifice. I was about to turn back when I noticed a door behind the Christ's throne, to which he motioned. Until that point it had been a normal pathworking in which I was slightly aware of my physical body in the background. Opening the door I could see nothing beyond it but pitch darkness, and so being forever inquisitive I stepped through into nothing.

Upon moving for a short distance I was suddenly aware that I had lost all contact with my physical body. This was not like a deep meditative state wherein the concentration is of such an intensity that the physical senses have faded into the background, nor of a full 'astral projection' which utilises one of the etheric bodies, but rather a full awareness just as in everyday life, but 'bodiless.' (A person using the technique of astral projection is limited to the sensual structure that the etheric body uses.)

I immediately tried to turn back, but turning my 'consciousness' back round, found that there was nowhere to go back to. I was surrounded by complete darkness in all directions and a total absence of anything, for not even darkness existed, let alone directions. There was absolutely nothing but my centre of consciousness and it was as though nothing else existed. I was aware I had a wife and children whom I loved dearly, yet knew that I reacted with them through a physical body, and that without a means to interact with them, for all intents and purposes they did not exist; there was complete nothing and it was as if the whole universe (inner and outer) had been obliterated. It is hard to put this into words – what do you do when there is absolutely nothing – where do you go when there is absolutely nowhere to go to? I searched for my faith, but even this had been obliterated. I had absolutely nothing; I *was* absolutely nothing but a small centre of mind in the darkness. Everything had gone as if it had never existed.

For those who seek occult experiences just for the experience (and there is nothing wrong with that, for we all learn by experience) I can tell you that this is not an experience that you will want, for having absolutely everything dissolved is unpleasant in the extreme. I recalled the experience I had achieved in the sphere of Tiphareth before this had happened and while knowing that to a certain extent it had been a creation of mind, I held on to the hope that there had been some reality to it, and having nothing left but hope, journeyed on. How long this took I did not know, for even time had ceased to exist and likewise I did not know in what direction I was heading for there was no direction to go to. But I could feel that my consciousness was moving and I held onto HOPE with the whole of my being for it was all that I had left.

Eventually I began to perceive that the darkness was slowly changing into a pinkish grey which grew brighter as I continued. It was almost like a mist but then again was not. Having something now to focus my consciousness on other than hope, I became aware of a sort of direction once more, and focusing on what could be called a downwards direction or back from where I had come/moved, I was now aware of great lines of force. These were many in number but they did not appear to be of any geometric pattern or even on the same level as each other. I suddenly knew with complete certainty that the whole of creation was a complete illusion created by the mind of God. In some strange way what I was 'seeing' was a part of God's thoughts creating the structure on which the whole of creation, or what we call reality, is based. At this point all worry disappeared and I entered a state of the deepest calm and bliss. I had travelled beyond (I thought at the time) the structures of manifest creation, and no longer being subject to it suddenly found myself in a state of what Buddhists know as nirvana or perfect bliss. At this point I knew that I could remain 'here' forever and that my physical body, wherever it was, would just die. However, I made my choice and after one other experience was returned to my physical body.

Afterwards, I knew that I had travelled through the sphere of Daath but had not realised what was happening at the time. Later still, I realised that the lines of force that I saw are in fact circular, but such is the immensity of them that from my viewpoint at that time they appeared as lines stretching into the distance.

This I hope goes some way in demonstrating the difference between the first three planes and the remaining four. In working with the Chalice imagery our aspiration is to reach to plane one and beyond into the Unmanifest. I do not believe it is too important once you leave the Round Table of the Masters and progress upwards to experience this separating level, or even to attempt to, but an awareness of its existence is important. Planes one, two and three are above form, in contrast to planes four to seven, and if you do experience this separating level fully I hope the account of my own experience will make the initial part less harrowing for you. You may experience plane two manifesting as flowing circles of force while plane three may appear to be full of intersections and angular force, and this is because you are now operating at a level above form which is difficult for normal consciousness to comprehend. Another point that is worth mentioning is that the black current that travels back up through the current of white light that descends would just fade into nothingness if the white light had not been brought down first. This is well worth pondering.

There are those who think that attaining such a 'high level' experience is the sign of great spirituality but I can assure you that this is not the case. As I have stated previously, each level is as holy as the other. It is just that there are fewer complexities inherent in the preceding planes, and so consciousness feels more liberated when operating there. As to the ability to perceive them, this is more down to the psychic structure of the operator than a sign of a more spiritual person and it is just as likely to indicate that a level in the psychic structure of the operator has probably not formed correctly when they came into incarnation, which is something to consider! There are also ways that the psychic structure can become damaged in early development, particularly in very young children, which will give the same ability as can be got from the various occult exercises that aim to develop such ability. The most 'spiritual person' will always be one who can operate on plane seven, experiencing all yet harming none with his or her actions.

Another point to consider while working with the seven planes of consciousness is 'does one plane evolve into the proceeding plane?' The answer to this I believe is 'no.' They all exist to a certain extent independently of each other and could be considered as separate places; in fact it is we who change as we progress through them.

While working with this material I made a very strong contact with what I would call an Elven figure who resides on the sixth plane of consciousness and with whom I merged auras. One of the things that she showed me was the Planetary Being at the level of the fifth plane. To the inner eye it appeared as a sphere of many different sparkling, flaming lights and I was aware of a potential for a grid-like pattern to be imposed upon it, which it could hold or contain. To my surprise the Elven contact then revealed how the psychic structure of her own kind fitted into the Planetary Being on plane six and how the human psychic structure, which was much more complex, fitted into the Planetary Being. She showed me how we would both perceive plane seven, and how although the embracing sphere contained both our environmental perceptions, we would see two different places. This imagery reveals much, for we do indeed share the Planetary Being with many other forms of life, but at different levels.

It is perhaps at this point that we should return to a consideration of the Planetary Being. We have seen how during the formation of the seven planes in potential, the Planetary Being came into creation at plane four which is the first plane of form as we know it. Now this is a very difficult point to both explain and understand. Our present viewpoint in manifest existence on plane seven teaches us that concrete form creates consciousness, whether in the development of the brain or in its subsequent conditioning by environment, but the truth is that consciousness creates form and not the other way round. If you consider the physical world, science teaches us that creation is a matter of atoms in space and attractions between them, and that although our conscious minds and perception of scale interprets things as solid, science will show that this is not the case.

Now each plane has what we can term an etheric body attached to it which is created by the consciousness of the preceding plane. We can think of it as the oversoul of the preceding plane and its methods of consciousness-creating thought patterns which weave forms and structures in the all-surrounding 'ether.' It is to these structures that matter is attracted on the succeeding plane and they will indeed govern the extent to which the consciousness abiding there can develop. Thus the Planetary Being is subject to the etheric patterns of planes One, Two and Three created by the Lords of Flame, Form and Mind, and these Lords create the basis of physical reaction, chemical reaction and motion respectively throughout the universe. It is according to these laws that the consciousness of the succeeding plane must act. The fourth plane will then impart what we could call the law of the element of Air in its broadest sense on plane four, plane five will create the element of Fire in its broadest sense, plane six will create Water and plane seven will create Earth. Thus our Planetary Being is subject to the laws imposed by the Lords of Flame, Form and Mind but will itself create the laws controlling the elements of Air, Fire, Water and Earth. Perhaps it will be helpful to give an image of this.

Think of the deepest dark of space and then envisage one of the planes as a living thing, perhaps a flat disc, milky white in colour, floating within space. Upon the surface of the disc we can envisage patterns and lines of force flowing from one side to the other, and to simplify things we will see them as gold in colour. We instinctively know that these lines of force are the thoughts of the oversoul of the disc. Eventually the lines of force start to etch a pattern in the surface of the disc, and the pattern glows with a golden light. Where these lines cross we can feel other conscious entities emerge at the intersections, and they create their own lines of force upon the surface of the disc which we will see as silver. We know that these gold and silver lines of force represent both the thoughts of the oversoul of the disc and its inhabitants, which it has created by contemplating aspects of itself.

As we watch, we see a pattern emerge that eventually becomes harmonious, and the etched lines become deeper until they cut a pattern right through the disc floating in space. Now see that a light is shining from above the disc, and see the light pass through the lines that have been etched through it. Just like a torch beam passing through paper in which a pattern has been cut out, it creates an image of a similar disc below the first. The first disc has the lines it created itself and the lines added by its 'children.' But the next disc's oversoul has a conscious entity that can interact with the lines created by the first disc *as a totality*. In other words, all lines are merged into gold, not gold and silver, and so the patterns it creates through its thoughts are immediately more complicated. Now as we watch, the oversoul of the second disc starts its own contemplations and we see its own gold lines flow across its surface, following the patterns of the first disc. However, where in the first disc we saw only one line etched across its surface we now see two, and so the intersections of the lines become more complicated. They become centres of consciousness and start to add their own lines of force/thought to the pattern which again we can envisage as silver, and so the process is repeated.

This image is the best that I am able to provide and I hope that it goes some way to giving you a feeling for how the Planetary Being develops through planes four to seven, and of how different inhabitants of these planes develop, one of whom is the 'Elven' consciousness mentioned earlier. In reality each disc would appear as a sphere and the preceding sphere would be contained within it so that all spheres occupied the same position, but to visualise this just complicates matters, and demands much of the concrete consciousness. We have said that consciousness creates form and not the other way round and if you look at the universe from this viewpoint you will see that it is indeed a wondrous creation, not of form, but of the different consciousness of many beings. However it is important to keep in mind the difference between human consciousness and the consciousness of those who are the 'creations of the created.' There is an important distinction, which is that humanity has a link to the centre (the Great 'I am who I am') and also to the Great Sea of All Being/Non Being.

I am now passing beyond what I have seen and experienced on the Inner planes while working with this material so far. To write anything else would begin to push this work into speculation which is an avenue that I do not wish to travel. The alternative would be to revert to direct dictation from the Inner plane communicators after the manner in which *The Cosmic Doctrine* was originally written, and which I have tried to avoid. However, who knows, maybe the journey will open up to reveal a few more miles yet, or maybe the next steps are waiting to be trodden by you. I do hope so. Good luck to one and all. May the Spirit move within you and guide you in your progress.

1   The first three exercises are adapted from material developed by Gareth Knight, an old friend and one time teacher, and are used here with thanks for his kind permission.

Lightning Source UK Ltd.
Milton Keynes UK
UKOW01f2327091017
310712UK00001B/42/P

9 781908 011862